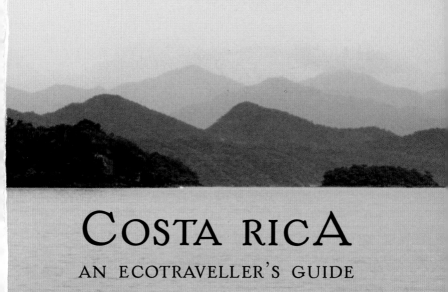

COSTA RICA

AN ECOTRAVELLER'S GUIDE

COSTA RICA

AN ECOTRAVELLER'S GUIDE

BY HANNAH ROBINSON

Interlink Books

An imprint of Interlink Publishing Group, Inc.
Northampton, Massachusetts

First published 2006 by

INTERLINK BOOKS
An imprint of Interlink Publishing Group, Inc.
46 Crosby Street, Northampton, Massachusetts 01060
www.interlinkbooks.com

Library of Congress Cataloging-in-Publication Data
Robinson, Hannah.
Costa Rica : an ecotraveller's guide / by Hannah
Robinson.—1st American ed.
    p. cm.
Includes bibliographical references and index.
ISBN 1-56656-617-7 (pbk.)
1. Ecotourism—Costa Rica—Guidebooks. 2. Natural
areas—Costa Rica—Guidebooks. 3. National parks and
reserves—Costa Rica—Guidebooks. 4. Costa Rica—
Guidebooks. I. Title. G155.C67R63 2006
917.28604'52—dc22

                                    2005022439

ISBN 10: 1-56656-617-7
ISBN 13: 978-1-56656-617-9

Printed and bound in China

*With thanks to Philip Davison for giving invaluable
suggestions on the manuscript, to Eric J. Olson, PhD,
Earthwatch principal investigator and "instigator" who
introduced me to tropical forest ecology in the field, and to
the Klingenstein Fund for providing an Earthwatch education award. Photographs on pages 208, 209 and 271 are
courtesy of Michelle Wurth.*

To contact the author: hannahrepresents@yahoo.com

Contents

1
The Northwest

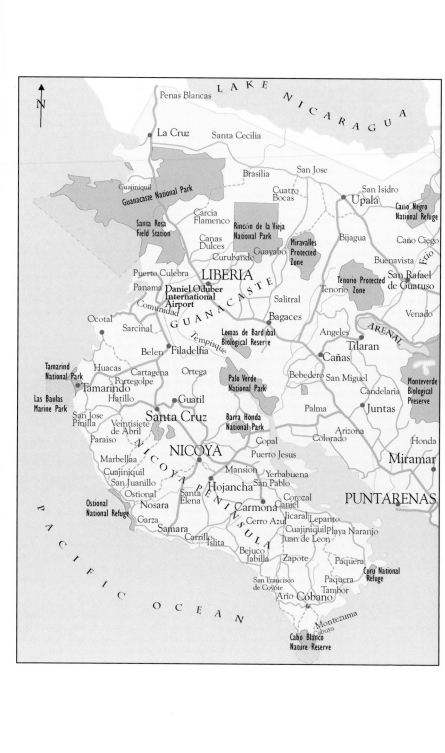

Trees arch over the roadway, leaves rustle, and a troop of spider monkeys deftly skitters across the treetops, some mothers carrying infants. They cautiously peer into the canopy, their long tails secured to tree limbs. Below, dense clusters of sulfur and green pierid butterflies sample the warm road mud for minerals, and there are so many blossoms falling from a frothy cedrela tree (*Cedrela odorata*) that it sounds like it's raining.

This is the Guanacaste area where you can surf, snorkel, dive, watch nesting sea turtles, and immerse yourself in deciduous tropical forests, green over green. Outside the forests, umbrella-shaped trees dot the baking cattle pastures that were cleared of forest three hundred years ago. Huge cenizaro (*Pithecellobium saman*) and conacaste or "ear fruit" trees (*Enterolobium cyclocarpum*) provide shade for white Brahman cattle and create perches for snake-eating laughing falcons, Hoffmann's woodpeckers, rufous-naped wrens, and white-throated magpie-jays. Most visitors come for the beach resorts on the Nicoya

Human Exploration

A fluted spear point from the Guanacaste-Nicoya area is the only evidence that nomadic hunter-gatherers moved through the Guanacaste area on their way to cross the isthmus of Panama in the process of populating South America from the north. According to Patagonian carbon dating, this occurred at around 10,000 BCE.

These mangroves in the Pacific have pneumatophore roots that breathe for them (preceding page). Restored Guanacaste forest (above).

Volunteers

Earthwatch is one of several organizations that offer ecotravellers a way to get up close to the research side of conservation while exploring Costa Rica. "Volunteers" pay (or get grants) for the chance to work with scientists for about two weeks on research projects. Projects in Costa Rica at this time range from investigating rainforest caterpillars in La Selva, to gathering data on leatherback sea turtles in Las Baulas National Park, Guanacaste, and monitoring the interactions between dolphins and tourists at Gandoca-Manzanillo Wildlife Refuge on the Caribbean side of Costa Rica.

Earthwatch investigator Dr. Eric Olson with researchers (top, above right)

Peninsula (pages 34–50) than the national parks, attracted by the white sands and the six-month dry season from November to April. But the region offers a huge restored forest in the Guanacaste National Park (pages 5–28), indigenous Chorotega crafts, volunteer ecology opportunities, and steam-vent-studded volcanoes for ecotravellers to discover. The wetlands of Palo Verde National Park also fill with a quarter of a million waterbirds and woodland migrants (many from North American gardens) during migratory season (pages 28–33).

To experience more of the region's vivacity, slip into natural time: get up with the howler monkeys at dawn and hear them set out to browse and sun themselves. Even more activity occurs after dark, when animals feel it's safer to wander, so don't miss shining your flashlight around to see if you can spot cute opossums nibbling in fruiting trees or blossom bats pollinating heavily scented night-blooming flowers.

Guanacaste National Park

Guanacaste National Park is one of the world's success stories in terms of large-scale wildlands restoration. One half of all Caribbean and Central American land was once covered by the type of tropical deciduous forest found here. It resembles rainforest during the wet season, but dries to a crisp for six months of the year, losing most of its leaves. The Pacific forest has now been cut back to a mere 2% of these lands in order to clear them for agriculture. However, the Costa Rican government, with visionary tropical ecologist Daniel H. Janzen, has reversed the trend in this park. International conservation organizations and individuals have provided the funds to convert farmland back to forest. Guanacaste National Park is now the only entirely self-sustaining tropical dry forest anywhere. You can still assist in the land purchase of the

Toxic Intelligence
Mantled howler monkeys (*Alouatta palliata*, below), are as successful as more intelligent capuchin monkeys. Howlers eat leaves, fruit, and flowers and do not compete directly with aggressive capuchins, who would outsmart them. Howlers have a feeding pattern of sampling small quantities of younger, less toxic leaves from among some highly poisonous species. Kenneth Glander found that howler monkeys will avoid the toxic alkaloids and cardiac glycosides found in 146 individual *Madero negro* trees this way, eating only from three other *Madero negro* trees, which are the only ones without toxins—the other trees could kill. The howlers remembered which was which even though the trees looked the same. Glander has hypothesized that this need for complex discrimination and memory among primates may have resulted in the evolution of higher intelligence.

Big Bang

The dry season of the Guanacaste is filled with brilliantly colored blossoms (right) synchronized in a "big bang" from January to March. The flowers are timed to come out before the leaves, at the start of the rainy season. This is associated with a boom in herbivores, including ants and caterpillars. Golden Cortés (*Tabebuia ochracea*) and trumpet-vine trees (Bignoniaceae family) are among the bloomers. These are pollinated by animals, including 53 species of hummingbirds. The strategy overwhelms any animals that consume pollen and fruit, ensuring survival of at least a few viable seeds. Frangipani (*Plumeria rubra*, opposite page) is called Flor de Mayo in El Salvador because its flowers unfurl just before the rains come in May.

Rincón Rainforest by contacting the Guanacaste Dry Forest Conservation Fund, care of Professor Daniel H. Janzen, Department of Biology, 415 South University Avenue, University of Pennsylvania, Philadelphia, PA 19104.

Land that was pasture for hundreds of years has been added back to the park through a carefully planned restoration program, and the amount of protected land continues to grow. This restoration involved some hand-seeding and planting, coupled with careful fire management and a hunting ban. Most of the recovery, however, is due to the rapid natural regrowth of this tropical forest. Cattle are allowed temporarily to reduce the smothering tall grasses that were once introduced for ranching, so that restored native species have the chance to emerge. Lands from the most recent buy-backs include one large farm that hid Oliver North's Iran–Contra landing strip near the park entrance.

Huge areas have been restored. From the Santa Rosa observation tower, you can look across a vast expanse of forest wilderness rolling away from one horizon to another, seeing nothing but trees where pasture used to be. In newer sections you can see fast-growing native saplings poking back through the nonnative grasses. Nearby, crowns of twenty-year-old pioneer trees are closing the light gaps overhead, and saplings of slower-growing semi-deciduous canopy trees are establishing themselves in the shade below.

The Guanacaste is now large enough to support a viable genetic base of all its organisms, from jaguars and Baird's tapirs that depend on huge territories, to forty humming-bird-sized hawk moths that migrate west to east high over the mountains every year.

The forest is distinct from those found across the rest of the Costa Rica because it is in a rain shadow on the leeward side of the Guanacaste volcanoes, sheltered from the prevailing, moist Atlantic trade winds that dominate December through May. During this dry season, animals can be found clustered around waterholes in the parching heat, beneath bare branches.

Trapliners

Nocturnal sphinx moths, bats, and hummingbirds level out their food supply by learning the location of long-term low-producing "steady state" flowering trees. These include sleepy hibiscus, *Malvaviscus palmanus* (above). Over many months, the nectar seekers "trapline" a route that can cover several miles between each source that they remember. Calabash trees, (*Crescentia alata*), coral trees (*Erythrina* sp.), and wild coffee species use this "steady state" strategy, in which a few flowers open every few days, keeping the total amount of food needed by the plant low, but the length of time flowers are available high. This keeps the herbivore level low, while maintaining a good level of specialist poll-inators.

Frangipani (Plumeria rubra, *left*)

Horse Followers

The epiphyte-laden calabash tree (*Cresentia alata,* above, and gourd, right) has an unusual distribution. You only find it where horses range. The species appears to have been dispersed by wild horses, extinct land sloths, and extinct elephant-relatives called gomphotheres, up to ten thousand years ago. These mastodon-like species were wiped out when megafauna went extinct. After that, limited dispersal by agoutis and tapirs kept calabash trees from becoming extinct, but the calabash did better for the last five hundred years after horses were reintroduced by the conquistadors. The otherwise poisonous fruit ripen after weeks on the ground. Horses are the only species to relish the gooey mess, and after digestion, disperse the seeds in a viable form. You may spot traplining bats coming to pollinate the blooms at night.

There are ancient petroglyphs carved in stone in several locations, signs of pre-Columbian cultures that eventually became city communities.

The park shelters about 300 bird species, 140 mammals, and 3,000 plant species, some of these "strays" from other habitats, and some specially adapted to this area.

You may spot thicket tinamou, banded wrens, black-headed trogons, and scrub euphonia. Tiny as they are, the euphonias are among the most colorful birds. Flocks of yellow-naped amazons (*Amazona auropalliata*) and other dry forest parrots may be seen and heard flitting between seed-laden trees early in the morning. During the dry season the parrots tend to be lower to the ground and are much easier to spot among the leafless trees than in the evergreen rainforest canopy elsewhere.

During the wet season from May to October, the forest flushes with food that spurs an enormous burst of diversity. This season spans two summer peaks, not one, when the sun's rays are vertical and at their strongest. A vertical sun that casts no shadow only occurs in the tropics, which is why the heat can be so intense in this region. With a vertical sun, the photons are concentrated into a much smaller land area, and the impact of this tremendous amount of energy creates a change that becalms the wind. This event is called the doldrums. You can sense a mini-doldrum each day when the tropical sun is at its highest, even if it is not vertical, and the weather goes into a short lull. Long sleeves, a hat, and plenty of water to drink are essential to combat the solar rays.

Focus on Wildlife: Guanacaste Nature

The Guanacaste is known for its gorgeously colorful, elephantine caterpillars. Furry or spiky, mirrored or eye-spotted, quiet or strumming, these caterpillars are like nothing you have seen before. It's worth a moment to be charmed and beguiled by these not-so-little nocturnal beasts, because they offer a

Assassins

Assassin bugs (*Apiomerus pictipes*, opposite page on calabash) kill ants and bees by injecting flesh-eating saliva through their beaks. They put sticky resins on their legs to increase their chances of catching prey. Assassin bugs follow the scent of bee pheromones to find the spout-entrances to nests of stingless bees (*Trigona fulviventris*, above) at tree bases. An attacked bee releases an alarm pheromone that brings out defense bees to hover threateningly over the assassins. However, the unphased assassin bug simply picks off each bee one by one, and can kill the entire nest over time. Some species of assassin bugs, known as "kissing bugs," carry chagas disease. This is a serious tropical heart and brain disease affecting humans. The disease is caused by the parasite *Trypanosoma cruzi* that is found in the feces of carriers, not their bite, and is absorbed through scratches.

Wild bromeliad pineapple relative (left)

Cantil

The cantil (*Agkistrodon bilineatus*) is a dry forest beauty. It is a poisonous pit viper related to the cottonmouth, and captures frogs, mice, and lizards. Its venom is less toxic than that of the dangerous and common rainforest hognosed pit viper (*Porthidium nasutum*). Watch out for snake coils on verandas and bunk house floors by day or night.

window into the bizarre and amazing relationships of the tropical forest. In June and July, about three to six weeks after the end of the dry season, a major flush of new leaves unfurls and a caterpillar boom begins. Field ecologists are studying the intricate relationships involved in their survival. By carefully analyzing the data of these caterpillar populations, one can begin to appreciate how an entire forest network coexists.

At the peak caterpillar boom, you can stand under the canopy and listen to what appears to be the patter of rain, but is actually made by caterpillar droppings (or *frasse*) raining down on the forest floor. Around the Santa Rosa field station, experts have found 3,140 species of

butterfly and moth caterpillars, mostly nocturnal, including that of the much studied and widespread saturniid (or silk) moth *Rothschildia lebeau*, the symbol of this national park.

Plants and caterpillar predators have evolved crazy ways to succeed, creating a game-theorist's paradise. Plants even recruit wasps in various ways to help them remove or disable these huge chomping caterpillars before their leaves are stripped bare. The aroma of plant sap helps to protect the host plant: wasps recognize the aromatic profile of caterpillar burp mixed with sap and remove the caterpillar. The color of the caterpillars serves as a defense: wasps avoid the most brightly colored species. Some wasps patrol plants visually, possibly looking for leaf damage caused by their prey and certainly looking for palatable caterpillars. This may be why some moth caterpillars fend the wasps off by storing some of the plant's toxins in their skin and spines. However, the beautiful silk moth

Geometry
Snake-imitators (top) are caterpillars that appear to have snake eyes, mouths, and harlequin-patterned skins. This one has a small mirror above its tail that wiggles when it has been disturbed, perhaps imitating the quiver of a Neotropical rattlesnake tail (*Crotalus durissus*, below top). One caterpillar folds into tight geometric squares (below) to elude capture by birds, whose eyes seek out round patterns.

Fast Food Outlets

The ant plant *Acacia collinsii* (right) is the star of TV documentaries because it employs ants as security guards in return for shelter and food. Ant plants are like a fast-food chain for ants: their stems offer little cups of nectar supplemented with amino acids and their leaves display beads (orange Beltian bodies) filled with high-energy oil (bottom). The meal is packed "to go" for the guardian ants to pluck and take away to feed their brood. Acacia ants, such as *Pseudomyrmex ferruginea*, nest inside the hollow paired thorns (top right), one queen producing a colony that has about 12,000 workers alive at any one time. Any intruders get removed or stung with a painful mix of formic and other acids. The ants effectively defend the plant from caterpillars, beetles, humans, and horses. The plant perfumes its flowers with ant repellent to allow pollinators to visit.

common in the Guanacaste, *Rothschildia lebeau*, is palatable whether it feeds on toxic leaves or not. One of this moth's parasitic wasps patrols for the scent of its caterpillar's food source, being hard-wired to identify the food and from this to search more closely for the caterpillars.

Some plants use ants to deter caterpillars. They offer nectar from leaf stems to attract ants and adult parasitoid wasps that eat caterpillars. The nectar reward that the ants receive encourages

them to patrol the branches for caterpillars and other herbivores, which they cart away for a high-protein snack.

The intricacies of caterpillar life may not be immediately apparent to the eye, but these symbiotic, coevolved relationships deserve attention. Caterpillars are most easily sighted during an evening hike after the rainy season has started.

Caterpillars are not the only creatures to participate in such complex interdependencies. Many tropical species have creative ways of getting around the thick forest, where the same species are scattered few and far between. The huge riverside wild cashew, or acajou (*Anacardium excelsum*), recruits bats as dispersers. Its fruit stalks sweeten and become soft when the nuts are fully ripe. This attracts bats that cart them off, stalk and nuts attached. The bats drop the toxic seeds after eating the resinous, nu-

Vegetarian Spider

A species of jumping spider (below left) is a predator that verges on vegetarianism. It feeds on acacia ants and their brood, but Dr. Eric Olson has shown that it also eats a significant amount of inanimate Beltian bodies (see opposite page). This is an incredible leap for an animal whose brain and eyes are wired to seek out moving prey.

Some species have evolved different tricks. A moth caterpillar (top left) has evolved camouflage that looks like the leaves and spines of acacia branches and uses ant-appeasing behaviors. Rufous-naped wrens (*Campylorhynchus rufinucha*) borrow the ant security guards, building their nest in ant acacias, often close to a wasp's nest. The ants bite and the wasps sting animals that try to raid the wren's nest. They even select the most aggressive ant species in an effort to stymie capuchin monkeys. The ant *Pseudomyrmex nigropilosa* is a cheat: this ant takes over the acacia shrub temporarily, eating the food offerings and quickly breeding young, but does not protect the plant—it moves on to another plant before its rapidly weakening host dies.

Common Language

The ultimate caterpillar defense is to turn a predator into a protector. Ants normally kill caterpillars for food. But when caterpillars make noises that mimic ant dialects, they can persuade ants to be their bodyguards or at least to leave them alone. In the case of blue, copper, and hairstreak butterfly species, their caterpillars recruit ants by stridulating (making grating noises) in ways that mimic the ants and which ants understand. Responding to their alarm call, the ants then defend the caterpillars from other enemies, such as wasps. In return, the ants are fed nectar and amino acids that drip from glands dotted on the snowy spots of the caterpillar's body and spiky tail. Even the caterpillar pupae stridulate to keep the ants informed. If you stroke the branch on which the caterpillar is sitting, it will stridulate with its specialized noises. In this species' case, the reason for this reaction is unknown.

tritious stalks in flight, dispersing the acajou effectively.

Other dispersers include orioles, cotingas, and some parrots and toucans that seek out fruit especially during the dry season. *Stemmadenia donnell-smithii* and related species (called *huevos de caballo* and *cojon de puerco*: horses' eggs and pigs' testicles) have juicy, paired fruits that are dispersed by 22 bird species. Strong-smelling fruit, such as the hog plum (*Spondias mombin*), are dispersed by bats, coatis, and monkeys.

Evergreens are found in the slivers of *bosque humedo*, the humid forest that covers the streams, lowland crannies, and volcanic foothills. These damper microclimates become cool refuges for animals during the dry season. Here, look for long-tailed manakins (*Chiroxiphia linearis*) and even the diurnal weasel-like omnivorous tayra (*Eira barbara*), which are among the wide variety of species that feast on the common fruit of *Ardisia revoluta* from the understory. Meek-looking flycatchers such as the greenish elaenia (*Myiopagis viridicata*) and bright-rumped attila (*Attila spadiceus*) splash yellow in the dappled shade, while their songs add a new vocabulary to our world.

Along the light-filled banks of the streams around the kapok (*Ceiba pentandra*) and sandbox trees (*Hura crepitans*), you may see Muscovy ducks (*Cairina moschata*), rose-throated becards (*Pachyramphus aglaiae*),

Turds to Tails

Insects do strange things to avoid being eaten. Several leaf hopper species (below) evade capture by looking like bird droppings, complete with seeds. Other insect nymphs of beetles (above left) appear so bizarre that predators cannot figure out what they are and leave them alone. The citrus swallowtail caterpillar (above) looks like a bird turd complete with white uric acid, but it inflates two orange horns when threatened. These exude a pungent oily odor designed to warn off potential munchers. Some caterpillars can produce ant pheromones that are adjusted to communicate with the ants. For example, some predatory caterpillars mimic the aroma of an ant larva, so they are left alone while they eat nourishing ant larvae within the nest.

which locally lack red throats, and crane hawks (*Geranospiza caerulescens*). Crane hawks watch for nestlings, mice, and lizards from forest edges. Kapok trees produce a profusion of air-filled fibers that carry their seeds over the forest canopy. The fibers are used by various communities to stuff cushions and toys. These trees grow into huge canopies, the base of their trunks identified by the plank buttresses that unfold below spine-studded branches. They are "big bang" flowering trees, with bats, hummingbirds, bees, wasps, songbirds, beetles, opossums, tayras, and squirrels visiting the blossoms, though bats are the primary pollinators. This species is also found in West Africa, suggesting that it has its origins in Gondwanaland, the supercontinent that included all the present southern hemisphere

Detox

Some Guanacaste caterpillars detoxify host plant defense compounds before they eat them. One silk moth caterpillar (*Rothschildia lebeau*), can adapt to thriving on a toxic, carcinogenic mangrove, the manzanillo (*Hippomane mancinella*), which exudes sap capable of blinding humans. The caterpillar detoxifies its food with multifunctional oxidase enzymes in its gut. *R. lebeau* females (top right) seek out species from nine unrelated families, each of which has a unique phytotoxin. (This way, she stays a step ahead of a parasitic wasp that has genetically imprinted the smell of at least one of these food sources in order to find her caterpillars.) The young caterpillars adapt to each plant, and once adapted, older *R. lebeau* caterpillars cannot switch food sources. Trogon bird parents carefully remove caterpillar guts before they feed their brood. This gets rid of the poisonous wastes in the gut that could harm their nestlings.

continents, thus connecting present-day South America and West Africa. The trunks of sandbox trees have a swollen base and are studded with pyramidal spines. Both trees only grow in sunny locations.

The long-tailed manakin is a gorgeous black bird with an undulating tail longer than its body, a sky-blue back, and a red crest. During "cartwheel" courtship dances, two males face off: The males trade places in a choreographed dance, in which one moves forward while the other flutters upwards and backwards in a circular display, landing on the vacated perch of his rival. The female chooses the most elegant male as her mate.

Activities and Places to Stay in Guanacaste

Santa Rosa Field Station

Guanacaste National Park is currently set up for research and organized education, centered at the Santa Rosa field station. The research focus at Guanacaste National Park contrasts with more public trails and guides found in Monteverde. Yet independent travellers are welcome and will find that this fascinating dry forest is made even more interesting by the researchers that eat together with visitors in the central mess hut.

Visitors to the Guanacaste National

Park can stay at the Santa Rosa field station (tel 506-666-5051, fax 506-666-5020, www. acguanacaste.ac.cr). Researchers and groups receive priority. To reach the field station, head north of Liberia on the Interamerican Highway and after about 20 minutes turn left to Santa Rosa. You can also find accommodations at Hacienda los Inocentes Wildlife Conservation and Recreation Center (tel 506-679-9190 or 506-265-5484, fax 506-265-4385, www.losinocenteslodge. com, info@losinocenteslodge.com) north of the park border.

The field station is operated as a park base, with shared dining for park employees and visitors, surrounded by research bungalows, bunk houses, shower facilities, clean toilets, potable water, phone booths, and laundry rooms. Wildlife is everywhere. A tapir mother and baby once routinely visited the toilets at night to drink, and jaguar spoor can sometimes be spotted on the muddier tracks. Tents can be pitched at the campsite or in quieter areas under the large trees, and howler monkeys will probably be the morning wake-up call. A raised tent platform should be built first to avoid flooding during the wet season.

Costa Rican employees live on-site or come into the park by bus each day to fulfill the research and service duties associated

Doll Houses

The Ichneumonid wasp (*Enicospilus lebophagus*) lays its eggs on silk moth caterpillars at night. The wasp larva tries to move to the salivary gland, which is one of the few locations where the caterpillar's immune responses cannot encapsulate it. Eventually the silk moth larva spins a cocoon (below right). It is at this point that the wasp larva breaks out of the gland and eats the pupating, defenseless caterpillar from inside out, killing it. When fully grown, the wasp spins its own cocoon inside the caterpillar's (center in photo below), pupates, and then a single wasp emerges instead of the moth. In a bizarre twist, in some moth species, there can be up to four additional cocoons (left) made by successive parasites, producing a Russian doll of cocoons. These wasp parasites (strictly called parasitoids) can be valuable: they are now used in biological crop protection.

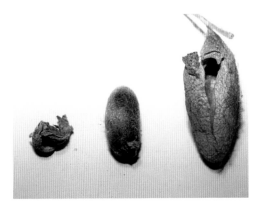

Outwitters

The common guapinol tree (*Hymenaea courbaril*) is also called "stinking toe." Its sap feeds the weird peanut-headed bug (*Fulgora laternaria*, opposite page), and you are likely to find them together. Just before the wet season, this virtually evergreen tree drops its leaves and usually within two weeks blooms with new leaves. This process allows its new leaves to toughen before the onslaught of herbivorous caterpillars that boom just after the rains start. The pod of its legume is so thick that the seeds cannot sprout without the help of gnawing agoutis (*Dasyprocta punctata*) to free them. Fortunately the agoutis cache a few cracked seeds that are ready to grow. *Rhinochenus stigma* weevils eat their fill of the seed but then are trapped inside the pod, leaving some of the seed as a scent offering to attract agoutis. The weevils are freed when the agoutis gnaw through the pod.

Some bugs are beautiful (right), others are ugly (opposite)

with this park. The park provides valuable employment for families who used to farm the land as *campesinos*, and who now spend their time doing everything from running the kitchen to inventorying potential medicinal plant species in a major computer database managed by INBio, the national biological resources research company. Some of the associated research is funded by international universities and some is sponsored by INBio as part of comprehensive bio-prospecting activities. The integration of a significant level of local employment was envisioned by Dr. Janzen in his plan for park restoration, which he felt would be essential to its long term success. (You may spot Dr. Janzen working in the area, resembling a shirtless Santa Claus.)

The Casona Battles

Santa Rosa field station is found in the relatively flat lowland forest around the restored hacienda, or *casona*, of Santa Rosa. The hacienda was the original reason for creating a park in 1971, though since then, Santa Rosa National Park has been folded into the much-expanded Guanacaste

National Park and renamed. The name change perplexes many Costa Ricans, who revere the name of Santa Rosa as a symbol of national independence. This is because the Santa Rosa farmhouse is a testament to two major battles for Costa Rican independence and democracy, one in 1856 and the other in 1955.

The hacienda is reminiscent of the lofty and larger Osaka Castle in Japan, as both stand on a stone mound and have beautifully sloping rooftops and chunky wooden rooms, contributing to the feel of a garrison. The hacienda is modest, dusty, and remote, yet more Costa Ricans visit this site than any other in their country. The history is directly relevant to United States citizens: the first battle was fought by Costa Rican expeditionary forces against an American, William Walker. After Walker led an insurrection in Nicaragua, he invaded Costa Rica at Santa Rosa. His goal was to annex Costa Rica as a slave territory of the United States or to form his own republic with five other nations of Central America. This was mixed in with the proposed creation of a Pacific–Atlantic waterway spanning Lake Nicaragua and the San Juan river, backed by US financier Cornelius Vanderbilt. The battle of Santa Rosa ensued,

Adam and Eve
The peanut-headed bug (*Fulgora laternaria*, above and below left), is a strange but gorgeous bug. It is a relative of cicadas, a homopteran. It is easily overlooked because it often sits on mottled bark under powdery pale gray forewings, but it can unfold the underwing eyespots to startle predators when threatened, and you may find around lights at night. The most bizarre part is its head, which resembles a peanut. No one knows what this protruberance is for; perhaps it imitates a lizard's head for defense. Legend says that if a girl is stung by this bug (which is not known for stinging), she has to sleep with her boyfriend within a day or she'll die.

Petroglyphs

The jaguar image was a major symbol in pre-Columbian petroglyphs, jade, and gold figures. This stone petroglyph of a jaguar (right) has a full stomach of various animals. The image's head is to the right, and the front and back limbs are the vertical reliefs.

The stone is located above a bat cave in the Guanacaste National Park, easily accessible from Santa Rosa casona. The bats in this cave include insectivores, nectivores, frugivores, and possibly blood-lapping bats. 65% of cattle on farms across Costa Rica are bitten each night by the common vampire bat (*Desmodus rotundus*). These bats are capable of running on all fours after fluttering close to their target. Travellers are adequately protected by windows and mosquito nets. Cattle can be protected from vampire bats by using nets and vampiricida, a bat poison-laced anticoagulant.

and Walker was pushed back to Nicaragua by valiant Costa Ricans. The retreat was made possible by a young drummer boy, Juan Santamaria, who became a hero of Costa Rica when he gave up his life to set fire to the building where Walker hid and flushed him out. After another round of action near Lake Nicaragua, Walker gave himself up to a US warship. He eventually met his end in Honduras after naming himself president there.

The second battle of Santa Rosa was part of an attempted coup in 1955. This occurred after Costa Rica had abolished its army in 1948, in favor of spending the resources on education. This time a Costa Rican militia had to be drummed up to beat back the Nicaraguan mercenaries of dictator Anastasio Somoza. The mercenaries tried to overthrow the Ferrer government with the backing of some Costa Rican politicians. The successful action of the militia, just outside what is now the entrance to the Guanacaste National Park, turned the tide. Despite air cover from Somoza's air force, the Costa Ricans won.

Trails

The most accessible forest walkway in the park is the 1km/0.6mi loop Sendero Natural or "nature trail" that starts to the left of the hacienda and rapidly immerses you in a variety of forests. You can also take this easy gravel trail at night to spot the active nocturnal animals. A large pre-Columbian petroglyph of a jaguar rests intact where it can easily be seen via a small stone bridge over a bat cave. A few more petroglyphs are scattered in the river below. (You can jump down to see the bats roosting. However, do not enter the water as these three bat species may carry a deadly virus communicable to humans.)

On the other side of the park, on an accessible boulder field northwest of Maritza Biological Station, by Orosi Volcano, 800 petroglyphs can be explored.

Other than Sendero Natural, the significant network of forest paths around the Santa Rosa field station is well-known only to researchers who have a detailed map, which is not sold in stores. Pathway entrances may be hidden from casual

Groomers

Shine a flashlight along a roadside by fields and open forests at night and you are likely to see the rose-colored glow of common pauraque eyes (*Nyctidromus albicollis*). This nightjar calls loudly at night in April. Its huge gaping mouth is designed to scoop up beetles and moths in brief flight, aided by long bristles that fan out from the beak. To groom these essential hairs, the central claw on its foot has evolved into a deep comb structure.

Restored tropical forest (below)

Tree Chickens

Ctenosaurs (*Ctenosaura similis,* female above and male opposite page) are common. These huge lumbering lizards are found anywhere from the ground to the treetops. They are varied in color and are similar to green iguanas (*Iguana iguana*) except that the ctenosaur can be told apart by the ring of cone-shaped scales on its tail. Iguanas are vegetarian; ctenosaurs eat a mix of veggies and baby animals. They are hunted outside conservation areas.

visitors in order to protect research activities and keep the animals wild.

A trail system for recreational hiking has not yet been established, although there are several 4WD access tracks used to reach the beaches and volcanoes. You can walk along these as well, but the walk could be quite long and the high temperatures are not moderated by shade, so it is better to get to outlying destinations by rental vehicle or taxi, either of which can be booked from Liberia, even if you are staying at Santa Rosa. If you are part of group with research links, you may be able to borrow one of the bicycles owned by field station staff. Check with the field station first for permission before driving down the restricted-access roads.

Naranjo Beach

Naranjo Beach is world-famous for Witch Rock, which curls great waves for surfers. However, watch out for severe rip currents. If you get caught in a rip current, swim parallel to the shore until the current's power dissipates, then swim back in. There are no lifeguards. Don't confuse this beautiful beach with Playa Naranjo on the Nicoya

Peninsula: this one has no resorts or hotels.

Olive ridley turtles (*Lepidochelys olivacea*) nest on the beach occasionally, sometimes in small *arribadas* (mass nestings).

There are two campsites, one at La Playa and one at El Estero near the estuary to the north, which is nearer Nancite Beach. Bring your own drinking water; the well water at La Playa should only be used for washing.

Naranjo Beach is 6km/4mi long, located at the end of a 4WD track 11km/6.8mi southwest of Santa Rosa field station. The route may be impassable during the wet season.

Nancite Beach

5km/3mi north of El Estero campground is Playa Nancite, the site of turtle *arribadas*, or mass nestings. Check with the Santa Rosa office before you go; the access is restricted to protect the turtles.

It is best to drive to Naranjo Beach and then walk to Nancite Beach—it takes six hours to walk from the Santa Rosa field station, through swampland, so the trip should not be taken lightly. Follow the directions above to Naranjo Beach and then continue

Ankle Care

Chiggers (*Eutrombicula*) are minute larvae of red mites whose bites produce pyramid-shaped eruptions that itched around our ankles for days. The chigger drops off almost immediately, after injecting saliva with protein-digesting enzymes designed for lizards, their normal hosts. The human body responds by encysting the saliva, without success, which then generates an ongoing reaction. Repel them effectively by dusting socks with powdered sulfur and avoid areas of vegetation favored by lizards. Applying alcohol is helpful in limiting secondary infection and cooling the irritation.

Crackers

Charles Darwin was
intrigued by the loud
clicking sounds produced by
the flying male Guatemalan
cracker, (*Hamadryas
guatemalena*, above), or
calico butterfly. Their veins
are adapted into sound
organs. The noises are
produced to chase away
other males from their home
territory. Look for these
sipping the sap of feeder
trees. Pierid butterflies
(below right) need various
mineral salts to make viable
offspring, so they sip mud.
The *Historis odius* butterfly
(right) drinks fruit juice,
sap, and dung. Look for
them resting on tree trunks,
imitating dead leaves. The
caterpillars eat cecropia
leaves (*Cecropia peltata*)
despite the *Azteca* ants that
are housed in the plant's
hollow limbs to defend it.
The caterpillars stay on
tiptoe to avoid the ants.

north along a small trail. Look for jaguar
spoor on the beach in the morning.

The offshore currents produce ideal
conditions for *arribadas* of olive ridley and two
other turtle species. This is one of two major
nesting sites for these small turtles along the
Pacific coast of Costa Rica, the other being
along Ostional beach northwest of Nosara on
the Nicoya Peninsula. The turtles arrive
somewhat unpredictably all year, and particularly between August and November in pulses
that tend to occur as the moon wanes into a

Liberia (above) offers a small Regional Museum where you can see stone carvings of animals from ancient times.

new moon. A handful of *arribadas* can occur during one season. 350 to 150,000 nests can be filled with eggs in one month, though the numbers are declining significantly.

Turtle watchers must follow several guidelines, or the turtles will turn back to the sea. The females are remarkably sensitive to any noise or moving shadows and you should stay inland from any incoming turtles. Remain completely quiet and use starlight, not flashlights, when looking for them. Once the female starts laying, you can come in close without disturbing her and use a weak red flashlight to watch the eggs being laid.

You are unlikely to see white-nosed coatis (*Nasua narica*) here. This is because white-faced capuchin monkeys (*Cebus capucinus*) have become more aggressive in their behavior on the isolated cove. Their occasional raids of the young in coatis nests changed into an all-out hunt that wiped out all coati juveniles in the area.

Valuing Education

The Costa Rican army was abolished in 1948, and the country has dedicated its funds to education rather than defense. Although school is free and compulsory, a few children cannot attend due to the remoteness of their homes. Most, like the child below, receive an excellent basic education.

Matapalo

A hive of activity is found around matapalo, or strangler fig, trees (*Ficus* sp., right). These houseplants and forest giants are not only major fruit sources that attract a host of monkeys, peccaries, agoutis, and Amazonian parrots, but their nooks and crannies are also home to whip scorpions (below), sac wing bats, day-active *Gonatodes* geckos, anole lizards, *Polistes* paper wasps, *Trigona* stingless bees, and millipedes. The matapalo starts life as a microscopic seed eaten away by fungi high up on another tree. It then sends down aerial roots, eventually outliving its support.

Cuajiniquil

The fishing village of Cuajiniquil is located near the Bahia Junquillal Wildlife Refuge and campground. The refuge is now within the Guanacaste park system. Try snorkeling and turtle-spotting around the bay, and keep an eye out for jellyfish.

Maritza Biological Station

Maritza is a secondary station of Guanacaste National Park east of the Interamerican Highway. The primary, fully-serviced settlement is at Santa Rosa now that the two parks have merged. This is not a primary ecotravel residence, as food is not generally available at Maritza. For visitors with research interests, it is possible to book accommodation in the bunk houses. Maritza is in the foothills of Cerro el Hacha, Orosi Volcano, and Cacao Volcano.

Creepy whip scorpions do not sting (below)

The Sendero Cacao trail leads to the cloud-forest-veiled summit of the 1,659m/5,442ft Cacao Volcano. The 18km/11mi trail takes about nine hours round-trip through old pastureland and rainforest, with a distant view of Lake Nicaragua and its resident sharks. Until recently, these sharks were considered freshwater sharks, but it has been found that they enter the lake from the east, along the San Juan River rapids.

The easier way to approach within 2.5km/1.5mi of the Cacao Volcano summit is by 4WD to the remote Cacao Field Station, which is 14km/8.7mi from Quebrada Grande.

To reach Maritza from San José, drive north on the Interamerican Highway 42km/26mi and turn east at the Cuajiniquil signpost (away from Cuajiniquil). Maritza Station is 17km/10.5mi up this dirt road.

Orosi Volcano and Llano de los Indios

Petroglyphs are scattered across the boulder scree below Orosi Volcano, 1.5km/0.9mi northeast of the Maritza Biological Station in the Pedregal section of the park. These can be reached by trail from the station. These are pre-Columbian images dating from 500 CE. At one time, this community's

Jumpers

The jeweled green and copper colors are gorgeous camouflage for the female top-of-the-canopy jumping spider *Eris aurantia* (below left). The strikingly garbed male performs a dance for the female by buzzing his tail like a cell phone on silent vibrate. You are likely to see the male *Lyssomanes* sp. jumping spider among the understory vegetation around you in the dry forest. It dances for females by moving its legs in a semaphore pattern of signals (below). Jumping spiders are not known to be venomous. They are curious and have excellent vision and intelligence for their size.

Pioneers

Cecropia trees (*Cecropia* sp., right) are the most common pioneer species, and you will soon learn to recognize their umbrella-like leaves. They grow quickly to establish themselves in light gaps in open disturbed areas of the forest. Cecropias favor speed over defense. Instead of killing half their predators by producing energy-demanding tannin defense compounds, cecropias use the energy for growth instead. You are likely to see Cecropia trees with holes in the leaves as a result, but the trees grow too fast for the chewers to compromise them. Biting ants make their homes within each branch node and protect the tree from browsers.

trading and communications connections may have extended south into South America and north into Mexico.

The Hacienda los Inocentes Wildlife Conservation and Recreation Center is an ecolodge located north of the park border on the edge of Orosi Volcano (506-679-9190; see page 17).

Rincón de la Vieja National Park

Guanacaste National Park sits on the foothills of the Rincón de la Vieja volcano detailed in chapter four.

Palo Verde National Park

Birdwatchers flock to the raised platforms set up in this park to watch the incredible variety of waterfowl during their migrations. In January and February, the crocodile-filled Tempisque River basin floods, attracting more migratory waterfowl than anywhere else in Central America.

There are a quarter of a million individual birds at the height of the migration, including 60 migratory species from North America. The 300 species participating in the migration include ducks, spoonbills, and herons, and, in the drier woodland, banded wrens and black-headed trogons.

Birds are food for the endangered American crocodiles (*Crocodylus acutus*), which here are rarely more than 13ft/4m, one half their potential length. Their size is limited because they were severely hunted until a few decades ago, and so the specimens surviving today tend to be young. The more common spectacled caiman (*Caiman crocodilus*) grows to 8ft/2.5m. Both are found in Pacific and Caribbean lowland swamps, rivers, and mangroves, here among the mud turtles (*Kinosternon scorpioides*).

The Organization of Tropical Studies, OTS (OET in Spanish), runs a field station in Palo Verde National Park to study its fifteen types of floodplain, chaparral, and dry forest habitats. OTS leads excellent guided walks and boat tours that can be booked at the field station where you can also stay (www.ots.ac.cr).

One way to view birds during the migratory peak is to travel by boat from Puerto Humo and Bebedero through the flooded river system for about 6km/3.7mi to the Tempisque River dock (506-671-1072; 506-671-1290 for the Tempisque Conservation area in Bagaces. OTS and many San José tour companies also offer boat tours). At this time of the year, however, birds are widely spread out, unlike in the dry season when they cluster, and a better approach may be to see the nesting birds clustered on Isla de Pajaros. Anhingas, roseate spoonbills, glossy ibises, egrets, and storks seek the protection of this island for their nests. The surrounding wetlands provide nesting sites

Jabiru

The jabiru (*Jabiru mycteria*) is a waterbird that has a prehistoric flying silhouette that looks like a dinosaur with an upturned snout. It is enormous, with a wingspan over 2.7m/8ft. Its wings and body are white, distinguishing it from the black flight feathers of the smaller wood stork (*Mycteria americana*). The jabiru is as majestic as it is ugly, with black bare skin on neck and head, trimmed with a lower red band of skin that swells as its crop fills. The nest trees stink from exuberant parents regurgitating their meals of mice, fish, and lizards for their chicks.

Priceless

The roseate spoonbill (*Ajaia ajaja*) comes from one of the most ancient bird families, evolving perhaps 60 million years ago. It is part of the ibis and spoonbill family and uses its bill paddles like a metal detector, with sensitive nerves in the spoon that trigger snapping closure when they detect small fish and snails. Their feathers were used for hat ornaments by Europeans and North Americans. By 1910, the feathers of four roseate spoonbills were worth more than an ounce of gold. Hunting completely decimated rookery after rookery in the United States, with a few left in Central and South America. Their numbers are now starting to increase again.

for jacanas, limpkins, grebes, rails, bitterns, and gallinules. You can reach within 46m/50 yd of the island by boat during the wet season (call 506-671-1062 to book a boat with the park administration). There is kayaking around the island, or you can walk from the park headquarters along a trail that leads to a lookout across from the island. In the wet season the trail can be flooded.

There are several trails throughout the park. Sendero Querque starts at the hacienda where guides are based, and leads through mature dry forest to the Sendero Cerros Calizos. You can reach a good lookout by taking the Sendero Cactus west from Sendero Cerros Calizos. During the dry season you can watch wildlife from this trail at the cistern. Look at the fig trees for roosting bat colonies.

The park gets its name from palo verde trees (*Parkinsonia aculeata*) that grow in marshland, decked with bindweed (*Ipomoea*) and interspersed with rushes. Palo verde have chlorophyll not just in their leaves, but in their branches and trunk surfaces, allowing them to photosynthesize even when their leaves have fallen. Most trees lose their leaves in the dry season from November to March, like those in the Guanacaste National Park. One difference between parks is that Palo Verde roads are less accessible during the wet season.

Don't be surprised if you see cattle in the park. In Palo Verde, cattle have been used since 1991 to control introduced jaragua grass, although grazing is restricted and occurs primarily during the peak of the wet season. Before ruminants were introduced, annual fires were used to clear the way for new growth, a holdover from pasture management practices. However, this tall grass burned so hot that woody species were eliminated, preventing the regeneration of the natural forest.

Rancho Humo is an ecolodge, with a restaurant overlooking the Tempisque River and easy access to Palo Verde. The lodge offers guided tours of Barra Honda, Palo Verde, and Guaitil (tel 506-255-2463, fax 506-255-3573). There is a small airstrip nearby. Bagaces is 30km/19mi and 1.5 hours away.

With advance booking, you can arrange excellent tours and boat rides, bunkhouse accommodation, and meals at OTS (tel 506-524-0628 or 506-542-0629 or 506-524-0607, US tel 919-984-5774, fax 919-684-5661; www.ots.ac.cr, paloverde@ots.as.cr).

The park headquarters are a kilometer away from OTS, 9km/5.6mi from the park entrance, and also offer basic accommodation and meals (tel/fax 506-200-0215, or contact the Tempisque Conservation Area office in Bagaces at 506-671-1062 or 506-671-1290). Bring your own bottled water.

Lomas Barbudal Biological Reserve

Located just north of Palo Verde park, this plunging series of river valleys, dry forest, gallery rainforest, and savanna provides a beautiful backdrop for this relatively

Nightlife

It is worth taking a guided night walk to spot as many creatures as you can. Use the reflection of your flashlight, aimed from your eye-level, to see retina reflections from mammals and spiders. Creatures of the night include caterpillars (above), the northern cat-eyed snake, (*Leptodeira septentrionalis*, below left), and night-blooming scented flowers (top two images) visited by bats (center).

*Gulf of Papagayo beach
(right)*

undeveloped, small but important reserve, which is surrounded by drier farmland. Over time, there are plans to link this reserve with seven other conservation areas including Palo Verde to provide a sustainable base for all wild organisms in the area.

You can see the remarkable synchronized mass flowerings of golden Cortés trees (*Tabebuia ochracea*) here. This occurs when trees burst into mass bloom in one or more "big bangs" towards the end of the dry season, usually during March, which last less than a week. These bursts produce a glut of communal seeds that overwhelm predators and ensure that some new shoots survive. Cortés wood is one-and-a-half times as dense as water. It is one of the hardest and most durable woods of the Neotropics and as a result is used to make bowls and furniture. Stingless bees pollinate Cortés blossoms, while hummingbirds and xylocopids rob the nectar without pollinating. All areas of Costa Rican dry forests are home to bees whose hyperactivity has given them the name "killer bees." But these are only one of the 250 bee species and thousands of butterfly and moth species found in the park, including a large number of stingless and solitary bee varieties. Lomas Bardubal bees are said to amount to one-quarter of the world's bee species.

Listen for the "chachalaca" calls of the plain chachalaca (*Ortalis vetula*) as they creep through the undergrowth looking for fallen figs. The chachalaca is among the 130 bird species in this reserve, including jabiru storks, toucans, trogons, king vultures, endangered great curassows, and lineated woodpeckers. The waterbirds here include wood storks and black-bellied tree ducks.

Howler and white-faced capuchin monkeys frequent the park, and a long-term white-faced capuchin research project is in place to document how behavioral traditions form in these monkeys. Other mammals are harder to spot, but include white-nosed coatis, collared peccaries, and deer.

The reserve has many streams filled with tropical fish that decorate aquaria back home. You can snorkel to watch convict cichlids (*Cichlasoma nigro-fasciatum*) and green mollies (*Poecilia gilli*) in their wild homes at the Cabuyo "*poza*" or swimming hole.

The Visitor Center is 7km/4.3mi from the Interamerican Highway: turn south at the 221km marker, 17km/10.5mi northwest of Bagaces. Another entrance is located further to the south, about 3km/2mi northeast of the Palo Verde entrance station. Pick up trail maps from the Friends of Lomas Bardubal office in Bagaces.

Nicoya Peninsula

The long dry season and beautiful white beaches have helped make the northwest of Nicoya Peninsula Costa Rica's top resort

A Tico proprietor and her baby at Bar Acapulco on the beach just beyond the village of Puerto Soley, located in the northern Guanacaste area near La Cruz.

destination. The peninsula sits between the the Gulf of Papagayo to the north and the Gulf of Nicoya to the south and east. Although there are some coral reefs, most diving is around rock pinnacles that feature huge pelagics and manta rays, with a scattering of reef fish. There is turtle watching at Playa Ostional near Nosara and along Playa Grande near Tamarindo. *Arribadas* ("arrivals") of Pacific ridley sea turtles (*Lepidochelys olivacea*) come in unpredictable waves several times a year to Playa Ostional, peaking July through November. Leatherbacks come to Playa Grande in the Las Baulas National Marine Park from November to April. The opening of Costa Rica's second international gateway, Daniel Oduber Quiros airport near Liberia, has made the area more accessible. There is also an airstrip at Tamarindo and other peninsula outposts for local flights. The extreme pace of the boom has crammed three quarters of the country's hotel rooms into small pockets of coastline, and this has generated significant environmental degradation despite conservation laws.

Bahia Culebra, Playas del Coco, Flamingo, and Tamarindo are some of the destinations where sun, sand, diving, fishing, golf, and coastal wildlife are to be found. Hotel Punta Islita and Florblanca offer luxury ecotravel accommodations and authentic activities. Some visitors gravitate inland to Guatil, a small village 11km/7mi east of Santa Cruz, known for its stalls displaying the region's Chorotega pottery. The pottery is the specialty of the region's Chorotega people, whose pre-Columbian jade carvings and ceramics have fascinated archeologists.

The peninsula itself, beyond the beaches, has been deforested for cattle ranching since colonial times, so there are

Shelter Booster

The Nicoya Peninsula supports many fishing boats (left). The fish stocks are hatched in the mangroves cloaking the coast. Red mangrove roots shelter fish fry and are also home to corals, sponges, oysters, crabs, and octopus. These all depend on the highly branched root system for protection. The organism that triggers branching of red mangrove roots is a wood-boring isopod *Sphaeroma terebrans*. This creature leaves holes and kills roots, but overall may chew its way to creating an entire ecosystem by stimulating much more branching of the roots than would otherwise occur.

Bluffers

Many house plants come from the dry tropical forests and rainforests of Costa Rica (right). Many of the spotted colors and Swiss cheese holes that appeal to us probably evolved as a defense rather than for ornamentation. A plant with colored spots and stripes mimics patterns caused by a deficiency in key minerals. Herbivores will then avoid it. Herbivores also avoid leaves that have deep holes or white marks where the most succulent leaf parts lie, as this signifies to a scanning browser that the most highly nutritious areas have been chewed by an earlier visitor, and another plant would be a better bet. In this case, however, the predator has been fooled.

only a few small but fascinating conservation areas to visit. As you move south from the drier flat northern plain (which used to be dry tropical forest before being made into pasture land), emerald hills rise up, surrounded by patches of moist coastal forest filled with evergreens and weeping palms. Mangroves line the Gulf of Nicoya, which is dotted with small, wild islands.

Activities and Places to Stay on the Nicoya Peninsula

Barra Honda National Park

Barra Honda is the site of some ancient calcite caverns good for spelunking. The caverns have been hollowed out by water acting on a 60-million-year-old ocean reef formation. The reef created the limestone that later uplifted to form the mountain of Cerro Barra Honda. Travertine marble can also be found above ground at Las Cascadas, a further 8km/5mi. The limestone gives clues to the prehistory of the area: part of a mastodon fossil was recently found in a riverbed nearby.

Keep your eye out for dry-forest animals: howler monkeys, white-faced capuchin monkeys, coati, armadillos, and a variety of birds including orange-fronted parakeets. Look for the round, prickly fruit of the monkey's comb on the ground. This fruit contains enough animal hormones to act as natural birth control, depressing the population of herbivores, including monkeys, and thus giving some relief to the tree.

Nicoya Cave was used as a burial place about 2,000 years ago. Evidence from this site demonstrates that the practices of peoples in Costa Rica at this time were linked to those of contemporary peoples in South America and to later cultures in Mexico.

These are among the most pristine caves open for exploration anywhere in the world. The only cave that is accessible to the ecotraveller without specialized equipment is La Terciopelo, named after a fer-de-lance snake that was once found dead in this cave. You need to make a reservation at least a week in advance, as two guides are needed to belay you down into the cave safely. Once you are roped up, you descend a cable ladder vertically for 40m/100ft into

Chorotega

Beautiful ceramics dating back to 1000 BCE have been found in the Guanacaste, including ritual figurines, stamps, glazed bowls, and motifs featuring bats, jaguars, turtles, and birds. The plumed serpent (and tail of the quetzal) symbolized spirit flowing through matter. The Chorotega found in the Guanacaste today were strongly connected with Olmec and Aztec cultures, from which they apparently had fled, displacing original Guanacastans. A rich trade of pottery and jade developed, based around village and city living, with an agriculture of maize, cotton, and cacao. Pottery was burnished until it shimmered like a mirror. As the theocracies to the north became more militaristic, the value placed on jade symbolism declined. However, the Chorotega culture continued to evolve, the only culture within Costa Rica with a written language and Mayan calendar.

Surf's up!

the magical world of "shark's teeth," "popcorn," and "fried egg" calcite (calcium carbonate) formations. Calcium carbonate is the same substance that forms eggshells, bones, coral, and marble. One of the guides will show you the vast chamber of beautiful stalactites and stalagmites. In La Terciopelo, the musical notes of "The Organ" can be struck, resonating because these stalactites and stalagmites form hollow structures similar to pipes. The hollow pipes are of increasing length, and when tapped in succesion, make a natural musical progression of audible notes. Bats are relatively uncommon in the caves except in Pozo Hediondo (Stinkpot Hole), named after the odor of guano they produce. Endemic species in the cave system include a blind fish and a blind salamander. There are 42 caverns to consider, 19 of which have been explored, including Santa Ana and the Hall of Pearls, Mushroom Hall, and snow-white La Trampa (the Trap).

The park trail system leads to the caves and beyond, and also to a dramatic lookout, or *ventador*, from Cerro Barra Honda, 445m/1,459ft above sea level. This is about 3km/2mi from the end of the dirt road and start of the trail (fork right to Sendero Cevernas). The limestone on this mountain has eroded into remarkable forms, some very sharp and convoluted. From here you can look across the Gulf of Nicoya to Chirra Island.

To reserve a tour or get permission to visit one of the caverns using your own equipment, call Parque Nacional Barra Honda (506-685-5267, 506-233-5284, or 506-671-1062) or contact the Tempisque Park Service, the overall area coordinators. You can camp in the park for a nominal fee or stay in Nicoya.

The Gulf of Papagayo

The Gulf of Papagayo has over two dozen dive sites for reef fish and large pelagic fish within easy boat reach of Playa Hermosa and Playas del Coco. Flamingo Beach is a hotspot for marlin sport fishing and boating activities. Unfortunately, Flamingo Beach and Bahia Culebra are associated with some of the most concentrated hotel development and environmental problems, so please choose carefully if you decide to stay in the area rather than go to a more eco-friendly destination on the peninsula. Angel fish, manta rays, white tip reef sharks, and schools of grunts and yellowtails abound. Bat Island, or *Murciélagos*, is further to the north and tends to attract bull sharks, pompano, and wahoo. The rock pinnacles of Catalina Islands are home to huge manta rays, as well as marlins and mahi-mahi. Coco-nose, eagle, and manta rays are best seen between March and

Scavengers

Brown pelicans (*Pelicanus occidentalis*, below) are the only species of pelican that hunts with dramatic vertically plunging dives. After capturing the fish, they rise to the surface and drain two gallons of water from their pouch. Then they point the drained bill up and swallow the catch. They are often robbed of their catch by bold gulls before they get the chance to swallow. Brown pelicans are often found around boats and garbage, but are generally looking for scraps rather than stealing from fishermen's live catches.

North–South Switch

Central American wooly opossums (*Caluromys derbianus,* above) are among the marsupials found in South and Central America and Australia. The Virginian opossum migrated to North America when the Costa Rican land bridge was formed. Opossums originated with armadillos, tree sloths, and anteaters in Gondwanaland, the supercontinent of South America, Africa, India, Australia, New Zealand, and Antarctica.

November. Whale sharks, bus-sized beauties that are not dangerous, may be seen in the region. Spinner dolphins, humpback whales, and even orcas may also be spotted. Bill Beard Diving Safaris offers PADI, NAUI, NASE, and IANTD Nitrox courses and operates out of Playa Hermosa (US toll-free tel 877-853-0538, toll 954-453-5044, fax 954-453-9740; www.billbeardcostarica.com, costarica@diveres.com) and Rich Coast Diving offers PADI-certified dive boats from Playas del Coco (tel 506-670-0176, US tel 1-800-4DIVING; www.richcoastdiving.com, dive@richcoastdiving.com). The Four Seasons has just opened a resort at Peninsula Papagayo, among the many resorts with dive options.

Tamarindo Wildlife Refuge, Playa Grande, and Las Baulas Marine Park

Giant soft-shelled leatherback turtles, *las baulas* (*Dermochelys coriacea*), may be seen nesting on Playa Grande and Playa Langosta (Lobster Beach) in Las Baulas Marine Park from late October to February, just north of the Matapalo Estuary near Tamarindo. Leatherbacks are the largest turtles in the world. Their average weight is 350kg/772lb and length is 1.5m/5ft, with one male measuring over 3m/10ft long. Playa Grande is one of the major sites for this turtle to nest on the east side of the Pacific Rim.

Las Baulas National Marine Park was established to protect the turtles in 1993 and is one of the most accessible turtle watching sites in the North West. This park, and the smaller Tamarindo Wildlife Refuge around the adjoining Matapalo Estuary, offer trails through mangroves and dry forest, where crocodiles, monkeys, and

True Colors

Many butterflies, including the malachite butterfly (*Siproeta stelenes,* below) have colored scales on their wings. However, many species such as the blue morpho have uncolored, clear scales that create brilliant colors another way: these scales diffract light waves into intense colors when a sunbeam hits them at a specific angle, rather like a prism. The type of diffraction grating used by butterfly scales to produce color has been dated back at least 350 million years by a University of Sydney researcher looking into the seed-shrimp *Myodocopid ostracod.*

Bubble Fishing

The peninsula waves (right) hide much. Look out to sea and you may spot one of several species of shearwaters at work, highly strategic hunters that collaborate with dolphins to net their dinner. First, dolphins occasionally swim aggressively in superpods, in which they can force fish shoals upwards, away from the safer darkness and into the solid ceiling of the ocean surface. The dolphins then cut off a splinter-group of panicked fish by blowing air to form an encircling "bubble net." The fish form a tight bait ball that is their only defense as they reach the surface. Then, huge numbers of shearwaters and other hunters join the dolphins in a feeding frenzy. Although the bait ball appears to be a huge meal, when attacked it dissolves like a bead curtain into scintillating evaders. Those that survive eventually descend back to the depths. The bait ball strategy exemplifies new theories of evolutionary biology and mathematics, which claim that it is an advantage for individuals to collaborate.

200 species of birds may be spotted. You can rent a boat from Tamarindo to explore the mangroves.

Night access to the beach is limited to a specific number of visitors who must go with licensed guides, so book your tour with your hotel or with the Matapalo Conservation Association, which opens at 6 PM east of Las Tortugas. Call the Parks Service, 506-643-0470, for more information. For turtle watching details, please refer to page 25.

The protection of the turtles here has switched the turtle economy from egg-poaching to turtle-guiding and -guarding activities. Unfortunately, turtle numbers are plummeting just as tourist numbers are soaring, and the gene pool is now so small it may be unsustainable. It is projected that leatherbacks may go extinct within the next twenty years if emergency measures are not put in place. This is because long-line fishing practices drown this species of turtle as they follow migration routes through commercial fishing grounds. In addition, light pollution scares females away, and egg poaching actively continues in other areas. Plastics in the ocean are a major hazard for leatherbacks, because the turtles confuse plastic for the jellyfish that they normally eat.

Turtle conservation focuses on research and on increasing the hatchling survival rates of each nest. Researchers carefully excavate nest eggs and move the eggs to a protected area guarded from poachers or predators. These eggs are rebuilt into a nest that duplicates the original, because the layers and orientation of each egg are vitally important to the development and sex of the offspring. Conservation workers watch the eggs until they hatch, and then release the hatchlings and help them to the ocean. Saving even a single hatchling can make a difference at this point.

El Mundo de la Tortuga is a turtle museum with information about turtle conservation and ecology that is worth a visit.

There are many places to stay in Tamarindo, fast-growing with hotel development that is, unfortunately, not necessarily in tune with environmentally sensitive policies. Some smaller hotels are delightful. See www.tamarindo.com.

For ecotravellers who want an authentic experience in Tamarindo, the Sueno del Mar Bed and Breakfast right on the beach of

Land Seekers

Tropical frogs are moving their life cycles gradually from water to land. Unlike most North American frogs, which lay eggs in water, many Costa Rican frogs perch their eggs on leaves, where the eggs then hatch into tadpoles. Some leafborne eggs are laid above water so the tadpoles fall into streams below. Others hatch directly on land into minute froglets. A few are carried by their parents to well-defended bromeliad reservoirs. One poison dart frog even feeds her canopy-dwelling tadpoles with her own infertile eggs.

Phrynohyas venulosa (below left) hangs around outdoor plumbing and is among the amphibians with a toxic arsenal. When threatened it exudes a poisonous mucus that is, at the very least, a nasty skin irritant. The giant toad (*Bufo marinus*) can produce an aerosol spray from its parotid glands that is toxic enough to kill a dog.

Survivors

The nocturnal giant cockroach (*Blaberus giganteus*, right) is a soft-shelled forest star. Cockroaches are so sensitive to vibrations that they are aware of earthquakes long before we detect them. The two cerci, or rear appendages, that you can see are thought to explain one reason for cockroaches' special success and their intact survival as a species for 300 million years. Cockroaches use their cerci to sense what is going on behind them, feeling vibrations that alert them to food or danger behind, and with their antennae working in front. The cerci are linked to a nerve ganglion in the tail, so that their impulses do not need to get to the brain before the cockroach can react. This makes for lightning reflexes.

Playa Langosta has a natural focus. Start your eco-adventure from this Spanish colonial style home and *casitas*, surrounded by nature. Soak in the picturesque pool overlooking the waves, snorkel (with supplied equipment), explore the San Francisco estuary with a guide, go horseback riding, or simply soak in the atmosphere of this delightful paradise. The rustic breakfasts here are well renowned. Tamarindo is only minutes away, and turtle-watching, diving, and land-based excursions are within easy reach. This small hotel is in demand, so book well in advance. (tel/fax 506-653-0284, www.sueno-del-mar.com, innkeeper@sueno-del-mar.com)

Tamarindo can be accessed by air or by road in a couple of ways. You can fly in to Liberia international airport and drive, or fly directly to the Tamarindo air strip from San José and Liberia. You can travel by road from Liberia via Guardia, Filadelfia, Belén Huacas, and Villa Real. The other road route is via Santa Cruz via Villa Real. The second route may still be significantly unpaved, so check out your options before you decide which way to go.

Ostional Wildlife Reserve

Small olive ridley turtles, or *lora Lepidochelys olivacea*, may crowd the beaches around Norasa, protected by the Refugio Nacional de Vida Silvestre Ostional. Playa Ostional to the north joins Playa Nosara and Playa Guiones to the south to create one of the nine sites in the world where their *arribadas* occur. Half a million turtles massed at Ostional in November 1995 during one of the largest known *arribadas* in recent history. An *arribada*, or "arrival," is a synchronized mass nesting event occurring several times a year. Another *arribada* site is found at Playa Nancite.

Some *arribadas* occur three to four nights after the full moon, but others occur out of the lunar cycle and the triggers are complex and therefore difficult to predict. They occur year-round but peak between June and

Turtles in Danger

Tons of plastic grocery bags that end up in the oceans are mistaken by leatherback turtles for jellyfish, their main food. Their walnut-sized brains cannot process the new threat quickly enough to survive. Many then eat the plastic, resulting in death from gut blockages or drowning. Leatherbacks descend to an incredible 1,220m/4,000ft to find the jellyfish. They also migrate across long-line fishing grounds, and become caught in the commercial catches; egg poaching is also an ongoing threat. Local light pollution from resort hotels is also extremely disturbing to all turtles, which nest under cover of complete darkness and now rarely return to beaches that are developed, including Playa Tamarindo. No flash photographs or regular flashlights are allowed on Playa Grande at night to keep this beach inviting. It is the last nesting site in the vicinity.

Dead trees (left) provide nesting sites for many bird, insect, and mammal species

Mangroves

Mangroves detoxify thousands of tons of pollution, provide breeding grounds for a large percentage of commercial fish species, and colonize salty lands. Snorkel-like black mangrove *Avicennia* roots (see page 1) breathe the air and can grow above oil pollution. The stilt prop roots of red mangroves (*Rhizophora harrisonii*) reduce wave energy above the mud surface. Mangrove tree crabs (*Aratus pisonii*) live in the canopy and *Pseudomyrmex* ants live in the hollow twigs. The fluted buttresses of tea mangroves (*Pelliciera rhizophorae*) stabilize the mud, their branches protected by *Azteca* ants. Red mangroves are viviparous (right), with pre-shooted seeds designed for colonization. These float intact to new lands. When they arrive on land after their ocean voyage, the seed spikes respond to the change in osmotic pressure between salt and fresh water, and switch from horizontal boat to vertical, rooting anchor.

December. Once the synchronized event begins, the little turtles come in droves, day and night, swarming slowly up the beaches and crawling over one another to reach the upper part of the beach where females choose to nest.

Significant poaching resulted in plummeting numbers of turtles, made worse by major coastal development. In 1987, the problem was turned on its head by allowing Ostional residents to harvest eggs during the first 36 hours of each *arribada*, after which time the eggs were protected. This improved the situation for both the turtles and the villagers in the longer term. Now, each family is limited to 200 eggs a season, and the eggs can only be sold at bars licensed to carry them. The local population is motivated to protect the hatchlings, as these secure their future income. Occasionally other species of turtle nest around Ostional, including huge leatherbacks (*Dermochelys coriacea*) and Pacific green turtles (*Chelonia mydas*). Turtle watching guidelines are detailed on page 25.

You can rent a boat from Santa Marta to travel up the small Montaña and Nosara Rivers to look for the wildlife, including 100 species of birds. The ranger station (506-680-0167) is in Ostional village, and you'll need to register here or with the turtle cooperative in order to visit the beach (Asociacion de Desarrollo de Ostional, or ADIO, 506-682-0470). Volunteers may find projects to participate in. The Sea Turtle Research Station at the University of Costa Rica runs research programs at Playa Ostional (506-682-0267).

However, check the status of the reserve before you depart. The locals and scientists have been feuding divisively over the practices associated with the use of turtle funds. This is despite the success of the overall conservation efforts that places this among the most effective turtle conservation stories.

Access is via Nicoya, or there is an airstrip at Bocas de Nosara. Along the coast between Nosara and Cabo Blanco is the recommended ecotraveller's nature spa resort, Hotel Punta Islita. This luxury lodge offers a wide range of ecoadventure options with a unique Tico ambiance due to its Costa Rican ownership. River kayaking, eco-safaris, sunset panga rides, and cultural excursions to the local community are part of the way of life here. There is also a spa, beach club, 1492 restaurant, and private outdoor jacuzzis and plunge pools to relax and rejuvenate guests, while surrounded by nature. (tel 506-290-4259, fax 506-232-2183, www. hotelpuntaislita.com, info@ hotelpuntaislita.com.)

Cabo Blanco Biological Reserve

This reserve is relatively inaccessible to the public, although there are some forested trails along Sendero Danes and Sendero Secuo that lead to the beach. It is

Diving in Tamarindo

Diving and snorkeling along the Pacific coast can be a fantastic experience; you'll find a scattering of gorgeous reef fish and many large schooling fish. The better diving options are generally to the north in the Gulf of Papagayo. The Agua Rica Diving Center in downtown Tamarindo offers snorkeling and dive tours, including to Catalina Island (tel/fax 506-653-0094).

Unfortunately, many coral reefs have been completely wiped out by extreme natural and human-induced effects, including storms, coastal development, and runoff from deforestation and fertilizers. The level of sediment can be high. The dominant coral, *Pocillopora* sp., has disappeared from many sites, but successful experiments with transplanting live *Pocillopora* into damaged sites show that restoration is feasible.

Red tides of toxic algae have increased in intensity along the entire Pacific coast of Costa Rica. The phytoplankton and cyanobacteria *Pyrodinium bahamense* var. *compressum* and *Gymnodinium catenatum* create toxic waters and are eaten by shellfish. These can cause paralysis when the shellfish are consumed by people. The water itself is also toxic and should be avoided when these algae are present.

Nicaragua

Some wonderful ecotravel destinations are opening up just across the border in Nicaragua. Morgan's Rock Hacienda and Ecolodge is north of Guanacaste and is a surfside ecolodge with management connections to Lapa Rios in Corcovado. (tel 506-257-0766, fax 800-866-2609, www.morgansrock.com, info@morgansrock.com)

a historic reserve in that it was the first one in Costa Rica, founded in 1963.

If you can form a group, you can stay at the San Miguel Marine Research Center (tel 506-645-5277 or 506-645-5890). This is a marine station founded by the US researchers who started the San Luis Ecolodge. A minibus from Montezuma runs three times a day to Cabo Blanco and back.

North of Malpaís and close to Cabo Blanco is the intimate luxury ecohotel, Florblanca Resort. Its nature-centered focus is ideal for ecotravellers interested in an exotic getaway with a Costa Rican flair.

Florblanca offers half-day guided hikes of the Cabo Blanco Nature Reserve, as well as surfing, fishing, a yoga and Pilates studio, a gym, horseback riding, and bike rides. The resident guide is a trained biologist and there is an excellent open-air restaurant. To get there, you can drive or fly to Tambor airstrip from San José. (tel 506-640-0232, fax 506-640-0226, www.florblanca.com, florblanca@racsa.co.cr).

Curú Wildlife Refuge

The small area of Curú Wildlife Refuge contains so many diverse habitats that it has an amazing nineteen species of bats alone. (Most of the bats are frugivores; the primary species is *Artibeus jamaicensis*.) During the dry season it can be easier to spot wildlife than in the wet season, when leaves obscure the line of sight—although it can get very hot.

The best waterholes to spot game such as white-tailed deer (*Odocoileus virginianus*) are at Organos and St. Teresa Arriba, and the best waterhole for birds is El Tanque. Spider monkeys (*Ateles geoffroyi*) were re-introduced to this refuge in 1992 to join the already present howler monkeys and white-faced capuchins. A 500-meter-wide wildlife

Right: Brown pelican

corridor was drawn up in 1994 connecting this refuge with Cerro Frío. This is part of an important plan to link the mosaic of fragments found in this region and increase the sustainable base for many larger-territory species.

Curú beach is a good site for rock pools and snorkeling. In addition to algae, you can find coral (*Portites astereoides*), anthozoa (*Pacifigorgia* sp.), and hydroids (*Lytocarpus nuttingi*). The fish include the exquisite Cortez damsel (*Pomacentrus rectifranum*), Cortez rainbow wrasse (*Thalassoma lucansanum*), and spotted rose snapper (*Lutjanus guttatus*).

Close to Curú Wildlife Refuge, north of Paquera, is Bahía Luminosa, a very reasonable small hotel founded by a retired mariner. The hotel offers diving, snorkeling, boating, and nature activities. This haven for boating and ecotravellers overlooks Bright Bay, after which it is named. Fish from your catch and from local fishermen is cooked divinely in the restaurant or served sushi style. Fly to Tambor or drive from San José via Puntarenas car ferry. (tel 506-641-0386, tropics@sol.racsa.co.cr, www.bahia-luminosa.com, marine fVHF channel 16)

Isla Tortuga is 3.2km/2mi offshore of Curú. Day cruises to the island for snorkeling, beach fun, and pampering depart from Bahía Luminosa or Puntarenas. Puntarenas cruises and sailing adventures are run by several companies including Calypso Cruises (tel 506-256-2727, US tel 1-866-978-5177; fax 506-256-6767, www.calypso cruises.com, info@calypsocruises.com).

Gulf of Nicoya

The River Tempisque spills from Palo Verde National Park into the mangroves and mud flats of the Gulf of Nicoya. Look for white

Ear Fruit
The legume seeds of the
endemic curly "ear fruit"
(above) of the Guanacaste
tree (*Enterolobium
cyclocarpum*) are eaten by
parrots, peccaries, tapir, and
cattle. Paradoxically, this
process is necessary for the
seeds to germinate: without
passage through the gut to
thin the imprisoning seed
coat, the seeds remain
dormant.

ibises, roseate spoonbills, anhingas, jabiru, and wood storks among the waders, but beware of the crocodiles. Mangrove hummingbirds are endemic and may be seen with mangrove vireos, mangrove warblers, and scrub flycatchers. Red mangroves (*Rhizophora harrisonii*) have stilt roots and Pacific mangroves (*Pelliciera rhizophorae*) have fluted buttresses and nectar-laden flowers visited by hummingbirds. (The incredible concentration of migratory waterbirds is discussed in the preceding section on Palo Verde.)

The Salina Bonilla near Colorado is a salt evaporation system that attracts sea and shorebirds at high tide and to roost. Wilson's plovers and black-necked stilts nest around the dikes.

Guayabo Island, Pajaros Island, and Negritos Island form a biological reserve with restricted public access. The ferry route from Puntarema to Paquera goes close enough to Guayabo Islands for a chance to see breeding boobies, brown pelicans, frigate birds, and wintering peregrine falcons. Frigate birds can also be found nesting at Chira Island.

Bird Coast: Costa Pajaros

The shoreline of the northeast side of the Gulf of Nicoya between Puntarenas and the Tempisque River is so crammed with waders that it is called the "bird coast." Two-thirds of the way north is La Ensenada Lodge (506-289-6655, www.laensanada. net) on accessible wetlands where you can spot frigate birds, pelicans, brown boobies, and ibises. This salt and fruit farm offers a multilingual guide, boat excursions to Pajaros Island, birdwatching along the Costa Pajaros, and horseback riding.

2

Monteverde

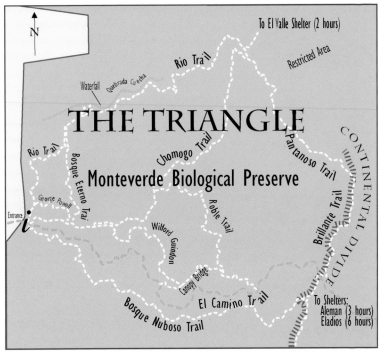

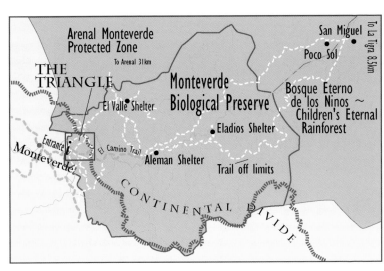

You will only find the total
green effect in light gaps, as
seen in this photograph of
Monteverde. This gap is
created when a big tree falls,
allowing light into the deep
understory, which stimulates
green growth below the
canopy. Most mature
rainforest, by contrast, is
dark. Under usual conditions,
it takes an effort to spot the
animals you expect to see:
they have adapted to hide
from predators. Patience,
quiet, and good listening
skills are essential to see
more.

*The San Luis area below
Monteverde offers quiet
birdwatching lanes
(previous page)*

Watch exquisite endemic hummingbirds sip from purple orchids.
Swing on a canopy bridge to spot
monkeys and treetop animals. Listen to the
wooden-bell-like calls of wattlebirds. Stop to
take in the panorama of velvet emerald
foothills. And soar on zip lines across the
canopy from one hilltop to another. All this
and more can be found in Monteverde.

The richness and diversity of draped
mosses, tiny orchids, bright bromeliads, and
epiphytic ferns in Monteverde is
outstanding. (Epiphytes are non-parasitic
hitchhiker plants that live on branches and
trunks.) One tree by a Monteverde canopy
walkway supports several dozen orchid
species. In fact, the epiphyte load is so high
that branches are often shed by trees when
loads become too extreme, opening up
more light gaps and increasing the variety
of plant and bird species. Emerald
toucanets, black guans, black-faced
solitaires, prong-billed barbets, and slate-
throated redstarts can be found in

Monteverde, as well as the resplendent quetzal, the forest's most sought-after bird.

The name Monteverde is synonymous with all that is successful about ecotravel, a model of the best that can be accomplished by combining community and conservation. Each year, tens of thousands of visitors explore the wild trails, canopy bridges, and zip lines of this huge cloud forest, while helping to ensure its longevity.

Focus on Wildlife: the Resplendent Quetzal

The three-foot, green tail feathers (left) of the resplendent quetzal (right) are so intense that they were once used to adorn Mayan headdresses. Quetzal sightings, a birdwatcher's dream, are now common from March to June when the quetzal is breeding. Quetzals eat wild avocados, insects, and lizards. Travellers to the cloud forests of Monteverde may spot this bird around wild avocado trees. There are 66 species of avocado tree in Costa Rica. The trees are protected in some parts of the country, including Monteverde, but elsewhere their survival is threatened, because their timber is highly desirable.

Many legends are told about quetzals. The names of the main gods of the Mayans and of the Toltecs, Kukulcan and Quetzalcoatl, are derived from the quetzal root word, which means "feathered serpent." This phrase describes the sine-wave created by the quetzal's tail as it flies through the cloud forest. According to a Guatemalan legend, large flocks of all-green quetzals flew down to a battlefield during the European conquest to keep vigil over the slain Mayans. It was here that the quetzal's breasts were stained blood-red for all time.

Quetzal feathers are no ordinary color. The incredible natural engineering of their

Bellbird Migrants

Listen for the notable sound of the three-wattled bellbird's (*Procnias tricarunculata*) wooden "bonk." This call echoes through the high-altitude (4,000 feet above sea level) rainforest during the breeding season from March to June. Later in the year, one can hear the bellbird at lower altitudes—both bellbirds and resplendent quetzals are altitudinal migrants. The courting dance of three-wattled bellbird pairs is initiated by a jumping male. The pair then changes places ritually. Ornithologists believe that bellbirds spend so much time singing and dancing because they have such easy access to abundant, fatty, sweet fruit that they need not devote much time to looking for food. Their low-protein diet means that the young take a long time to mature, necessitating greater secrecy about nest location. Only the female cares for the young.

microscopic feather layers fuels a whole travel industry and helps keep Monteverde alive. Color in nature comes from two major interactions. The first kind is seen in the quetzal's red breast, where colored pigments absorb some wavelengths of light (green) and allow others to pass through and be reflected (red). The pigment electrons resonate at the exact quantum frequency of some wavelengths of light, which it absorbs. The wavelengths that pass through out-of-sync with the molecular frequencies are the ones we see. This is called subtractive color and is found in paint pigments. This type of pigmented color was found in the fossil of a red armored fish dating to 375 million years ago.

Under a microscope, green quetzal feathers are not like the red ones: they are unpigmented and gray. This is because the iridescent green and blue of the quetzal's wings, collar, and tail are from structural iridescence, the second major source of natural color. Structural color is breathtaking because it is more intense than sunlight. In the quetzal feather, air bubbles alternate with keratin protein layers that are spaced apart by an exact multiple of the width of a blue or a green light wave. As a result, the gray-colored thin layers reflect just blue and lime-green light when sunlight hits at the right angle. Not only that, but these waves are also reflected in such a way that the peaks of the light waves are aligned, so that they add together and the light is amplified into a brilliant, dazzling array of color brighter than anything else around. This effect cannot be reproduced in photographs, digital or otherwise. The iridescent color of soap bubbles, peacock tail feathers, giant clams, blue morpho butterflies, and hummingbird gorgets are all produced in this way using thin-layer constructive

interference. A related structural effect also scatters light to produce the blue of the sky and the duller blue of some bird feathers. Interference-produced color has a more sumptuous quality than other colors. Seed-shrimp fossils at least 350 million years old show evidence of this type of color, and it probably dates back even further.

Monteverde: the Preserve

Monteverde Preserve is 10,500ha/26,000ac and was formed in the 1970s from a reserve originally established by Quakers to protect the watershed of their dairy farming community. The preserve is managed by the Tropical Science Center (tel 506-645-5122, fax 506-645-5034, www.cct.or.cr). Dairy farming continues here hand-in-hand with conservation—you should certainly visit Monteverde Cheese Factory during your stay. The division of land into farm plots began when Quakers moved to Costa Rica from the US in 1952, during the Korean War. The preserve owes its existence to the vision of George and Harriet Powell, who were able to galvanize US citizens and conservation organizations to help create it. The Tropical Science Center also coordinates many high-level international research projects on rainforest species and ecology that take place here (check out the

Gingers

Spiral gingers including *Costus wilsonii* (this page) are related to the regular ginger family Zingiberaceae. Look for the spiral whorl of their leaves. *C. wilsonii* flower cones are covered by red or orange bracts through which yellow flowers peep. Spike gingers (*Renealmia* sp.) (opposite page) are in the Zingiberaceae family and have clusters of flowers and bracts that splay out in spiky bunches. The leaves alternate from the long tall stems. Yellow spike ginger (*Renealmia ceruna*) has a ginger or camphor scent and is attacked by rolled-leaf hispine beetles and other caterpillars that drill holes through the rolled immature leaf, producing evenly spaced holes that decorate unfurled leaves.

excellent website at www.cloudforest alive.org). Its research center is near the Monteverde entrance. The organization depends on entrance fees and private donations and receives no government funding. Largely as a result of their work, Monteverde is a success story for research and conservation action. The presence of the preserve is also of significant economic benefit to the community. Donations to support maintenance of the preserve and to build a land acquisitions fund can be sent to the Tropical Science Center (CCT PO Box

Bar Hopping

Hummingbirds provide taxi service to hummingbird flower mites. These little arachnids live entirely off flower nectar and a dusting of pollen. They jump actively onto hummingbird beaks to get from one flower to another. The mites "pay" for their ride by cleaning pollen from the hummer's nasal passages, helping to maximize oxygen flow to its heart, which beats up to 1,260 times a minute. The mites then use flower scent to tell them when to move from the nasal passage of the hummer onto their next temporary flower home.

8-3870, ZIP 1000, San José, Costa Rica or, within the US, to the Friends of the Monteverde Cloud Forest, PO Box 1964, Cleveland, OH 44106, friends@cct.or.cr).

The humidity that bathes this ridge forest of Monteverde comes from the Pacific trade winds. The breezes sculpt elfin canopies along the east side, enrich the 1,680m/5,510ft Tilaran crest with a nutrient-wafting mist, and cause a rain-shadow on the western slopes. Birds of the top elfin forest include highland tinamous, black-and-yellow silky flycatchers, and

Leaf Rollers

Lobster claw *Heliconia tortuosa* and smaller *H. monteverdensis* (right) are found in Monteverde. These are the lobster claw variety of heliconia, with huge red bracts and yellow flowers. *H. tortusa* is found all over Costa Rica, but *H. monteverdensis* is local to this forest and has slightly smaller bracts and paler yellow flowers while looking very similar. Juvenile leaves come in rolls (above).

ruddy nightingale-thrushes. Although the endemic golden toad (*Bufo periglenes*) is still featured on postcards, you won't see it during your visit. This eye-catcher became extinct, along with half of the species of frogs studied in Monteverde, in a recent, great frog die-off that extended worldwide and baffled biologists. So far, two of the multiple likely causes identified are a virus and a pesticide, so make sure to clean your boots well as you go from one forest to another to prevent contamination.

The best ecotravel sites can also be counterproductive because their increased access to wildest nature draws crowds of people. Monteverde's popularity might be frustrating for those that want to get away from the madding crowd and truly immerse themselves in nature. Some have even dubbed the reserve a "crowd forest." However, the area does offer deep wilderness experiences, found either by travelling beyond the "Triangle" of the most-traveled Monteverde trails or in nearby, quieter

reserves, such as Sendero Tranquil and Santa Elena Reserve, which also offer guides. You can also stay outside Monteverde and Santa Elena—at the nearby community of San Luis in the ecolodge, for example, which is far enough from the scattering of commercial Monteverde hotels to be truly immersed in nature. San Luis Ecolodge offers simple living in bunk houses or high-quality private ecolodge suites overlooking the bird-filled forest, while being close enough to Monteverde Reserve to arrange guided visits.

Wherever you stay, the rough roads to Monteverde make the trip seem longer than it is and transforms one's visit there into a frontier experience. The Monteverde community has resisted paving the road, and this has helped keep traffic under control. However, this also means that anyone visiting Monteverde needs to plan on a multi-day trip and be prepared for a jarring ride. If you are based in San José and want to visit a cloud forest in only one day, go to the Los Angeles Cloud Forest instead (see page

Delicate Cargo

The wet-season flower of the rattlesnake plant (*Calathea insignis*, left) has a beautiful pollinating mechanism precisely designed to keep its pollen alive just long enough—only a few hours—for fertilization. Euglossine bees feed at these flowers. When it visits the flower, the bee unfolds its tongue, exposing a groove into which the flower then daubs pollen. When the bee flies away, it folds back its tongue, keeping the delicate cargo safe until it reaches the next flower, which is then pollinated. Rattlesnake plants are known as *marantas*, or prayer plants, and are often kept as house ornaments. Prayer plants can open and close their leaves according to their shade needs. This process is regulated by a swelling at the base of the leaf, which bends the leaf according to the rate of water-loss. This mechanism is often triggered by intense sunlight.

Quaker Tea

Aroids abound in the
rainforest, including the
familiar houseplant, white
sails (*Spathiphyllum wallisii*,
top). Aroids are plants that
have a spathe or spear for a
flower, surrounded by a pale
leaf bract. The huge
elephant-ear plant (below)
you'll see in Monteverde was
used by Quakers for tea,
although it was later found to
be carcinogenic. Related
Xanthosoma species are
pollinated by beetles, and
have evolved to produce a
beetle pheromone to ensure
success. When ripe, the flower
base undergoes a chemical
reaction, heating it at night
and producing an alkaloid
that mimics the sex
pheromone of the female
beetle, attracting male
beetles.

85). Another increasingly popular alternative is to go to the large Santa Elena reserve
a short drive away, which has fewer visitors
but is almost equal in fascination and
variety. Nearer Monteverde is the smaller
but animal-filled private Sendero Tranquil.
Each option is detailed in this chapter.

Monteverde Trails: the Triangle

Only one hundred visitors are allowed into
the Monteverde reserve at one time, so get
there early to avoid waiting in line. You can
walk through the huge reserve on your own,
but the best approach is to go with one of
the professional guides. To reserve a guide
for Monteverde, call the Monteverde Conservation League (506-645-5112) rather
than booking from your ecolodge—some
ecolodges have arrangements with private
guides who may be inferior to the league's.
If you have a particular interest, make sure
to select a guide in advance who is
specialized in that area; such an option
won't be offered unless you specifically
request it. Some of the guides have an
impressive specialized knowledge of certain
subjects, including botany, birds, and local
history. You'll pay according to the level of
their expertise.

Bosque Nuboso, Pantanoso, and Río
trails form the triangle of well-maintained
paths that encircle the most accessible part

of Monteverde. The central divide passes across it roughly north–south.

Sendero Bosque Nuboso and Canopy Bridge

Most people walk along the base of the Triangle, the 1.9km/1.2mi trail from the biological station. This is Sendero Bosque Nuboso, or the "cloud forest trail," which travels through the cloud forest, or what ecologists call tropical lower montane wet forest. The wet continental divide is at the end of the trail. Close to the start of the trail, wild avocados attract resplendent quetzals (*Pharomachrus mocinno*) during the start of the so-called dry season, which in these high mountains is still foggy and damp compared with the western lowland slopes. As you go east along the trail, you will encounter habitat gradients as the moisture increases.

The understory bursts with the creamy yellow flowers and orange bracts of endemic lobster claw (*Heliconia monteverdensis*). This species is slightly smaller and darker than the other, more widespread species of the orange-bracted lobster claw found throughout Costa Rica and now in gardens all over the world (*H. tortuosa*).

Sloths

Two-toed sloths (left) and three-toed sloths consume more of the Central American leaf canopy than any other vertebrate. If you weighed all the mammals in this rainforest, 70% of this mass would be contributed by sloths. Three-toed sloths are hard to spot, as their fur is loaded with green algae, providing excellent camouflage. They fertilize their primary host tree with dung and urine about once a week, clambering slowly to its base; this ensures optimum nitrogen cycling for the home tree. Sloths move slowly in order to reduce their metabolic rate to about half that of similar-sized mammals. A mother teaches her young her own unique pattern of feeding from about forty different leaf species, as well as where each feeding and resting tree is located. She also feeds the baby with leaf cud inoculated with bacteria needed for digestion. Sloth territories may overlap, but each maternal line has learned such specific feeding strategies that their feeding patterns are non-competitive.

Bromelaids

Costa Rica has over 170 bromeliad species, the richest in Central America. Bromeliads, which include the pineapple plant and Spanish moss, generally have a central whorl of leaves and usually are epiphytes. *Guzmania nicaraguensis* (above) is a common hummingbird-pollinated bromeliad. Bromeliads are among the epiphytes that, with mistletoes, cover three quarters of cloud forest trunk surfaces.

Look for epiphytic begonias (*Begonia estrellensis*) and hydrangeas (*Hydrangea peruviana*) growing on the trees as you reach the ridge. The strangler figs *Ficus hartwegii* and *F. crassiuscula* can be seen along the trail, providing a huge amount of fruit for frugivorous birds, bats, monkeys, and mammals, which you can watch for. These animals are essential to dispersing seeds in areas that have been cleared, as well as for the forest's longevity as a whole.

A quarter of the way along the path you will come across the more uniform trunks of the secondary forest that used to be pasture. This is made up of fruit-producing, leathery-leaved cow's tongue (*Conostegia oerstediana*) and yellow flowered, prickly, red-fruited burio (*Heliocarpus americanus*). These are common in forest light gaps and old pastures. Cow's tongue is a member of the widespread cloud forest and lowland rainforest understory family of melastomes. All 269 Costa Rican melastome species have netted leaf veination that looks like ladders. Female bees hold the anthers of cow's tongue flowers and use their flight muscles to vibrate a cloud of high-protein pollen onto their bodies from the nectar-free flowers. Sixteen species of birds and several bats seek out and disperse the juicy purple berries.

You can also see burio, a member of the Linden family, which grows so quickly that its soft wood is similar to balsa. Its wood is used to make crates for shipping easily bruised tropical fruit by air. The gluey bark secretions are used to bleach local sugar and remove its sediment.

The Nuboso is an interpretive trail, and if you stop at each sign the trail will take about 1.5 hours. Booklets explaining each stop are available at the west entrance store.

Crossing the canopy bridge is a highlight of the trip. The entrance to this suspension bridge is obscure and can be found by going along Sendero Bosque Nuboso for 1km/0.6mi from the entrance, then turning left and east up to an almost hidden footpath, turning left on the multi-use road and walking 0.5km/0.3mi, then turning right onto the trail that leads to the bridge. There are several trail options to explore around the bridge. Turning left just at the entrance to the bridge leads you to Sendero Wilford Guindon and back to the entrance. Turning left a short walk after the bridge leads you up Sendero Roble, which returns you to the entrance if you turn left onto Sendero Chomongo. Bearing right after the bridge will lead you

Cow's Tongues

The melastome family is a major group of berry shrubs that colonize light gaps. There are twelve *Conostegia* species in Monteverde (below). One is called Maria; another is called cow's tongue, named for its bristly leaves. You can identify melastome by their parallel net-veined, opposite oval leaves and their pretty, small, pinwheel flowers. An arboreal mammal, the rice rat (*Oryzomys devius*), pollinates one melastome, *Blakea chlorantha*. This hemiepiphyte, with small, green, tubular flowers, is found across the cloud forests of Central America. The rat's face is dusted with pollen as it laps nectar from the flowers, which it holds with its dainty forepaws. Such relationships between pollinating small mammals and specific flower species have only been found here, in South Africa, and Australia.

Bamboo Ark

Bamboos (right) house up to 21 bird species, nine specializing in bamboo seeds, twelve in bamboo-based insects. A further sixteen birds are common around bamboo stands. Fiery-throated hummingbirds build their nests in the fronds. There are 40 species of bamboo native to Costa Rica, with *Chusquea longifolia* common in light gaps.

back to Sendero el Camino.

Sendero el Camino is an access road that parallels several trails near the main entrance. It can be used as a trail itself in order to see bird and butterfly species that prefer open sides of the forest. Look for black guans, collared peccaries, and white-faced capuchin and howler monkeys.

Sendero Pantanoso and Connecting Trails

Sendero Pantanoso, "swamp trail," takes about 1.25 hours (1.6km/1.0mi) to hike one way. The south end of this trail is found at the east end of Sendero Bosque Nuboso. Turn left and north at the T-junction to join Sendero Pantanoso and walk across the 1,600m/ 5,248ft continental divide and across the wooden walkway through swamp forest. You will need to return to the field station along Sendero Río (1.9km/1.2mi) or Sendero Chomogo (1.8km/1.1mi), which are both left turns west at the end of Sendero Pantanoso.

You can also go beyond the Triangle of trails by heading northwest along Sendero Valle. Here you can see rare magnolias (*Magnolia poasana*), an ancient sub-canopy tree species with huge flowers pollinated by beetles, found here only along Sendero Pantanoso and on Cerro Amigos. Look for the area's sole conifer species, *Podocarpus* sp.

Sendero Río passes through second-growth forest. Check for Baird's tapir tracks (*Tapirus bairdii*) towards the end of the trail. The tapir is an herbivorous horse-relative whose predators are humans and jaguars; its tracks resemble the club symbol in a deck of playing cards. A 213-foot triple waterfall can be seen from a side trail 0.75km/0.5mi from the main park entrance. The wild sapote (*Pouteria fossicola*) is found near the waterfall, with huge buttresses that support the tree with wide, flat bases. This is related to the marketable sapote fruit *P. sapota* and the chicle tree that was used to produce chewing gum commercially until synthetic derivatives replaced natural production. Look for the large seeds on the trail gnawed by agoutis, squirrels, and pacas. Wild avocado trees at the west end of the trail attract resplendent quetzals during the early part of the dry season.

Sendero Chamogo takes about 1.25 hours to climb across the highest ridge in Monteverde reserve, reaching 1,680m/

Guan Tree

Guettarda pasana (below) produces four-petalled, fragrant flowers. Hummingbirds and skipper butterflies (below left) visit the flowers of this coffee relative. When you find these characteristically frilly flowers on the path, look up for black guans (above) feasting on the black fruit, March–June. This huge turkey-sized bird moves slowly through the forest canopy eating wild avocado, *Guettarda*, and *Cecropia*. One of the *Guettarda* visitors is the Brazilian skipper, or canna-leaf roller, *Calpodes ethlius* (left), which is a strong, small butterfly. Its caterpillars eat *Canna flaccida* leaves

Hummers

Look for the endemic coppery-headed emerald hummingbird (*Elvira cupreiceps,* male shown opposite), around nectar-filled hotlips (*Psychotria elata,* above). Surprisingly, hummingbirds in Costa Rica don't usually feed from the numerous canopy-tree blossoms. Instead, they seek sustenance from the epiphytes supported by these trees, and the heliconias and flowering bushes that grow in light gaps below them. Hermit hummingbirds forage using long curved bills. Small, short-billed hummers visit small flowers with little nectar, competing with bees and other insects that chase them away about one-third of the time.

5,510ft over 1.8km/1.1mi. At the end look for Baird's tapir tracks. Around the pathway, spot the scarlet *Stenorrhynchos* orchids at ground-level and the purple fruits of hot lips (*Psychotria elata*). These flowers are sought after by birds and are pollinated by hummers, including fiery-throated hummingbirds (*Panterpe insignis*), which weave nests in the trailing bamboos. These scintillating hummingbirds have longish bills but nevertheless reach nectar in the longer tubes of fuschia and centropogon flowers by using holes pierced by bumblebees and slaty flowerpiercers, or by piercing their own holes.

As you walk along, look for the gnarled roots of the oak trees (*Quercus corrugata*) where pacas (*Agouti paca*), large guinea-pig relatives, hide in shallow burrows. These nocturnal rodents are protected here in Monteverde, but are hunted outside the conservation areas for their meat.

Sendero Brillante

If you want to walk along the continental divide, take the Sendero Brillante trail. Reach this by walking east from the main entrance along Sendero Bosque Nuboso to the junction (1.9km/1.18mi). At this T-junction, turn right to Sendero Brillante. It is a short walk to the view from La Ventana. The track then continues on to the Brilliante shelter high above the San Luis valley, but from La Ventana onwards it is restricted for use by researchers. Along the crest you will experience the luminous elfin forest, sculpted into smooth-topped dwarfs by relentless Caribbean gales. One tree to poke through the canopy is *Clusia alata*, anchored by its stilt roots. Stilt roots are found in ten percent of trees of this altitude, less common in other types of rainforest where the wind is less extreme.

Cistern Community

This flatworm (top) is among 250 animal species found in bromeliads. Euphonias rear their chicks in nests made on bromeliads, and many frogs, crabs, and snails depend on the aquatic cistern for part of their life-cycle. The two-inch snail (below) is carnivorous, devouring other snails.

Monteverde Trails: Beyond the Triangle

Several trails go beyond the Triangle into the far reaches of the Monteverde Cloud Forest Preserve and into the huge area of the Children's Eternal Rainforest to the east. One of these is El Camino, that ends in name only 2.0km/1.2mi from the west park entrance and becomes the Camino a Peñas Blancas.

The more remote forest is subtly different, as one notices on exploration. For example, the local palmito "heart of palm" tree (*Prestoea acuminata*), related to commercial pejibaye, is more common in this hard-to-reach forest because it has had more chance to grow without being removed for consumption.

Alemán shelter, "the Germans," is 6.8km/4.2mi and three hours away along the Camino a Peñas Blancas and requires a small fee for overnight stays. Take the left fork from the shelter downhill to the Eladios shelter, 5km/3mi, along the Peñas Blancas river valley. To continue on the rough trail towards the Poco Sol field station, 14km/8.7mi, you will need advance permission to enter the Children's Eternal Rainforest (by phone 506-645-5003 or 506-645-5200, or email, acmmcl@sol.racsa. co.cr). The field station has its own extensive network of trails, a waterfall, hotsprings, and bunk house accommodations, and is about 30km/18.7mi from La Fortuna. The nearest village is La Tigra.

Sendero el Valle is at the north end of Sendero Pantanoso and, after about two hours' hiking through secondary forest, leads to El Valle shelter.

You can reach the foothills of Arenal volcano on the relatively new Sendero de las Dantas. This trail, about 32km/20mi long, extends northeast from the shelter, but takes about two days to complete, ending near the

Forest Ice Cream
There are many activities in the rainforest for children to enjoy. This young superman is working his way through a blindfold walk to hear, smell, and touch the surprises around San Luis Ecolodge. Both children and parrots love the pulp of guabas (above). Not to be confused with guavas (which in Costa Rica are called *guyabas*), guabas (*Inga* sp.) are cultivated in order to shade coffee trees. You can also find them growing wild on the edge of rainforest areas. Open the "ice cream pod" to enjoy its seeds, which are coated in delicious, sweet, citrus-tasting pulp.

Arenal Observatory Lodge 20 km/12mi from La Fortuna. You'll need a guide for this difficult, steeply undulating, and muddy trail, which has a net gain in elevation of 1,400m/4,592ft. Call the Monteverde Conservation League (506-645-5003, 506-645-5112) for reservations.

Monteverde Reserve Access

A stone-paved road jars passengers on their way to the scattered Tilarán mountain ridge communities, the main village of Santa Elena and the smattering of houses and craft works that constitute Cerro Plano and Monteverde villages. On the map, Monteverde appears close to San José, but in fact the 184km/114mi journey takes four hours. Take the Interamerican Highway to the 149km marker just before the Lagarto River bridge and turn right. Drive 43km/26mi up the unpaved road, following signs for Monteverde. There are two other routes to Monteverde via Tilarán, available

Working Together

The common bush tanager (*Chlorospingus ophthalmicus*) is the leader of mixed-flock cloud forest birds. The flock effectively flushes out insects and provides added lookouts for predators. Each mixed-flock species gleans food in slightly different ways, avoiding competition while increasing cooperation. Woodcreepers, warblers, woodpeckers, wrens, treerunners, and tanagers are often found in these flocks.

to those with good navigation skills and 4WD—both beautiful, traffic-free alternatives, if you want to see Arenal and its lake on the way. However, travelling via these routes requires an extra day.

Public buses to Monteverde leave San José Monday to Saturday and return Tuesday to Sunday. This bus has been known for theft targeted at tourists and their bags. Buses depart from Puntarenas and reach Santa Elena, scheduled daily both ways (506-222-3854, Tilirán Transportation).

Monteverde experiences a mixture of sun and fog. Expect some rain every day from May to October and a "little summer" reprieve during July—the rest of the time you'll find sunny weather interspersed with thin fog on the ridges. The total rainfall is around 760cm/300in a year, significantly lower than on the Caribbean lowlands.

Activities in Monteverde

From the cheese factory to craft stores, there are many activities to enhance your visit. Check with Monteverdeinfo.com for more details (tel 506-645-7070, fax 506-645-6060).

Selvatura

Monteverde's latest addition to the zip line world is combined at Selvatura with a butterfly garden, hummingbird gallery, and rainforest frog and snake exhibits to make a wonderful all-in-one rainforest immersion. You can eat at the restaurant as well. Canopy zip lines take about three hours, with the canopy walkway spanning eight treetop bridges. (www.selvatura.com accepts online reservations)

Skywalk and Skytrek

Zip lines are used by researchers to study the hyperactive part of the rainforest, the canopy. However, Monteverde's Skytrek zip

Oskars

Many rainforest canopy seeds have only six weeks' viability. These climax species can, however, grow in low light; their spindly saplings can stay in a state of suppressed growth for decades under the canopy, ready to shoot up as soon as light levels increase after a tree or branch falls. These saplings are called Oskars, after Gunter Grass's fictional character, the boy who did not grow up.

Pioneer species, such as *Cecropia*, respond to rainforest conditions differently. Their seeds remain dormant, waiting for bright light, as they cannot survive in dim conditions. As soon as the scorching tropical sun hits, their photo-sensitive seeds sprout. They can withstand hotter conditions and sink their roots deeper than climax species. Their growth provides necessary shade and branches on which climax seed dispersers sit.

line is not so much a scientific experience as an adrenaline rush. The zip lines are strung from hilltop to hilltop over the canopy, which in the valleys can be over a hundred feet below. Gravity pulls the strapped-in participant to each hilltop station. The entire trip takes about two hours. The ride is truly challenging, pushing the limits of one's instincts for self-preservation while fostering a deep respect for the immense diversity of the forest below.

If you would like more time to see and wonder at the canopy, take the Skywalk, which does not involve a zip line ride. Run by the same company and leaving from the same site, Skywalk covers a slightly different route and includes a couple of suspension bridges, so you can experience the canopy from above more slowly, without speeding by on a zip line. Skywalk demands an initial vertical climb up a crane stairwell to access the first bridge, so those with a problem with heights may find this difficult. Guides lead the Skywalk and

Canopy bridges (above) and zip-line tours are a major way of experiencing the rainforest, yet they are not regulated. Check that the system is in good shape and that wires are doubled to make them fail-safe. If not, then don't go.

Air Plants

Air plants, or *Tillandsia*
(right), are bromeliads that
form colonies which can
subsist on starvation levels of
nutrients. They survive by
concentrating the scarce
minerals and even amino
acids that are dissolved in the
fog that blows and drips onto
them. They brew some
nutrients from the waste
products of the larvae, snails,
and tadpoles attracted to their
central aquaria. Debris and
organic compounds pass into
the air plants across ultra-
absorbent trichome cells on
the leaves. The microscopic
trichomes are shaped into
mushroom domes that we see
as a white dusting on the
leaves. Some tillandsia have
set up shop for ants to live in
their bulbous roots and absorb
large amounts of nitrogen
and other minerals the ants
bring in from a wide area.
Each starved tillandsia flower
cannot produce enough
nectar to reward a pollinator
effectively, so they cluster
together to offer a
smorgasbord of sipfuls.

provide excellent help in sighting the nests,
plants, birds, and animals in the forest.

Skytrek is about a 20 minutes' drive
from Santa Elena. It is in a slightly
different, drier forest system than the
Monteverde cloud forest. You can arrange
a pick-up from most Monteverde and
Santa Elena accommodations. The private
reserve covers 228ha/663ac. (tel 506-645-
5238, fax 506-645-5786, www.skywalk.com,
www.skytrek.com)

Canopy Tour

The Canopy Tour is above Cerro Plano near
El Sapo Dorado on the Cloud Forest Lodge
reserve (tel 506-291-4465, US tel 305-433-
2241, www.canopytour.com). Their older
zip-line canopy tour competes with the
longer, very popular Skytrek and Selvatura
rides.

Orchid Garden

A visit to this miniature garden is
recommended. You'll experience a wonderful
collection of minute and larger orchids on a

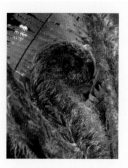

Tree Ferns
Cyanthea multiflora (left) and other gorgeous trunked tree ferns are called *rabo de mico*, or "monkey-tails," for their fiddlehead juvenile fronds (above). Most herbivores leave these plants alone, although hummingbirds use *Dicksonia* tree-fern scales to line their nests. Orchid growers use tree-fern trunks for potting media and epiphytic supports, but in the wild tree ferns do not gather epiphytes; they shed their fronds and the associated hitchhikers regularly. The worldwide horticultural demand for tree ferns has put many of them on the endangered species list. The bark is covered in aerial roots to grab as many nutrients as possible. Tree ferns pioneer light gaps, but they suppress competition when germinating by producing toxins harmful to other plants.

fascinating tour given by well-trained guides. The owner is Gabriel Barbosa, a world expert in orchids. This tour is one of the best ways to appreciate the intricate relationships on which this forest relies. Orquídeas de Monteverde is in Cerro Plano at Mr. Barbosa's home. (506-645-5510)

Butterfly Garden

Follow the signs from Hotel Heliconia in Cerro Plano to this screened garden. Here you can see one of Costa Rica's many live native butterfly collections. (506-645-5512)

Hummingbird Gallery

Just outside the entrance to the Monteverde Reserve is a photo gallery and hummingbird feeder site. The humming-birds that visit the feeders are worth a visit—their intense colors are so outstanding that you'll want to stand and watch for hours, mesmerized by your good fortune.

Finca Ecologica

This small reserve is on what used to be an orchard. It is located on the edge of Cerro Plano, within walking distance of many accommodations in Santa Elena and Monteverde. Here the large mammal life is

Herbivore Defense

"The world is not coloured green to the herbivore's eyes," said Daniel Janzen, the noted tropical biologist, "but rather is painted morphine, L-DOPA, calcium oxalate, cannabinol, caffeine, mustard oil, strychnine, rotenone, etc." As a result of these chemical anti-herbivore deterrents, less than ten percent of rainforest animals eat leaves straight off the trees. Even monkeys browse on small parts of each leaf before discarding them and moving to the next leaf species, to insure they do not eat a heavy dose if one is toxic.

Look for monkey debris (above) to find a monkey troop

Autograph tree or copey (Clusia sp.) opposite top right quadrant, is a common epiphyte genus found on rocks and canopies, its wheel-like fruit sought by birds. Cecropia sp. (opposite below left quadrant), with whorled leaves, is a gap colonizer.

more dense than in the rainforest, because this reserve is a transitional "edge zone" habitat offering a greater variety of easy-to-find foods. You are more likely to spot sloths, coatis, agoutis, porcupines, and monkeys in this secondary forest than in the primary rainforest. There are four short loop trails to hike, and the evening guided tour to see nocturnal animals is highly recommended. (506-645-5363)

Places to Stay in Monteverde

The small communities around Monteverde form a more or less continuous spread of small ecolodges and bunk houses centered around Santa Elena. Some offer private pick-up service from San José. Tourist buses go to Monteverde daily. (www.monteverdeinfo.com)

Santa Elena

Inexpensive pensions and backpacker dorms spill with friendly travellers. A selection of college-style restaurants, internet cafes, and Monteverde tour services are within easy walking distance.

Right in town, Arco Iris Eco-Lodge offers basic cabins, homey breakfasts, and friendly recommendations of the best guides to sign up with. Internet access. (tel 506-645-5067, fax 506-645-5022, www.arcoiris lodge.com, info@arcoirislodge.com)

Cerro Plano

El Sapo Dorado is an excellent ecolodge recommended for its eco-friendly policies and its cedar chalets with fireplaces and views. El Sapo Dorado runs a gourmet restaurant, open to outside visitors, offering excellent, healthy, and hearty dining. Close to Monteverde but set on its own hillside and reserve, this lodge has a special

Fig Wasps
You can take a green fig (top) and open it to reveal tiny creatures, fig wasps, each about a millimeter long. When fig trees produce a new crop of figs, an enormous gathering of these tiny female agaonid fig wasps appear. Squirming into the hole at the base of the fig, the females lose their antennas and wings. The fig wasp lays an egg on some sterile flowers, pollinates the fig, and then dies. Her babies consume 20–80% of the fig seeds. Juvenile males inseminate the female wasps before the females hatch. Only the females go free, flying off through a hole cut by the males in the fig. The males die inside the fruit.

Similar to but distinct from fig wasps, gall wasps (above right) create their own homes by turning on plant stem DNA. The stem expands into a gall that the wasps can eat.

relationship with Sendero Tranquil. A trail runs behind the lodge through El Sapo Dorado private reserve. Internet access. (fax 506-645-5010, www.sapodorado.com)

Monteverde

Arts-and-crafts style Monteverde Lodge is owned by Costa Rica Expeditions, a well-run ecotravel company, which can also provide combined deals with their high-end lodges or tent camps on the Osa Peninsula and Tortuguero. (tel 506-257-0766, fax 506-257-1665, www.costaricaexpeditions.com)

San Luis

The excellent San Luis Ecolodge is located south of Monteverde and below it in altitude, made closer by the new cement road that San Luis residents built with their own hands on rotating shifts, between farm activities.

For those that want to get away from the international crush at Santa Elena and into a more integrated Costa Rican ecology and campesino experience, this is the lodge to go to. It has recently changed hands and is now owned by the University of Georgia as a research station and ecolodge. Bunk houses pulse with students and families, cabins provide more private accommodations, and a ten-minute walk takes you to serene newer cabins overlooking steep forest. Lodge guests and student groups mingle with researchers and lodge organizers at the mess hall, which serves as a library, kitchen, and place to watch hummingbirds and relax. You can milk San Luis Ecolodge cows, arrange to stay with local families in the village, take dancing lessons, take a guided night walk, gather an intimate understanding of field research being performed on site, and visit the slash-and-burn plots to see how the rainforest used to be managed. (tel 506-645-8049 or 506-645-8051, fax 506-645-8050, www. ecolodgesanluis.com)

San Gerardo

Remote Albergue Ecoverde is run by a cooperative and is on a rainforest hillside filled with bird life on the other side of Santa Elena in San Gerardo. At night, depending on the weather, this lodge offers dramatic views of the red lava flows of Arenal Volcano. (tel 506-385-0092, www.agroecoturismo.net, cooprena@racsa.co.cr)

Sendero Tranquil Reserve

The private reserve closest to Monteverde is the Tranquil Reserve. It is a small, wonderful forest on the drier west side near the leeward

Liana Resonance
Lianas (above and below left) are woody vines that hang from the canopy. They are a variety of species and, surprisingly, grow from the ground. One acre of rainforest in nearby Panama was found to have 640 climbing lianas. Tropical trees are thought to shed lianas (which compete for light and bring them down) better than other forests because of the tropical forest's diversity. The diversity of tree species results in a variety of heights and shapes, which resonate dischordantly when the wind blows. This uncoordinated movement helps tear the vines from their branches. Some vines develop twisted, springy shapes so that they can stretch with the trees during tropical storms and survive.

Toucans

Unlike other toucans, the emerald toucanet *Aulacorhynchus prasinus* (below) is found in cloud forest and mid and high elevations. Its blue throat distinguishes it from the Mexican subspecies. The emerald toucanet eats *Clusia* (above) and other berries and a variety of small animals.

crest. This reserve is quieter than Monteverde, and visitors should book a guide in advance. The reserve is open from December through August. (506-645-5272 for reservations, or call Hotel el Sapo Dorado for pick up and reservations, 506-645-5010.)

Bajo del Tigre Reserve

The drier forest of Jaguar Canyon, Bajo del Tigre, is found within easy walking distance from Monteverde. The forest is on the Pacific side, which in Costa Rica is on the leeward side of the continental divde and prevailing water-loaded Caribbean wind. As a result, the forest is completely different than Monteverde, drier, with fewer epiphytes and understory flowers. This makes it less dramatic and tropical; it also has the feel of being closer to civilization. However, thirty tree species found in this unique habitat have been claimed as newly identified, and more surprises may be in store. Coatis, sloths, monkeys, nocturnal kinkajous, hog-nosed skunks, and armadillos can be seen here.

Listen for the "bonks" of the threatened three-wattled bellbird (*Procnias tricarunculata*). This is a remarkable bird, whose sound, which seems to come from another location than the bird itself, is so unique that you will remember it as characteristic of the cloud forest long after you return. The male sports three wormlike black wattles that drape from his white head, and accents the white and chestnut plumage he displays to females. He is difficult to spot at first, calling from high up in the canopy. Then he drops lower as the hen appears. When she approaches his sub-canopy perch, they engage in a ritualistic place-changing display. His voice and wattles are key lures. Once courtship is completed, he leaves her to raise their young alone. You are most likely to hear his characteristic wooden calls, which echo across the steep hillsides, from March to June. This is when bellbirds move up to elevations above 1,200m/4,000ft to breed. After this, and during the dry season, they move away from Monteverde to a lower elevation. This altitudinal migration is found among several Costa Rican species including large hawk moths, silver-throated tanagers, and scarlet-thighed dacnis. You

Mini-Orchids
The smallest orchid in the world, *Platystele jungermannioides* (above), can be found at the Orchid Garden in Monteverde. A visit is highly recommended. (For more information, call 506-645-5510.)

The seeds of orchids are so small that some may produce 3.7 million seeds per fruit. Vanilla bean is in fact an orchid seedpod and is grown in Costa Rica. Due to their seed size, orchids depend on symbiotic fungi to help them start their lives. These fungi extend a network of threads that feed water and minerals to the tiny shoots. The fungi even pierce the root cells of the orchid shoots to make the connection long-term.

New Slash-and-Burn Communities

Slash-and-burn agriculture (above), instead of being the way of the past, may become the improvement of the future. When carefully adapted and done in a way that retains surrounding rainforest, this may be the sustainable solution for new types of cash and food crops. This synthetic approach is being developed in areas of Costa Rica by Robert Hart, and at Lacandona in Chiapas, Mexico, by Lacandon Maya Indians.

A small patch of forest is cleared using machetes and then burned. The ash neutralizes and fertilizes the soil. It has been found that burning a patch of forest this size does not in itself deplete the area or lose topsoil, provided that the surrounding forest is retained. Even the essential mycorrhizal fungi survive. The clearing historically was planted with a mixture of maize corn, bananas (opposite), plantains, peppers, and starchy crops like manioc and sweet potato (above), with a possible medicinal garden. The plot is cultivated for three to five years. Each harvest declines by about one-half of the year before, as the soil gets leached by rain and the crops remove valuable minerals. Then the plot is left to grow back into the forest and renew itself. After about ten years, the bird community is the same as before the plot started. The advantage of this method is that it allows the surrounding forest to remain intact while supporting a community of people. The disadvantage of this older style approach is that the number of people supported is small, the need for a nomadic lifestyle is high, and cash crops are not produced.

However, when scientific knowledge of ecological succession is combined by Hart and others with updated slash-and-burn practices, diverse, fast-growing cash and food crops can be grown very successfully in rotations of up to fifteen years, without affecting the surrounding rainforest.

can find three-wattled bellbirds in the Talamancas and in the Guanacaste region as well.

There are several short trails in this forest, each less than 1km/0.6mi. One trail leads past bat roosts. To find Sendero Bajo del Tigre, walk down Sendero Arboretum from the "untamed garden" by the entrance, continue straight along Sendero Calandria, the bellbird trail, and straight onto the Sendero Escarpado, which reaches a lookout. Sendero Bajo del Tigre is a south turn about halfway along this last section. Despite the name, you are unlikely to spot a jaguar on your journey, although they are found in the Monteverde area.

To get to Bajo del Tigre forest, turn south on the Monteverde side of the CASEM building and take the track leading to the small information center, where books can be purchased and a map of the trails is available. (506-645-5305)

Santa Elena Cloud Forest Reserve

Founded in 1992 as a local high school's project, this large, stunning reserve provides excellent guides and pathways through extraordinary rainforest. Many find this reserve as impressive as Monteverde, but without the crowds. The forest here is less

Blue Morpho
Male morpho butterflies (above) have bright blue top wings, and may chase you away if you are wearing a bright blue color, mistaking you for another male morpho. Morphos slip in and out of light gaps in search of rotting fruit and sap. The undersides of their wings have several eyespots (top) used as startle devices to distract fast jacamars and flycatchers. When threatened, morphos also release a pungent scent from between their forelegs, to deter predators. Then they alight, close their blue wings and disappear into brown. Male *Morpho amathonte* keep their lives simple in order devote themselves to chasing females. They memorize only two sites, their source of rotting fruit and their nighttime roost.

Peppers

Costa Rica has many black pepper relatives: 113 *Piper* and 115 *Peperomia* species, all related to black pepper *Piper nigrum*. The candle-like flowers depend on Carollia bats for seed dispersal. When ripe, the drooping flowers stiffen into upright "candles," and the bats eat the seeds in flight. The flowers ripen in succession, providing the bats a continual food supply. Many of these species are found as houseplants, including *Peperomia hernandiifolia*.

The San Luis Ecolodge (above) nestles beneath Monteverde hills, where you can dance with villagers, explore a medicinal garden, and take part in milking the farm's dairy cows.

damp than Monteverde. The reserve is about 5km/3mi from Monteverde and is adjacent to the privately run Skytrek and Selvatura adventure zip lines. Reserve a guide and jeep pickup (506-645-5014), or catch the 6:30 AM collective taxi that leaves from Pension Santa Elena (506-645-5051). The office has more details (tel 506-645-5693, www.monteverdeinfo.com/reserve.htm, www.monte-verdeinfo.com)

Children's Eternal Rainforest: Bosque Eterno de los Niños (BEN)

This reserve started when Swedish school children purchased fifteen acres of rainforest for conservation. Their action inspired a worldwide conservation effort and created the largest private reserve in Central America. The 22,000ha/50,000ac reserve is managed by the Monteverde Conservation League, a private nonprofit association of Costa Rican and international groups.

This remote forest's trails and guides are not as well developed as those of other local reserves; it lacks the level of guiding services of Santa Elena or Monteverde. The San Gerardo Station is reached by hiking downhill for a couple of hours from Santa Elena Reserve. The bunkhouse there offers several trails. Poco Sol Station is south of La Fortuna, and has hotsprings and a bunk house.

A separate, very small section of BEN forest is within walking distance of Monteverde village. The Sendero Bajo del Tigre runs through this forest (see page 80). (Children's Eternal Rainforest tel 506-645-5003, acmmcl@sol.racsa.co.cr)

Mushrooms brighten the forest

Los Angeles Cloud Forest

The Los Angeles Cloud Forest is not in the same area as Monteverde. Nevertheless, it is listed in this chapter because this cloud forest, at about an hour's drive from San José, is much more accessible than Monteverde. You'll be thrilled by all you see in this forest, home to 210 bird species, as you follow the trail through brightly colored heliconias and fruiting fig trees.

This reserve is associated with Villa Blanca Cloud Forest Hotel and Spa, which was remodeled in 2004 as a green ecolodge, with eco-friendly cabins, recycling, and sustainable practices. Naturalist-lead tours reach the cloud forest and surroundings. There is a zip line, and you can also arrange for a night tour to see fascinating nocturnal animals. In March through June, there are special expeditions to see quetzals that depart at 6 AM and take four hours. The reserve is 20km/12.4mi north of San Ramon or 60km/38mi from San José. (tel 506-461-3033, www.villablanca-costarica.com/our-cloudforest.htm)

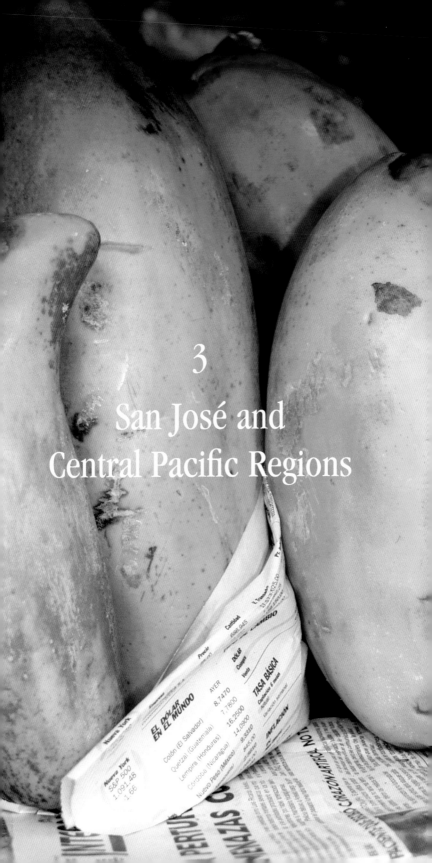

3

San José and
Central Pacific Regions

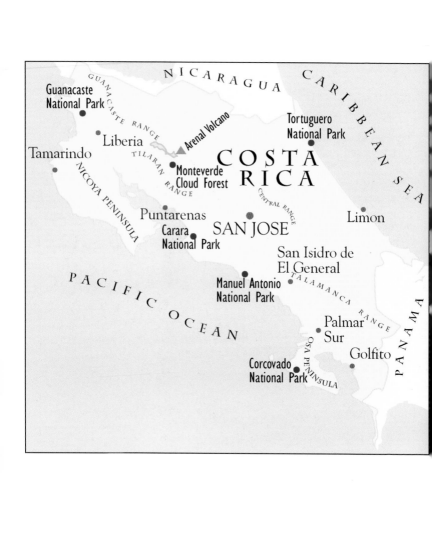

Sprays of maroon and cream orchids load the trees of the roadside bank in the mountains a half hour northeast of San José. Whorls of striped bromeliads stud the branches. Zebra butterflies and emerald green urania moths dip and soar around orange terrestrial orchids. A blue-throated emerald toucanet sails onto a perch. The side road winds through the surrounding dairy country, with fields bordered by lines of tree stakes that are taking root, providing more habitat for wildlife. The shade trees of the coffee plantations brim with yellow-throated brush-finches (*Atlapetes gutturalis*) and other birds, despite the near complete deforestation of this region. For travellers interested in exploring by car, the hilly

Costa Rican Holidays

January 1
April 11
Semana Sancta (the week before Easter)
May 1
July 25
August 2
September 15
October 12
December 24, 25, 31 (Christmas week)

Tropical Sun

Despite being in the northern hemisphere, Costa Rican "summer" occurs December–April, and "winter" June–November; the wet season, which occurs from July–November with local variations, feels cooler than the rest of the year. Since most of the rain hits in torrential bursts during the afternoon or at night, the green season can still be a wonderful time to visit.

The sun's rays hit Costa Rica vertically at certain times, unlike in temperate countries. This means two things: first, that the sun's rays are far more intense in the tropics than in temperate zones, and second, that Costa Rica has two summers. The first major summer occurs between January and March, and the second, little summer occurs during a drier interlude in the wet season, around July.

San José (above) is high enough on the central plateau to have cooler weather than along the coasts

countryside provides a charming backdrop en route to national parks and wilderness destinations.

These central highlands rise to the east of a comfortably cool and agriculturally rich tropical tableland. Most people live in this *meseta*, or plateau, with the population centered in San José. Although this is not prime ecotravel country, there are many destinations for wilderness travellers around the central cities, from the parks of the Pacific to some all-too-accessible rumbling volcanoes that mark the center of the country.

Each volcano has its own variety of volcano hummingbird (*Selasphorus flammula*), which potentially could be evolving into separate species, rather like Darwin's finches on the Galapagos. Male volcano hummers on Irazu have purple throat patches, or gorgets. On Poás and Vieja Volcanoes the male's gorget is red. Talamanca males have purple-gray gorgets. These hummers are common in highland areas, managing to elude the dominant fiery-throated hummingbird (*Panterpe insignis*), which is twice their size.

San José

San José, the capital, rests on the 915m/ 3,000ft Meseta Central and is well-placed as a central hub. Flights to Costa Rica usually arrive in this mountain-cool city, although some international flights arrive at Liberia in the northwest, close to the resort beaches. Other travellers come by cruise line or cross the border by road. Either way, San José is rarely an ecotraveller's primary destination, except as a stepping-off point for the transportation and ecotour options that are centered here.

A quarter of the country's land is now protected in public or private conservation areas, but there are major conflicts between developers and conservationists. In San José you'll immediately notice the black exhaust belching from the traffic that zooms around the tiny streets—pedestrians beware. This pollution is surprising: Costa Rica has strict environmental laws that supposedly require

Weather Guide

San José is tropical, but cooled by its mountains and cloudforests. The Caribbean side of Costa Rica is the wettest region overall, with the lowlands collecting damp tropical breezes from the warm Atlantic. The northwest Pacific lowlands have a six-month dry season from December to May or June, when the trees lose their leaves. Mountainous areas can be cool at any time of the year due to fog drip, and many mountain lodges have fireplaces that are great even in midsummer. The low Osa Peninsula is closer to the equator, and so the rainforest there is truly steamy. Fortunately, ocean breezes provide microclimates of cooling scattered throughout Costa Rica, so choose your accommodation site with this in mind (in each chapter of this book, you can read about specific recommendations in the descriptions of where to stay). Deluges are generally too warm for a raincoat, but an umbrella will come in handy. During an El Niño year, have enough flexibility in your schedule to work around flooding.

Costa Rica Transport

Personal itineraries and transport with Costa Rica guides can be arranged with Syracuse tours (www.syracusetours.com). Ecotravel tour companies include Abercrombie & Kent (US tel 800-554-7094, abercrombiekent.com), Butterfield and Robinson (US tel 800-678-1147, www.butterfield.com), Holbrook Travel (US tel 800-451-7111, www.holbrooktravel.com), and Swiss Travel (tel 506-282-4898 www.swisstravel.cr.com).

Tourist buses with regularly scheduled, reasonable tours, which can be used as your bus system include Fantasy Bus (tel 506-220-2126, www.graylinecostarica.com), and Interbus (tel 506-283-5573, www.costaricapass.com).

For public buses, A Safe Passage (www.costarica bustickets.com) enables you to board the public buses in Alajuela, which is a few minutes from the international airport, and is generally safer than bus stations in San José. Bus times are listed on their website. It's best to book eight days in advance. You can find public bus schedules and bus stop maps at the ICT office (the Costa Rica Tourism Board) in San José, below the Plaza de la Cultura, Calle 5, Avenida Central/2 (US tel 1-866-COSTA-RICA, and within Costa Rica: 506-222-1090, 506-223-1733, www.visitcostarica.com).

emission inspections for each car and truck every six months. The enforcement of this law is problematic, however. Local car owners will tell you that with a small, correctly placed fee, it is easy to pass the smog tests without any actual inspection of the vehicle. This attitude has also undermined the many laws set up to protect rainforests from deforestation, save turtles from egg poaching, and shield songbirds and macaws from the pet trade. Education, a national priority, is helping to change these corrupt approaches. INBio, Zoo Ave, and other organizations play a major role in teaching the value of conservation to school children growing up in a society where hunting is a tradition. The strong local traditions of hunting or capturing a variety of animal species, including baby spider monkeys, macaw nestlings, mellifluous euphonias, collared peccaries, and gorgeous ocelots are beginning to change. The Children's Rainforest in Santa Elena near Monteverde is testament to the positive changes that can happen when young people commit to conserving their heritage while it is still there.

For more on where to stay in San José, please see the resources chapter.

Transport from San José

To get around Costa Rica from San José there are several options: public buses, tourist buses, private vans, taxis, rental cars, and local flights. Of these, the rental car option is often assumed to be the best one by international visitors when travelling independently. In Costa Rica, however, you may want to reconsider. Road conditions change rapidly, and a significant number of roads are so cratered with huge pot-holes that regular driving is impossible. Road repairs are haphazard and the best road one year could be a nightmare the next.

There are not always signs to warn drivers of roads that have been completely washed away or of any car-sized holes, which makes night driving extremely challenging. If you rent a car and get a flat tire shortly after, drive to a gas station before you change it. You may be the victim of a flat tire scam, in which the driver is robbed as the tire is repaired. For all these reasons, it is usually preferable to engage a local driver; car, van, and taxi services are available. There are several charter van services in the San José area that cover the whole country.

Major ecotravel sites usually can arrange door-to-door transport for those starting in San José. Some research stations, including La Selva, have a scheduled private bus servicing the station on certain days, so inquire before you make your final arrangements.

Flower Service

Nocturnal cereus or wild pitaya (*Hylocereus costaricensis*, above) are pollinated by sphinx moths for the few hours that their night blooms last. One moth, *Manduca sexta*, visits between 10:00 and 11:30 PM. Sphinx moths "trapline" by travelling up to seven miles from one flower site to another, even if there are no flowers in between. The buds protect themselves by recruiting *Solenopsis* ants to ward off leaf and petal eaters in return for extra floral nectar.

Farmers' Market

Fruit spills from wagons in the San José mercado (above). Wild pineapple (opposite page, top) is similar to cultivated varieties (opposite page, below) that have juicier fruit lobes. Nance (opposite page, center), palm fronds, and fish are some of the other market produce offered, along with local cheeses, bread, fresh-squeezed orange juice, and much more.

Public buses are generally well-equipped coaches with comfortable seating. To signal to the driver that you need to get off, shout "*la parada*" before you reach your stop. Be careful: bus stations, particularly those in San José, are theft hot-spots. Watch your baggage at all times. These buses offer good service, but it is not advisable to use public buses if you are new to the country and travelling alone. Fortunately, San José bus stations have been relocated recently to shut down some of the stations in more notorious crime spots. The ICT office (the Costa Rica Tourism Board) in San José carries bus maps and schedules. For more information, see sidebar, page 92.

Taxis may be a cost-effective way to travel, even for difficult-to-reach locations or over long distances. It's worth checking prices and routes with the driver in advance.

For those beckoned by the romance of small planes, a network of air strips provides rapid access to outlying destinations, including places that otherwise require multiple transfers from bus to boat, such as Tortuguero and Barra del Colorado, and high-volume, lowland ecotravel destinations and resorts, including Quepos,

Puerto Jiménez, La Fortuna, and Tamarindo. There are two air services running from San José to these destinations. SANSA (506-221-9414) is located adjacent to the international airport; Juan Santamaria is based in Alajuela. A shuttle takes passengers from international arrivals to the SANSA area. NatureAir (506-220-3054) is based at the local airport Pavas, west of La Sabana. Both air services are close to San José (allow about 45 minutes from San José) and about fifteen minutes from each other. *Ticos* (the name Costa Ricans call themselves) advise that local air travel is best undertaken in the early mornings and not in the afternoons, when thunderstorms loom, reducing visibility and making small plane travel hazardous.

In terms of getting around San José itself, directions are often explained by landmarks rather than street addresses, so be prepared to give your taxi more than a simple street address for your destination.

Activities in San José
Mercado Borbon
One of San José's colorful tropical farmers' markets is on Calle 8 between Avenida 3 and 5. This market is so full of delicious tropical fruit, local cheeses, fresh herbs, and other produce that ecotravellers from temperate zones will wonder why they have never come across these delicacies before.

Cas is the Costa Rican guava (*Psidium friedrichsthalianum*). It makes a delicate fresh fruit drink, similar to lemonade, that is a delightful refreshment. *Refresco* or *fresco*, made of cas and other fresh tropical fruit pulp, sugar, and water, is a national drink. A variety of *frescos* are available throughout Costa Rica, bottled or from fountains, including *piña con leche*, exquisitely delicious pineapple in milk, and *guanabana* juice

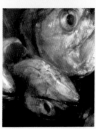

Alkaloids

In Costa Rica, high-quality coffee (top) is grown under shade trees (above, right). The shade trees provide fruit, fix soil nitrogen, and create nesting shelter for native birds, mammals, and insects.

Caffeine is an alkaloid, a class of addictive drugs used by plants as bitter defense agents to deter browsers. Nicotine, cocaine, and morphine are some of the 4,000 alkaloids found in plants. 45% of tropical plants contain alkaloids, while only half as many temperate plants do.

Nicotine affects humans as a stimulant, but to insects it is an insecticide: nicotine blocks insect enzyme systems and kills them. Nicotine was the first insecticide used by humans, as documented in ancient Egyptian hieroglyphics.

(accent on the second syllable), coming from the refreshing soursop (*Annona muricata*). You'll want to taste as many local varieties as you can. Other *fresco* flavors include *mora* (the tropical blackberry) and tamarind juice. Tamarinds are not native to Costa Rica, but can be found growing behind Tamarindo Beach and in other areas. The juice is made from imported dry pulp mixed with *tapa de dulce*, which is sugar produced by small rural sugarcane farms. Tamarind's invigorating taste comes from tartaric acid and it also contains calcium, iron, and B-vitamins.

Madrono (*Garcinia acuminata*) is local to Costa Rica and has rough, lemon-shaped yellow fruits that enclose deliciously tangy pulp and large seeds. Granadilla or passionfruit (*Passiflora ligularis*) is native to the Americas. Sip the juice and pulp from halved fruits, leaving the skin. The giant grenadilla or *granada real* (*Passiflora quadrangularis*) has edible, pulpy skin.

Peach palms, or *pejibaye* (*Bactris gasipaes*), are sold along the streets, boiled and ready for eating with a dollop of mayonnaise. Hearts of palm, or *palmito*, are prepared in Costa Rica from cultivated varieties of this palm tree, and there are several wild species that have been cut to an endangered level because of their use by local people. *Pejibaye*, a coconut relative, originated in the New World tropics and has been used as a staple starch for thousands of years.

Small yellow berries of nance (*Byrsonima crassifolia*) are packed with vitamin C. Look for wild trees loaded with the berries, or find them at the market. The aromatic flavor is wonderful, both when fresh and preserved.

One Costa Rican plum (*Synsepalum dulcificum*) contains an amazing taste enhancer that acts on our taste buds to reverse the signal produced by bitter and sour substances so that they instead taste sweet. This sweetener is known as miracolina, and is so effective that pharmaceutical companies mix it with bitter drugs

From Perfumes to Anecdotes

The heady aroma of queen of the night (*Brugmansia suaveolens*) is being analyzed as a perfume ingredient. This plant, native to Brazil, is related to *Datura,* which produces hyoscinescopolamine, used in a prescription motion-sickness patch to block nerve transmissions. Atropine, an important antidote to chemical weapons and to pesticide poisoning, is also derived from a species in this family. These plants contain many drugs affecting the central nervous system, and were used by Andes and Amazon Indians in hallucinogenic ceremonies. Because of these properties and their aromatic and beautiful flowers, the small tree has been spread throughout Central America.

Clearwings

Some butterflies have see-through wings to evade predators. *Greta oto* (below) is the most common clearwing among twenty species. This species is seen around San José and on mid-elevation slopes on both sides of Costa Rica. The butterfly mimics similar-looking, bitter-tasting butterflies so that predators are more easily trained to avoid them en masse.

The silvery caterpillar is called "little mirrors," or *espejitos*, for its sparkling dots. It becomes toxic by consuming night-shade family alkaloids. The male cannot synthesize the precursors of their sex pheromones, so they find daisy and borage plants with pyrrolizidine alkaloids and consume these pheromone precursors. They are then able to form multi-species leks, or groups of males, using these hormonal aromas derived from plants to attract females and prepare them to mate.

to make them palatable. In the markets, you'll probably see the relative of this fruit, the Sapodilla plum or zapote (*Puteria sapota*), a wrinkly, sweet fruit that resembles a mango, native to the area. Ripe fruit is available in market from wild sources. The related sapodilla medlar (*Manilkara zapota*) is even more prized, and comes from a tree that was used as a source for chicle, or chewing gum.

Work your fingers through the soft red and yellow spines of the rambutan (*Nephelium lappaceum*) to get to the delicate, juicy inner envelope that covers the inedible seed. Related to the lichee, the slightly less aromatic rambutan comes from Malaysia. Other nonnative fruit include star fruit (*Averrhoa carambola*), the watery yellow fruit native to Ceylon. These are filled with as much vitamin C as an orange, though they are bland in flavor. They are cultivated as ornamental trees and for the shape of their fruit. The large seeds of the Venezuelan fruit of *mamon* (*Meliccocus bijugatus*) are enclosed with a slippery, delicious flesh loved by children. The seeds can be roasted and eaten as nuts.

Agua de pipa, or coconut water, is offered along Caribbean beaches and should be from a freshly cut, immature coconut. The juice is rich in minerals and helpful for rehydration if you get sick. Ripe coconut milk can be

Legendmakers
The black witch moth (*Ascalapha odorata*) sometimes flies into homes to feed off fruit and roost. It can be seen in San José and mid to lowland areas. Mexican legends speak of it as a harbinger of death and as a house-borrower. The moth migrates huge distances including all over the United States, although it rarely breeds there. It has a purple band on the brown wings that creates an eerie glow.

drunk by putting a straw in the soft "eye" of a mature coconut.

The ideal time to visit Mercado Bourbon is very early in the morning, just after dawn, when you can explore the stands at their best and sample local varieties cultivated for their unique flavors. The market is not in a good neighborhood, so take a taxi. Ask your driver to meet you at a set time and place for your return.

Another market is held at the Feria Organica, northwest of the US Embassy, offering organic coffee, fruit, and vegetables Tuesday and Friday afternoons and Saturday mornings. San José also runs a Saturday morning farmers' market at Calles 7/9 and Avenidas 16/20. Mercado Central is near Mercado Bourbon and is at Calle 6/8 between Avenida Central and 1, and is closed Sundays.

Fruit from each of these markets should be washed in bottled water before eating. (You'll see at the market that the banana bunches are sometimes stored in the gutter.) Costa Rica has a good reputation for its clean water and public health policies. Nevertheless, bottled water is recommended even in cities and is widely available. In the lowland cities of the Caribbean, public water systems are impure.

Fake Aroma

Dutchman's piper (*Aristolochia grandiflora*, above and right), stinks of rotting meat, so don't sniff it close up. It has evolved to trap flies in its part-smooth, part-hairy gullet, where they pollinate the flower. Female carrion flies are attracted to the fetid smell, tricked into thinking it is a high-protein source (a carcass) in which to lay their eggs—only to be disappointed.

Gold and Jade Museums

Pre-Columbian gold gave Costa Rica its name. Costa Rica, or "rich coast," was named in 1522 by Captain Gil Gonzalez Devila for its dazzling gold, most noticeable in the ornaments worn by the indigenous Costa Rican peoples. Some of this gold was mined in the Osa Peninsula and then used by the pre-Columbian Diquis warriors. Other goldsmiths were members of the Corobicis villagers in the central highlands.

Diquis gold ornaments from the ancient southwestern communities of Costa Rica are on display at the Pre-Columbian Gold Museum in the Tourist Institute (Instituto Costarricense de Turismo). This is located at Calle 5 near the Avenida Central (Tuesday through Sunday, 506-223-0528, 506-243-4202).

Gold exhibits can be seen at the Jade Museum and National Museum. The Jade

Museum is found on the 11th floor of an office high-rise, the National Insurance Institute, east of the Barrio Amón at the north end of the Parque España (Monday–Friday, Avenida 7, Calles 9/11, 506-223-5800 x2584). This museum displays pre-Columbian jade, ceramics, and gold with many animal images of symbolic value.

The National Museum is housed in the Bellarista Fortress (Avenida Central, Calles 15/17, 506-221-4429, closed Monday). Here you'll find jade, gold, archeological finds, and colonial history exhibits.

Orchids

Costa Rica is an orchid-lover's world, and from February to May is the best time to visit. You can get a closer look at some species in several orchid gardens around San José; for smaller varieties, visit the orchid gardens in Monteverde, mentioned on page 74. The National Orchid Show in Zapote at the Republic Tobacco is held during March (506-223-6517, 506-224-4278, www.ticorquideas.com). Lankester Gardens is a renowned orchid and butterfly garden run by the University of Costa Rica and located 6km/3.7mi outside Cartago

Coatis

Coatis (*Nasua narica*, below), are large raccoon relatives that come out in the daytime in social groups, up in trees or roaming the ground. If attacked they defend as a group, all dropping out of trees at once to confuse the predator. Males wander around on their own, tail pointed heavenwards. At night females and young retire to a shelter tree, where they can feel the footfall of climbing jaguars and pumas (mountain lions) and be warned.

*Owls can turn their heads
180 degrees in either
direction, giving them an
all-encompassing gaze.
Costa Rican owls include
tropical screech-owls, pygmy
owls, and a burrowing owl
species.*

near Paraiso, south of San José. Here you can see blooms year-round (506-552-3247).

Butterfly Gardens

In the San Pedro campus of the University of Costa Rica, you'll find an insect museum with butterflies in the basement of the Artes Musicales building (Monday through Friday afternoons; call the faculty of agriculture at 506-225-5555 x318, 506-207-5647). To see more butterflies, visit Spyrogyra (just north of Barrio Amón, near the Jade Museum, southeast of El Pueblo shopping center), where you can watch blue morphos—though they are notoriously hard to get close to—heliconias and their mimics, and other beautiful species (506-222-2934, www.infocostarica.com/butterfly). Other butterfly gardens are scattered throughout

Costa Rica, the best being at La Paz Waterfall Gardens (506-225-0643, www. waterfallgardens.com). Another worthwhile destination offers San José pickups to Alajuela Butterfly Farm (506-438-0400).

Zoo Ave

This sanctuary is the most comprehensive and well-funded zoo of Costa Rican native species. It is also a haven for injured wild animals that were captured for the pet trade and can no longer survive on their own. Zoo Ave's major captive breeding program releases scarlet macaws and other endangered species back into the wild. Here you can see birds, including the gorgeous resplendent quetzal, as well as crocodiles and monkeys in jungle habitats.

Zoo Ave has played a significant role in conservation efforts and is well worth a visit. It's a bit of a drive out of San José, 15 minutes west of Alajuela and the international airport. (506-433-8989, www.zooave.org)

Snake Houses

For those interested in snakes, the Serpentario, Avenida 1, Calles 9/11 (506-225-4210), the World of Snakes, and a section of the aging Bolivar Zoo provide safe glimpses of a few poisonous and non-venomous snakes, reptiles, and frogs. The guide at the over-marketed shanty that makes up the World of Snakes actually provided inaccurate information on how to differentiate between venomous coral snakes and their nonvenomous mimics. So check your facts independently if you need to know what to be cautious about in the wild. Bolivar Zoo is at Calle 13 north of Avenida 9.

Habitat Park at INBio

San José area visitors are encouraged to visit a wonderful habitat park featuring Costa

Restoration Volunteers

Costa Rica is a hive of activity for environmental volunteering, from rainforest to reef. A small sample of organizations to consider include the following:

Earthwatch

This organization brings together volunteers with scientific field researchers engaged in environmental sustainability and wildlife studies, education, and action. Special educator programs fund teachers or teacher-student groups. (www.earthwatch.org)

Ríos Tropicales

Environmental education is the focus of this river conservation organization's volunteer activities. (tel 506-233-6455, www.rios-tropicales.com)

OTEC Tours

OTEC runs an extensive volunteer program with placements in many destinations within Costa Rica, including work with turtles, national parks, forest conservation, education, and more. OTEC is based in San José. (tel 506-256-0633 x311, fax 506-222-2605, www.volunteercostarica.com)

Curassows

The turkey-sized black male and brown female great curassow (*Crax rubra*, below) have gorgeous crests and stunning looks. They are declining rapidly because tropical forests are being opened up to hunting. The only remaining large population within Costa Rica is in Corcovado National Park, though wild curassows may be spotted at La Selva and Tortuguero. The curassow shown is the resident female at INBio Park in Heredia nar San Jose. The park includes a sculpture garden (above) with pieces by José Sancho.

Rica's diverse wildlife. INBioparque, renamed BioPark for simplicity, is a new development established by the education arm of INBio. INBio, the National Biodiversity Institute, was founded in 1989 and is Costa Rica's nonprofit, public interest, and private organization that specializes in mapping natural diversity, exploring its potential uses, and educating the public about conservation. The small park is located in Heredia, one of Costa Rica's oldest cities, and is a wonderful way of seeing a wide variety of Costa Rica's wildlife in a single afternoon. Its combination of outdoor habitats, live exhibits, and interactive museum experiences are in line with the newest thinking in wildlife and conservation education around the world. For that reason it's worth putting at the top of the list if you are staying in the San José area.

You can explore the bromeliad trail and the guarumo trail, where you can walk through small open habitats where wetlands, dry forest, humid rainforest, and central valley species live. Three-toed sloths, green iguanas, tanagers, and motmots come and go from the surrounding areas, and a tame great

INBio Database

Ana Huertas (left), a specialist at INBio, looks at INBio's insect archives. The agency is cataloging Costa Rica's vast biological resources. Newly identified species are discovered frequently. They are stored in climate-controlled cabinets. Their ecology and biomedical potential are explored through laboratory and field work. Scientists worldwide can access their records through the internet.

curassow stands on statues of wildlife by José Sancho.

Immerse yourself in the butterfly garden or take a dry-plunge into the lagoon by walking through the underwater viewing stations. Get a closer look at the intimate details of permanent living exhibits of poison dart frogs, a stingless bee's nest, a bullet ant community, gorgeous orchids and a variety of bromeliads.

The nation's decision to abolish a standing army in favor of spending the money on education has great promise for this country whose communities are living on very low income levels. People need to cultivate the land for survival, rather than for profit. The traditions of hunting and collecting wild animals as pets are unfortunately difficult to offset in a single generation. Yet a strong commitment to conservation and organic farming is also central to the beliefs of Ticos. Efforts by INBio, Zoo Ave, and other conservation organizations to educate local schoolchildren and their families about their natural heritage complement public

Bite-free Mosquitoes

Metallic giant mosquitoes (above) do not bite. These adults drink nectar and sap, like the majority of mosquito species, many of which are important pollinators. The larvae of the giant mosquito consume other mosquitoes. When in San José, you will probably meet the southern house mosquito (*Culex quinquefasciatus*). Ninety mosquito species are found in Costa Rica, though ocean breezes tend to keep them at bay. The nastiest biters are the rainforest blue devils (*Haemagogus* sp.). These can transmit yellow fever, though this disease is rare in Costa Rica. Mosquito habits are diverse: one genus even specializes in giant land crab burrows for their flight base and hatching center.

education in aiming to encourage Costa Ricans' appreciation of their own roots.

BioPark is open to the public in Heredia, a twenty minutes' drive west of San José (tel 506-244-4730, fax 506-244-4790, inbioparque@inbio.ac.cr, www.inbio.ac.cr/inbioparque.) It is located next to the research offices and laboratories of INBio.

Focus on INBio

A college trainee wafts a vial across a soft flame under the guidance of a white-coated researcher. She is sterilizing equipment to handle a new collection of extreme-temperature microbes just scooped up from the near-boiling hot springs of Rincón de la Vieja volcano. Multigallon stainless steel vats stand by, ready to brew biological samples and extract potential pharmaceutical breakthroughs. In the office above, Gantt charts map the health of the entire enterprise, project by project.

Bioprospecting

The lab is part of the bioprospecting arm of INBio, where employees are helping to look for potential uses of biodiversity. Could this species be the next biological control agent? The next miracle drug? Many antibiotics prescribed worldwide are based on natural products or their close derivatives, and the potential for a bioprospecting discovery in Costa Rica may lead to the next aspirin or Zocor. INBio's exploration focuses on the plant, insect, fungi, and microbial activity of novel compounds.

No single product has reached the market yet. Several samples being tested by partners are considered promising, however. Major agreements between INBio and pharmaceutical and biotechnological companies are set up on new terms that have been praised worldwide: the potential

Trays of preserved organisms (above) at INBio may hold the next major cure. Each specimen is attached to a minute bar code that is being scanned into a database by José Alejandro Herrera.

Bug Repellents

Research into malaria is proceeding at several Costa Rica institutions. Costa Rica is not a heavy mosquito country, but there are a few places where you will want to use repellent. DEET and the new lemon eucalyptus-based mosquito repellants field-test well. The US Center for Disease Control website advises that DEET should not be used at concentrations over 35%, because neurological side effects can occur at higher concentrations. A new water-based formulation is an improvement—it does not melt cameras like the original DEET did. The best alternative, the lemon eucalyptus repellant, marketed under the trade name "Off Botanicals" and other labels, seems to be less toxic and more pleasant to use than DEET. However, its lemon scent tends to attract some large bees, and it wears off more rapidly than DEET, so should be reapplied more frequently.

profits are shared between the company, INBio, and the Costa Rican government, so that Costa Rica establishes a sustainable basis for bioprospecting and contributes to the conservation of biodiversity. The partners cover research expenses, and local people participate in various phases of each project, enhancing their skills. INBio has fee-based agreements with multinational companies and negotiates royalty rates in these contracts so that any major finds generate profits shared with MINAE, the Ministry of Environment and Energy, funneling dollars from major discoveries back to national parks and local research.

At this point, bioprospecting is a relatively minor activity, still in its start-up phase and without much to show for the effort in terms of products. Tourism in Costa Rica generated $421 million in 1993 and forestry $28 million. In contrast, just over half a million dollars has been transferred by INBio to MINAE for conservation from the "10% up-front fee" of the research budgets with industrial partners; in addition, the bioprospecting projects with industrial partners have also contributed more than a million and a half dollars to the conservation

Passionflowers

Passionflowers cheat, mimic, zap, prick, recruit, and morph for survival—an array of evolutionary creativity. You will find them draping forest light gaps in a constant battle against *Heliconius* butterfly larvae.

Look at passionflower leaves and you will spot a great variety of leaf shapes between plants even with the same flowers. This appears to be an attempt to mimic the leaf shapes of common rainforest plants that *Heliconius* larvae cannot eat—passionflower plants with leaves resembling other plants are more successful because female *Heliconius* egg-layers avoid them.

Hermit and long-billed hummingbirds pollinate scarlet passionflowers, attracted by the color. *Passiflora vitifolia* (left) is nontoxic. The corona forms a circle of hairs that screens small marauding insects from the nectar cup. The only animals to reach into the flower are large enough to touch and pollinate the central post while they sip the nectar.

Smaller passionflowers are greenish with a musky odor that attracts specialized short-tongued wasp pollinators. Others are blue and full of perfume. *Passiflora foetida* is blue and white, stinks, and is toxic. These attract carpenter bees that feed their dehydrated nectar to their young, mixed with pollen. Female carpenter bees tag each flower they visit with their own scent marker. This acts as a repellent to other carpenter bees, perhaps because they indicate the blossoms will be low on juice.

Some passionflower leaves contain sugar molecules bonded to cyanide, called cyanogenic glycosides, plus cyanohydrins. When these compounds are digested, deadly cyanide gas is released. Each of the fifty passionflower species has a different set of glycosides, and *Heliconius* caterpillars have gut enzymes specially evolved to detoxify specific cyanogenic glycosides. *Heliconius* butterfly females selectively lay eggs only on the passionflower species that their offspring are adapted to detoxify.

Passionflowers recruit ant defenders as well. The ants are fed by nectaries dotted around the leaf stems, and the passionflower beefs up the nutritional value of the nectar by adding essential amino acids. These ants and wasps sting and bite flea beetles and heliconid caterpillars, killing twice as many as on plants without this high-octane reward and keeping the plant clear of herbivores.

Two percent of passionflower species also produce fake eggs at leaf tendrils. These are modified nectarines and are shaped like butterfly eggs to indicate to visiting female *Heliconius* butterflies that the leaf is already taken, so the butterflies will then avoid it.

All these strategies combine to allow passionflowers to thrive and outwit heliconia chompers, at least for a while.

Natural Work
The quest to explore our diversity involves old-world and new-world techniques. Koniko, trained in technical illustration, works in a rainforest lab to draw and paint live jumping spiders for a new book on spiders (top). Daniel Perez and Roberto Espinoza (above right) preserve botanical material for the INBio Plant Inventory and Internet Division.

areas and public universities of Costa Rica. The approximate economic value of the training of local scientists, the equipment, and infrastructure resulting from these deals exceeds $1.7 million. The potential royalties of major pharmaceutical or biotechnological discoveries would promote biodiversity conservation enormously. The world is watching this endeavor—a new model that potentially moves beyond the exploitative colonial model to a mutually beneficial one.

In addition to partnering with developed nations for bioprospecting, Costa Rica, along with other countries, plays an important role in finding remedies for diseases plaguing the developing world such as Chagas' disease and dengue fever. In order to be adopted by the population base, treatments for these diseases must be inexpensive and naturally derived.

In Costa Rica, dengue outbreaks in certain areas of the country are a big problem, although the government health services control the disease more effectively than in neighboring countries. Dengue incidence is on the rise around the world. The Gates Foundation has just committed $55 million to accelerate the development of a dengue vaccine. Low-tech, ecological methods of mosquito control are practical and promising. These include the use of fungi that kill the mosquito larvae. It is also possible that dengue could be controlled by a new method being used for malaria, with bacteria known as Bt (*Bacillus thuringiensis var israelensis*). Practical work in Peru shows that Bt can be cultured at reasonable cost in coconuts near mosquito ponds, then released to interrupt mosquito breeding, working effectively for two to three weeks.

Costa Rican research into Chagas' disease and dengue operates on several fronts. The National University, EARTH, and INBio have teamed up with international partners to look for solutions to Chagas' disease. INBio has received funding from Netherlands Development Aid (NEDA) to undertake its

Leaf Chemists

Santos and Hugo Guadamuz (below left) collect leaf miners (above) for a University of Bristol program. Leaf miners are so specialized in leaf chemistry that each plant species has a unique species of miner. The study of the chemistry involved may lead to new crop protection approaches.

Tool Users

White-faced capuchin monkeys (right) use eight different kinds of tools. They club venomous snakes to kill them, for example, and throw sticks at humans to keep them away.

Capuchins are slow breeders with a long adolescence that allows teens to learn a great deal from adults, including how to use tools. More capuchin males than females are born, but more female adults exist because of the mortality resulting from teen male aggression.

Capuchin monkeys chew aromatic vines and rub the pulp in their fur, deterring skin parasites. Each white-faced capuchin troop is lead by an alpha male. Capuchin monkeys eat a wide variety of foods including squirrels and other monkeys, though they favor palm nuts and disperse many seeds.

pilot project for biological control of the *Aedes aegypti* disease-carrying mosquito larvae.

Diversity Database

Four percent of the world's terrestrial diversity is located within Costa Rica's borders, although Costa Rica only occupies 0.04% of the earth's land area—making it the most diverse country for its area in the world.

To chart the country's biodiversity, an army of parataxonomists has been recruited from the rural populace to gather samples of Costa Rica's half a million species. These samples are then entered into a database. Many of INBio's parataxonomists are from rural families who have seen their farmland changed back into conservation areas, and are now able to earn their livelihood while benefitting the environment. This integrated approach, developing both economically and environmentally sustainable practices, has so far been very successful.

Row upon row of carefully boxed beetles, flies, and other insects fill the drawers of humidity-controlled rooms in the taxonomic wing of INBio. Each specimen has a bar code with which it can be found in INBio's database, which contains records of each specimen's originating location. In outlying field stations across Costa Rica, researchers continually upload digital images of carefully identified and preserved samples, building a web-based database of information like none other in the world.

Each species is cross-referenced to every relevant research paper. Anyone can access this material, from school students in Santa Elena, Monteverde, who initiated the Children's Rainforest conservation project, to antiparasite researchers in West Africa.

Carara Biological Reserve

The closest reserve to San José is small but diverse and close enough for a day trip. It is especially full of species because it lies in an "ecozone" that covers a range in altitudes and is located at the overlap between the deciduous northern habitat of the dry-season Guanacaste region and the southern habitat of tropical rainforest, with its longer wet season. Such a combination of habitats gives this preserve its ecological richness.

Listen for the squawks of scarlet macaws (*Ara macao*), then pick out their rainbow colors. In Costa Rica, you'll only find wild populations here, in Manuel Antonio National Park, and on the Osa Peninsula—a testament to the fragile but valuable role played by these conservation areas. You'll spot black and green poison-dart frogs (*Dendrobates auratus*) climbing over the forest floor under the heliconia-filled understory. On the branches close by, trogons sit quietly, their plumage glowing with color. Toucans flit from treetop to treetop, and there are white-faced capuchin monkeys, two-toed sloths, armadillos, and peccaries to be seen. Birdwatchers will enjoy the

Pets or New Species?

Squirrel monkeys are believed to have been introduced to Costa Rica by humans up to 30,000 years ago. Their distribution is so spotty that researchers believed it must have been associated with human occupation. However, new DNA and behavioral studies suggest instead that squirrel monkeys may have evolved into a separate species within Costa Rica over the course of several million years. Their behavior is non-hierarchical, non-aggressive and gender-neutral, unlike South American squirrel monkey species 600 miles away. Females cluster their births into a few short, synchronized weeks, protecting the troop as a whole from predators that can only attack a few babies at a time and so are overwhelmed. Females form alliances to watch for attacking predators. At night, they roost with birds at the end of palm fronds, which amplify the slightest twitch made by any marauding snakes or leopards.

The Afterlife

The burial sites of indigenous peoples in the Carara area show significant care in preparing for the afterlife. Slaves, wives, food vessels, and armaments were entombed with high-profile occupants. The civilization was most active from 300 BCE to 1500 CE and was associated with the Güetars from the central plateau. One of their leaders, Garabito, would later successfully resist the Spanish conquest for many years and was never captured.

prospect of sighting many endemic and regionally restricted species, including black-hooded antshrikes, beryl-crowned hummingbirds, Baird's trogons, black-bellied and riverside wrens, fiery-billed aracaris, and orange-collared manakins.

Guides can be booked through your accommodations or tour company and are able to take you to restricted areas. Contact Quebrada Bonita ranger station (506-383-9953) for more information. For more on where to stay in Carara, please see resources chapter.

Headquarters Trail

The 3km/1.86mi headquarters trail leads from the main entrance through primary forest with plank-buttressed kapok trees (*Ceiba pentandra*) and espavel (*Anacardium excelsum*). Espavel fruit are similar to cashews, with a fleshy, sweet stem that swells when the toxic seed is ripe. The stem is the edible part and is picked up and eaten by bats. The bats drop the seeds around their roosts, dispersing the trees over a wide area. Watch for blue-crowned and red-capped manakins around the bird ponds.

Tárcoles River Trail

The highlight of the trip to this trail is the flyout of scarlet macaws from the inner forest to the mangrove roosts at the river mouth, which occurs at approximately 5 PM and is best seen from the river bridge. Look down and you may see crocodiles (*Crocodylus acutus*) on the river banks, which disappear when the river bursts during the wet season and fills the oxbow lakes around it. Watch for roseate spoonbills among the waterbirds around the lagoon. The trail opens up into disturbed habitat, so the best birding spots are often at the start.

To reach the reserve itself, take the Interamerican Highway from San José via Puntarenas, then turn south on route 34. (The river trail turnoff is just inside the north boundary of the park.) Turn east after the Río Grande de Tárcoles bridge to the reserve headquarters, 3km/1.8mi.

Tarcol Lodge

Tárcol Lodge is located close to Carara on a muddy sand flat ideal for watching birds come and go along the Tárcoles River. From the lodge balcony, you can watch scarlet macaws flying to their mangrove roosts each evening, or magnificent frigatebirds, bare-throated tiger-herons, crane hawks, yellow-naped and Amazon parrots, ringed and green kingfishers flying around. Visitors can arrange guided birdwatching visits to Carara Biological Reserve or along the Tárcoles River and mangroves. You may see endemic mangrove hummingbirds (*Amazilia boucardi*) and boat-billed herons (*Cochlearius cochlearius*). (tel 506-297-4134, www.costa-ricagateway.com)

Gondwanan Heliconia

Thirty species of heliconia plants (not related to heliconia butterflies) occur in Costa Rica (left, spiral, hanging variety). Heliconias originated when Africa and South America were connected in a huge landmass called Gondwanaland. *H. imbricata* and *H. wagneriana* fill their boat-shaped flower bracts with water to prevent nectar-robbing by ants. The water is not rainwater, but an acidic water produced by the plant. *H. imbricata* carries a community of rolled-leaf hispine beetle larvae, isopods, and butterfly larvae in leaf debris. Red and yellow, upward-growing *H. latispatha* is pollinated by the rufous-tailed hummingbird *Amazilia tzacatl*, the most common hummer around. *Heliconia psittacorum* has a special technique to encourage cross-pollination by "bonanza-blank" nectar production: Nectar is over-produced at some times and not produced at others, in a feast-or-famine cycle. This pushes the visiting hummingbirds to dip into more flowers during the bonanza.

Passionflower Butterflies

Heliconius, or passionflower, butterflies are one of only two butterfly genera that consume pollen. These butterflies mix pollen with nectar on their proboscis (above), creating a slurry they can drink. This increases the lifetime of the butterfly to several months instead of the several days most species live. *Heliconius hecale* (above right) is the most widespread and can be seen flying around orange *Lantana* and other flowers collecting nectar and pollen. Its caterpillars eat passionflower plants and absorb the cyanogenic glycosides. Their guts can detoxify specific cyanide producers. The adults are poisonous; while it was once thought that they passed on the glycosides from the host plant, presently they are believed to manufacture their own defenses. See also page 109.

Manuel Antonio National Park

Scarlet macaws, green iguanas, ctenosaurs, two-toed sloths, three-toed anteaters, and coatis are easily seen in this small, three-peninsula, three-beach national park of tropical moist forest. Primary and secondary forests envelop visitors. However, every year there are malaria cases recorded in the central Pacific region, where the park and its neighboring towns are located, although this information is not widely circulated.

An endangered population of 50 ginger, biscuit, and white squirrel monkeys (*Saimiri oerstedii citrinellus*) is also found in the park at Manuel Antonio, along with white-faced capuchins and howler monkeys. Squirrel monkeys are delightful to watch, and prefer secondary to primary forest because of the abundance of invertebrates, their primary food, among the greenery. The recent decimation of disturbed forests has hit them particularly hard and they are on the verge of extinction, having retreated to a few conservation "islands" like this one.

Baird's trogons, tyrant hawk-eagles, gray-headed chachalacas, Solater's antbirds, and brown boobies are among the 353 forest and seabird species one may see here.

138 tree species include the coconut palm (*Cocos nucifera*); soft-wooded, fast-growing balsa (*Ochroma lagopus*); beach apple, or manzanillo (*Hippomane mancinella*); and beach almond (*Terminalia catappa*), which is eaten by the macaws. Manzanillo, an exceptionally toxic mangrove found behind the beach, should be neither touched or burned; its "apples" are extremely poisonous. Balsa wood is currently used to reduce static charges in supertanker lining, decreasing the chance of sparks that otherwise are a fire hazard.

The park is so popular that access is limited to 600 people per day. Visitors can wander along the trails that follow the coastline and also cut across to the far reaches of the park. Or they can go by kayak with Iguana Tours through the mangrove swamps and around the local islands.

The riptides at Playa Espadilla, on the west side of the park by the entrance station, are so dangerous that swimmers regularly drown there. The other beautiful beaches in this park are swimmable. If you get caught in a riptide, relax and swim parallel to the shore until the current dissipates. Then swim back. If you fight the current as it pulls you out, you are more likely to get exhausted and succumb.

The reef off Playa Manuel Antonio is best for snorkeling, with wonderful coral and reef fish. Snorkelers can see 78 reef fish species

Mimics

Heliconius melpomene (below left) is a Mullerian mimic that has converged to look almost identical to the most common Heliconid butterfly of Costa Rica, *Heliconius erato*. Convergent species look the same but come from different genetic lineages. In *H. melpomene*, the white hind-wing patch peters out far from the edge, unlike the full stripe in the *H. erato* species. Both taste bitter to birds, due to the toxic cyanogenic glycosides that it seems the adults produce. Because they look so similar, a bird only needs to learn to avoid this pattern once, saving twice the amount of butterflies. There are eleven local races of *H. melpomene*, which identically mimic eleven out of twelve races of *H. erato*. This racial change is controlled by only five genes. Surprisingly, these two butterflies are not closely related, and this mimicry probably evolved within the last 200,000 years.

Dolphins (above) are among the marine mammals seen in Ballena National Park

and 24 crustacean species living around 19 coral varieties. There are 17 species of algae and 10 sponge species found here.

There are a variety of places to stay nearby. The large luxury cabins of Tulemar near the park offer full kitchens and rainfall showers. (tel 506-777-0580, fax 506-777-1579, www.tulemar.com). For more information on where to stay near Manuel Antonio, please see resources chapter.

Access

To get to the park entrance, visitors have to wade a river, which can be chest-height at high tide. The park is bounded to the north by a sprawl of hotels and inns, many with gorgeous views over coves. Manuel Antonio National Park is 6.4mi/4km to the north of Quepos, a town named after indigenous peoples, which is easily accessible from San José. Public buses leave several times a day for Manuel Antonio or Quepos from San José or Puntarenas. However, it is safer to take the guided visits from Fantasy Bus (506-220-2126).

For those with not much time in Costa Rica, a visit to this park can be squeezed into a day trip from San José. It takes about four hours one way by car or is a quick flight from San José; flights depart several times a day to Quepos with pick up and drop off services from your hotel. Be wary of staying in the vicinity: Quepos has a reputation as a high-theft town, particularly at the less expensive accommodations. Camping is forbidden in the park.

Rainmaker Nature Reserve

In the Quepos biological corridor north of Manuel Antonio, there is a beautiful plunging conservation area of 1,500ha/600ac called Rainmaker Nature Reserve. Set on the western edge of the central mountain range, this reserve extends from tropical moist forest to cloudforest at 1,700m/5,600ft. A canopy walk and Damas Cave stalactite formations beckon you to explore. (tel 506-777-1250)

Ballena National Park

Ballena is Spanish for whale, and this marine park is a wonderful place to see whales while walking among the coconut and beach almond trees.

Spinner and common dolphins (*Stenella longirostrus* and *Delphinus delphis*) are visible from the beaches. You may also spot migrating humpback whales (*Megaptera novaengliae*), melon-headed whales (*Peponocephala electra*), and sperm whales (*Physeter catodon*), as well as other marine mammals.

Frigatebirds, white ibis, and brown pelicans breed on Ballena Island.

This is a relatively new marine park with exceptional diving opportunities. El Tombolo is a narrow peninsula, which used to be an island, linking Uvita Point at the north end of the park. Sponges, sea anemones, and corals are found off its edge. Some of the best dives in Costa Rica are around the island group of Las Tres Hermanas in the middle of the bay, and a

Dive Caño Island and Ballena National Park
Mystic Dive Center specializes in PADI, scuba, and snorkeling off the Ballena beaches, in the bay, and around Caño Island. The dive company is found at Ventanas Beach, south of Dominical at Ballena National Park (tel 506-788-8636,www.mysticdive-center.com).

Avoid the spines of the black sea urchin while diving

A color-coded forest research project

group of reefs grow around this area. Trigger fish, Caribbean snook, anchovies, and flying fish swim around the corals. Iguanas, basilisk lizards, and frigate birds breed on the islands.

The south end of the park at Playa Ventanas is about 21km/13mi from Palmar Norte, and 4WD is recommended. Ballena National Park is 190km/118mi from San José via San Isidro, and 228km/141mi via Quepos over a very rough road.

A good ecolodge to stay at near the park is Hacienda Barú Lodge and Wildlife Refuge at Dominical on the coast (tel 506-787-0003, fax 506-787-0057, www.hacienda-baru.com). While you are there, visit Oro Verde, a private nature reserve (no lodge) a few kilometers northeast of Ballena (www.costa-rica-birding-oroverde.com).

Juan Castro Blanco National Park

This park, set on the side of the active Platanar Volcano, is relatively unknown. Among its many highlights are the orchids and the resplendent quetzals that its cloud forest attracts. To reach this park from San José, drive to Alajuela and then to Ciudad Qesada (San Carlos). The park entrance is east of this town.

4
Mountains

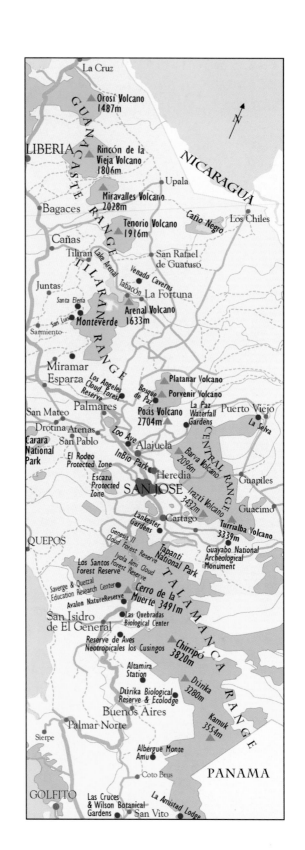

La Cruz

Orosí Volcano
1487m

GUANACASTE RANGE

LIBERIA

Rincón de la
Vieja Volcano
1806m

NICARAGUA

Miravalles Volcano
2028m

Upala

Bagaces

Caño Negro

Los Chiles

Tenorio Volcano
1916m

Cañas

Tilirán

San Rafael
de Guatuso

Lake Arenal

Venado Caverns

Juntas

Tabacón

La Fortuna

Santa Elena

San Luis

Monteverde

Arenal Volcano
1633m

TILARAN RANGE

Sarmiento

Miramar

Esparza

Los Angeles
Cloud Forest
Reserve

Platanar Volcano

Bosque
de Paz

Porvenir Volcano

San Mateo

Palmares

Poás Volcano
2704m

La Paz
Waterfall
Gardens

Puerto Viejo

La Selva

Drotina Atenas

Zoo Ave

CENTRAL RANGE

San Pablo

Alajuela

Carara
National
Park

El Rodeo
Protected Zone

InBio Park

Barva Volcano
2906m

Escazu
Protected
Zone

Heredia

SAN JOSE

Guapiles

Irazú Volcano
3432m

Guacimo

Cartago

Lankester
Gardens

Turrialba Volcano
3339m

QUEPOS

Genesis III
Cloud Forest Reserve

Tapantí
National Park

Guayabo National
Archeological
Monument

Iyola Ami Cloud
Forest Reserve

Los Santos
Forest Reserve

Saverge & Quetzal
Education Research Center

Cerro de la
Muerte 3491m

TALAMANCA RANGE

Avalon Nature Reserve

Las Quebradas
Biological Center

San Isidro
de El General

Reserve de Aves
Neotropicales los Cusingos

Chirripó
3820m

Altamira
Station

Dúrika
3280m

Dúrika Biological
Reserve & Ecolodge

Buenos Aires

Kamuk
3554m

Palmar Norte

Sierpe

Albergue Monte
Amu

Coto Brus

PANAMA

GOLFITO

Las Cruces
& Wilson Botanical
Gardens

La Amistad Lodge

San Vito

Eyecatchers
A *lluvia de oro*, or golden raindrop orchid variety (*Oncidium* sp., page 121), appears to mimic showy nectar-filled vine flowers to attract more pollinators. A huge number of orchids can be found in mountainous rainforests (left).

Giant rainforest trees surround you, buttresses higher than your head. Suddenly you feel the cool atmosphere getting warmer, smelling as pungent as just-struck matches. Hot fog wafts between the cool bamboo fronds in front of you, and a thudding sound kicks from beneath the ground. You're in volcano country, and despite being surrounded by rainforest, you have reached an area filled with steaming fumaroles, hot springs, and boiling mud pits. Volcanoes are among the attractions of Costa Rica's mountains, which also offer great orchids and an escape from the heat and humidity of the lowlands.

You'll find volcano action along the northern central reaches of Costa Rica's

Waterfall below Rincón de la Vieja

mountainous backbone. The cordillera is made up of four mountain ranges that stretch roughly from north to south: the Guanacaste Range, the Tilarán Range, the Central Range, and the Talamanca Range. The Talamancas spill over into Panama.

Costa Rica's active volcanoes are active geological chimneys where magma from deep in the earth spews upward, producing lava flows and hot ash explosions from the most active volcanoes. On the slopes, you can walk through rainforests dotted with steam vents, hot springs, and boiling mud cauldrons heated intensely by searing underground volcanic gases. The most visited volcano villages for inter-national visitors are around the active Arenal Volcano. Poás Volcano is very accessible from San José and also offers an orchid garden, making it a popular destination as well.

The wilder Talamanca Mountains in the south have the oldest and highest peaks in Costa Rica. Unlike their northern counterparts, these wild uplands are nonvolcanic, although active faultlines are present, so you may experience earthquakes as North and South America jostle for position with oceanic plates. Chirripo is the highest peak at 3,820m/12,532ft and is partly clothed in a type of alpine ecosystem called páramo, which extends up to 4,374m/15,526ft in the Andes.

La Amistad International Biosphere Reserve includes much of the Talamanca highlands, a wild area home to indigenous groups. This area is virtually inaccessible to visitors, although details to access the region are included in this guide. The best way to experience this park is by a lengthy visit to one of a handful of ecolodges with private reserves abutting the edges of the park on the Pacific side (see this chapter) or Caribbean side (see chapter five).

Orchid Feeders

A view of the central divide facing north (below), shows the prevailing fog-soaked winds moving from east to west (right to left). These damp Caribbean winds cloak eastern slopes with fog drip ideal for orchids. Northwestern slopes are drier and have fewer epiphytes.

Sit and Wait

The flowers of each of the orchids shown above and below are only a few millimeters in length. The orchid above, with flowers like half-open books, claps pollonia (pollen clumps) onto visitors. *Dracula* sp. (below left) orchids attract fungus gnats by mimicking fungi. Some *Masdevallia* sp. orchids (below, center left and right) have modified sepals so that they capture pollinators in their buckets. *Lepanthes* sp. orchids (below right) provide shelter with their leaf umbrellas to the small flies that pollinate them.

Orchid Gardens

You'll find many fascinating wild orchids in the mountains (see the second half of the chapter for more details). If you would prefer a more guided experience, several orchid gardens are worth visiting. The University of Costa Rica's Lankester Garden (506-552-3247) has a large orchid collection outside Cartago, east of San José. Rara Avis is an ecolodge that has cultivated orchids in their natural canopy environment for later enjoyment in homes (506-764-1111). The Monteverde Orchid Garden is run by one of the world's experts in orchids as a miniature research and education collection (506-645-5510). Some orchids depend on high altitudes or a particularly damp environment, so they will never make the transition to regular climates; preservation of their habitat is essential for their survival. Subalpine and alpine orchids that can only be grown in the wild include *Brachionidium*, *Fernandezia*, *Pachyphyllum*, and *Telipogon*

Cashing in on Color

Bandera Espanola (*Epidendrum radicans*, above and below left) is a year-round yellow-to-red orchid so common along some roadsides that it is almost a weed. Its lip signals to butterfly pollinators when they should not bother visiting by turning dark after pollination is complete. A group of flowers operates as a unit, with new yellow flowers attracting pollinators, against a background of older, darker orange petals. In other flowers, this usually signals that the yellow flowers carry nectar. But this orchid is cheating as it does not have nectar. The color is similar to introduced *Lantana camara* and native milkweed *Asclepias curassavica*, which carry nectar. Scientists believe the orchid is using Batesian mimicry to attract pollinating butterflies that have learned, from mimicked, nectar-laden flowers that look similar, to associate the color with nectar. However, the orchid does not use energy to produce a nectar reward.

Lantana camara (above right) is a great hedgerow butterfly magnet. It was introduced from the West Indies.

species. Look carefully around you when you are exploring and you may come across some gorgeous surprises.

Guanacaste Range

The access roads reach the lower Pacific slopes of the Guanacaste and Tilirán volcanoes. These areas of the volcanoes are drier, however, than on the Caribbean side or near the peaks, meaning that although they are the most visited, they have the least epiphytes and orchids. Orchid hunting is better at Poás Volcano.

The western slope forests of the Guanacaste Range have many giant figs with huge buttresses. The understory is open, and bamboos increase as you ascend in altitude. Golden-crowned warblers, ruddy woodcreepers, white-throated robins and rufous-and-white wrens may be spotted.

Large land crabs defend their burrows high on the sides of these mountains; the

Deforestation

Costa Rica is trying to balance the need for resources and logging income with the long-term benefits of conservation and ecotravel. Legal logging trucks (above) thunder through the roads by day. Some allege that these are replaced by illegal trucks at night. Ecotravel is one of the top three foreign income generators, significantly improving the chances that many national forests will be preserved intact.

crabs participate in a remarkable mass migration from ocean to mountainside. The crab burrows are also home to a unique species of mosquito. The male of this mosquito pairs up with a female when she is still in the pupating stage, grabbing onto the female with a specially adapted large leg paddle.

Rincón de la Vieja

Rincón de la Vieja, 1,806m/5,924ft, is visited less frequently than those mountains in the Tilarán and Cordillera Central because it is much further from San José, requiring several hours to reach by car. But its tall forests and steam pots are worth an expedition.

Rincón de la Vieja erupts unpredictably every few years, usually issuing to the north, creating dangerous pyroclastic flows. The lava flows are not visible, in contrast to those of Arenal. Its flanks are peppered with fumaroles, boiling hot springs or *hornillas* ("kitchen stoves"), and mud pots under the deep, tall, montane wet forest. Toucans and manakins flit around the forest, which is adorned with delicate bamboos. Las Espuelas, on the dry western slope, is the main entrance. To access the more humid forest, go to Santa Maria Hacienda to the southeast; both entrances lead to the same trail system. There are three beautiful waterfalls in the park, but don't drink the water.

The various volcanic hot spots are fascinating and can be found about halfway up the volcano, along an accessible trail that leads either from Las Espuelas car park or Santa Maria Hacienda. At Las Espuelas there is an information booth, with toilet facilities, camping, and picnic tables.

The trail to the summit is much more strenuous than those to the hot springs and leads to the cloud forest volcanic ridgeline, complete with the increased danger of eruption, extremely high winds, and exposure. There are several craters near the

summit. Wind-trimmed *Clusia rosea* provide
a sculpted treeline; scree and grasses replace
trees as you get closer to Von Seebach
Crater. This precedes Rincón de la Vieja by
3km/1.9mi. Be prepared to take two days if
the weather dictates, although the round
trip across the difficult terrain usually takes
about 8 hours for fit travellers. There is a
campsite 0.5km/0.3mi from the summit if
bad weather strikes. Horses will make your
journey easier: they are for hire at Las
Espuelas and can reach near the summit.
Guides can be arranged to navigate your
route through the park (506-666-5051).

Highland tinamous, black-and-yellow
silky flycatchers, and ruddy-capped
nightingale-thrushes can be found on these
remote peaks. Among the boulder and lava
scree you may spot rock wrens and Botteri's
sparrows.

Los Azufrales sulfur hot springs are
3km/2mi from Santa Maria Hacienda and
provide a wonderfully refreshing hot-and-
cold soak.

*Hot springs are created
underground when hot
gases heat plentiful
underground and surface
water. Fumaroles or steam
geysers occur when water is
scarce, and produce
steaming holes in the
rainforest floor that create
loud thudding sounds.*

Song Catchers

Flocks of the gorgeous blue-hooded euphonia (*Euphonia elegantissima*) are now rare because of the legal trade in caged birds. This species moves to higher Pacific and central elevations (above) during the breeding season, then down to the Caribbean slope. Lesser goldfinches (*Carduelis psaltria*) and yellow-bellied siskins (*Carduelis xanthogastra*) are also caught and caged for their mellifluous songs. All three residents are now difficult to find in the Cordillera Central and Talamancas.

To reach the Las Espuelas entrance, take the Interamerican Highway north from Liberia to the Curubande turnoff at 4.5km/2.8mi. Turn east towards Curubande for 12km/7mi, then up towards the volcano and the Las Espuelas/Las Pailas entrance on a rough stone road. The Santa Maria entrance is better accessed from Bagaces via Aguas Claras, rather than from Liberia.

Rincón de la Vieja Ecolodges

Several ecolodges are scattered on the lower slopes of Rincón de la Vieja, which, on the Pacific side, are in the dry forest region of Costa Rica. If you are looking for lush rainforest, these may disappoint you—the more arable lowlands around Curubande dry out for six months of the year. However, if you want to avoid the rain, this is the place and time for you!

In Curubande, Albergue de Montaña Rincón de la Vieja offers treetop trails across seventeen platforms, which require four hours, day or night, and are close enough to the Los Azufrales for a dip after your walk (tel 506-256-8206, fax 506-256-7290, rincon@ sol.rasca.co.cr). Hacienda Guachipelin also has a canopy tour in a canyon (tel 506-442-2818, fax 506-442-1910, www.guachipelin.com, www.canopytour.com, info@guachepelin.com). Posada el Encuentro offers bed and breakfast with a volcano tour and also camping in their rainforest, tent supplied (tel 506-382-0815, fax 506-666-2472).

Santa Maria Volcano Lodge (tel 506-235-0642, fax 506-272-6236) is on the lush Atlantic side towards the Santa Maria entrance, with greater access to wet rainforest.

Tilarán Range

Arenal Volcano

Arenal has been active since 1968. Volcano watchers hum around La Fortuna and Tabacón villages where tours, restaurants, and accommodation options blare their signs. If the clouds clear, it is possible to

Volcano Safety

Arenal is an active volcano that unfortunately claims lives every few years. In 2000, an unexpected pyroclastic flow killed a guide and severely injured a mother and child at an observation area designated as safe. When it erupted in 1968, Arenal's volcanic effects reached 5km/3mi west and killed 78 people. Now, the one-sided lava flow is pirouetting so that hotels built to watch the red and orange lava at night are gradually finding themselves out of view. Do not walk up the trails close to any volcano summit unless the volcano is dormant. Activity can change at any time, so be prepared to change your plans immediately if you hear sounds or unusual steam activity that may warn of an impending eruption.

Mud pots are created when sulfuric acid from the volcano dissolves the rock structure. This slippery mix of minerals mixes with water to make mud at several hundred degrees. The mud bubbles up to the surface, prodcuing ponds and cauldrons of bubbling activity around active trails.

Amps

Two thirds of the electricity
supplied in Costa Rica is
generated by Lake Arenal's
hydroelectric plant. The Costa
Rican Institute of Electricity
completed the associated dam
in 1979. The lake itself also
forms a wind corridor that
provides perfect conditions for
wind-generated electricity on
its hills (above), and for
windsurfing.

watch Arenal's lava flows at night from your
natural Tabacón jacuzzi. See "Volcano
Safety," page 131.

You can also watch the volcano at a
greater distance from some Monteverde
locations, detailed in chapter two.

For vulcanologists who don't mind the
risk, Arenal Volcano Observatory offers an
ecolodge on its slopes. (tel 506-257-9489,
fax 506-257-4220, www.arenal-observatory.
co.cr, info@arenal-observatory.co.cr). This
lodge was originally built as a scientific
research station for Smithsonian scientists.

Lake Arenal provides two-thirds of the
electricity for the entire country, having
been dammed at one end. The long lake
surface creates a wind tunnel, and windsurfing is fantastic on its extensive waters.
You can rent equipment at the lake.

Arenal Botanical Gardens just south of
Nuevo Arenal offers a collection of world
and native plants.

Places to Stay Near Arenal

Arenal Volcano is far from San José, so it's
helpful to stay at La Fortuna or Tilarán. You
can reach either by bus from San José; either
trip takes about a half a day. Good options
include the Cabinas La Rivera in La Fortuna
(506-479-9048) and Tabacón Hot Springs
Resort and Spa (tel 506-519-1900, US tel
877-277-8291, www.tabacon.com). If you're
prepared for another half-day trip, you can
continue to Monteverde from La Fortuna.
One shuttle from La Fortuna to Monteverde
(506-645-5263) is by boat and jeep. It takes
about three hours to reach Tilarán from La
Fortuna. Or, you can combine the entire trip
into one day's drive from San José to
Monteverde via Arenal, avoiding the
dangers of staying too close to the volcano,
while still getting a chance to see it.

Venado Caverns

Fifteen-million-year-old caverns host lime-stone stalactites and stalagmites, plus fascinating marine fossils and live cave animals. The caves are 45-minute drive northwest from La Fortuna.

Central Range

The Central Range, Cordillera Central, is scattered with oak-filled forest, all that remains after deforestation for dairy and vegetable farms. You will also see coffee plantations, the older style being planted under fruiting shade trees that attract and feed many wild birds.

Poás National Park

The 2,500m/8,200ft summit of Poás Volcano is easily accessible from San José by bus or car (37km/25mi), making it a popular day trip. It has enough vegetation around the peak to attract hummingbirds and provide good epiphytic habitats for orchids, unlike Irazu.

Arenal Volcano

Arenal is so active that its sulfur compounds seed a cloud layer (above). In this way the world's volcanoes act as a global cooling force: their production of cloud-forming aerosols and dust blocks sunlight. Although Arenal's clouds often mask the fantastic lava and rock that spew out unpredictably from Arenal's three craters, many visitors are rewarded with a view of the red-hot lava at night.

Torito

Large flowers of *Stanhopea costaricensis* (right) are called "little bulls" or *torito* for the horns on the flower lips. There are several as yet unidentified similar species found in the Rio Indio area. These are perfumed epiphytes with psuedobulbs and are pollinated by euglossine bees. The bizarre flower structure forces bees to fall through the flower, down the column onto the lip, in the process pollinating the short-lived flower.

The Poás area is the orchid-hunting volcano for first-time visitors.

The crater gets covered in clouds later in the day, so go early. Be prepared for cold weather. With its sister, Barva Volcano, Poás raised the entire central valley and has been active for 11 million years; in recent history it has been active every 40–45 years. Poás is unusual because it has nine craters that connect directly to a central magma chamber. The magma chamber is the source of pressure and heat; therefore Poás has more escape routes than other volcanoes and so tends to release pressure more effectively. Poás spewed a 4,000m/13,120ft plume of mud and steam in 1910, and in 1989 belched ash a mile high.

Visitors can look over the main crater, which is 0.5km/0.3mile wide and 300m/328yd deep and surrounded by fumaroles. The surrounding environment varies from barren ash to elfin forest. The extinct crater seen from Botos Lake trail (1km/0.6mi) is near a *Clusia odorata* forest that is particularly bonsai-like because of the effects of sulfuric acid rain from the sulfur in the volcano, as well as the extreme wind and cold.

Here you can see 26 different bird species, occasionally including resplendent quetzals. Listen for the song of the national bird, the clay-colored robin (*Turdus grayi*) along the luminous, mossy, elfin forest of the Escallonia trail (1km/0.6mi). Here you can see Poás magnolias (*Magnolia poasana*) and escallonia trees (*Escallonia poasiana*). Escallonia trees grow at the frost-line across Costa Rica mountains, above which few trees or tree ferns are found.

For those wanting to find accommodations close to the volcano, there are several options, including Lagunillas Lodge, which has extensive trails through a private forest and pastureland (506-389-5842).

To reach Poás from San José, drive to Heredia, then take the Barva-Birri road to Vara Blanca, where you should turn left. After about 6km/3.7mi, turn right to Poasito. Day tours are run from San José, and Poás is close enough to San José for a taxi to be economical if you have no car.

Bosque de Paz Cloudforest Lodge and Reserve

This is a well-loved and highly esteemed birding and wildlife lodge located between Poás Volcano and Castro Blanco National Park in a private biological reserve of 1,000ha/3,000ac. Over 300 bird species have been recorded here. Trails totaling 28km/17mi wind through primary and secondary forest across the continental divide, with altitudes ranging from 1,400m/4,592ft to 2,450m/8,036ft. Violet sabrewings, green-crowned brilliants, and purple-throated mountain gems are among the many hummingbirds you may see.

Fungi Feeders

Wild orchids use mycorrhizal fungi to feed them at least when young, controlling the fungi by releasing phytoalexin compounds. The fungi collect and break down nutrients into a form that the orchid can use, collecting these nutrients from a wide area by extending much deeper into the branches and crevices on which the orchid grows. In return, the orchids feed the fungi with sugars, and both organisms thrive.

Euglossine bees and their relatives (below) have metallic coats and seek out primitive scents such as oil of wintergreen, which is made from a naturally synthesized combination of aspirin and vinegar.

Tall Rainforest

Plank buttresses (right side of image) are triangular extensions located at the base of rainforest trees. Researchers have found these give less added support than was assumed. Instead, they are loaded with lenticels, like those found in mangrove snorkel roots. Lenticels are aerating cells that take in oxygen for the tree during the wet season, when the waterlogged roots cannot do so. (All plants need airborne oxygen to survive during periods of darkness.) Buttresses also act as dams during flooding, collecting high-nutrient debris above the thin, mineral-poor rainforest floor.

Listen for the "bonks" of three-wattled bellbirds, or the rusty-gate hinge tones of golden-browed chlorophonia (*Chlorophonia callophrys*). Rare solitary eagles (*Harphyhaliaetus solitarius*) sometimes soar overhead. (tel 506-234-6676, fax 506-225-0203, www.bosquedepaz.com, info@bosquedepaz.com).

La Paz Waterfall Gardens (Peace Waterfall)

La Paz Waterfall Gardens is a much visited and praised series of hummingbird, orchid, and butterfly gardens. The butterfly garden is very large, and the waterfalls add to the natural ambiance. The gardens are one hour from San José, near Poás Volcano, at 1,373km/4,500ft altitude. There is a restaurant on the grounds. (tel 506-225-6043, www.waterfallgardens.com)

Horses are available for hire for the more arduous treks

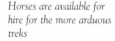

Irazú Volcano

This 3,432m/11,257ft volcano is the highest in the country and overlooks San José and Cartago (32km/20mi from San José). One can reach the moon-like summit easily during a day trip from either city. People sensitive to high altitudes may experience increased fatigue, and the summit may be unexpectedly cold. Eruptions in the 1960s rained ash on Cartago residents, the city that was once Costa Rica's capital. The volcano erupted most recently in 1994.

The slopes have been deforested to make way for dairy pastureland and so there are few orchids or hummingbirds to be seen, but the drive is beautiful nevertheless. Wild oaks, ravines, and fields reach to 3,100m/10,168ft. Halfway up you can walk in the oak and pine reforestation project in the Area Recreativa Jiménez Oreamundo, 8km/5mi west of Tierra Blanca.

As you continue up the volcano above the timberline, the habitat shifts into páramo, studded with a few large oak trees. You may spot the red flowers of endemic *Castelleja irazuensis*, or see any number of birds, including volcano juncos.

Mountain Crabs

Upland crabs (*Gecarcinus quadratus*, below) can be found high up on some mountains. They live in burrows around tree bases. They reached these altitudes after a long trek from the ocean where they hatched. During breeding season, the brown crabs return to the shoreline in a mass migration. Females change color and lay eggs while being washed by the surf, violently shaking their bodies to release up to 100,000 offspring.

Ferns color the trunks and the moist understory (right).

At the summit, short trails lead around four craters and one pyroclastic cone. The semi-dormant main crater has formed a lake tinged green with sulfur compounds and thermal bacteria. This is surrounded by fumaroles that release sulfur-laced steam.

You can get to Irazú by bus or car. Buses travel round-trip on weekends and holidays only, from San José and Cartago. By car, go east on the Interamerican Highway to the Taras intersection; turn left there (before Cartago) and then take your first left again, and follow the signs. A taxi may provide a reasonable round-trip rate.

Turrialba Volcano

Northeast of Irazu Volcano is Turrialba Volcano with three craters. Its last eruption was in 1866, and it was considered dormant, but it is active seismically and is dotted with fumaroles. This is the only volcano in the country where you can walk into the crater, though you do so at considerable risk. Its steep flanks are partially covered with montane rainforest. The Guayabo National Monument is located near Santa Cruz below the volcano, the most significant archeological site in Costa Rica. You will need a 4WD vehicle.

Volcán Turrialba Lodge

Volcán Turrialba Lodge is located close to the volcano and offers horseback rides into the volcano and a tour through the primary forest where quetzals, among 78 other bird species, may be spotted. You will need 4WD to travel here from San José, or arrange a pickup from the lodge. Due to the volcano's activity, tour companies no longer advise staying at the lodge. (tel/fax 506-273-4335, www.volcanturrialbalodge.com, info@volcanturrialbalodge.com)

Orchids like Fernandezia costaricensis *(above), an epiphyte with a fireworks-burst of crimson flowers, defy expectations. Other orchids (below) look like common lilies-of-the-valley.*

Rancho Naturalista

This ecolodge and 49ha/120ac reserve is in the Caribbean premontane forest near Turrialba Volcano; the lodge is located at 900m/3,000ft in elevation. Ecotravellers interested in birds will find much to delight them here.

Over 400 bird species are found along the 8km/5mi of trails, including dozens of tanagers, whistling wrens, brown-billed scythebills, and keel-billed toucans. The calls of great tinamou can be heard ringing from the undergrowth. 200 bird species can be seen from the lodge balcony, and hummingbird pools by waterfalls attract many species both from lowland rainforest, like the purple-crowned fairy (*Heliothryx barroti*), and from foothills or higher elevations, like the snowcap, an iridescent purple hummingbird with a laser-white hat, (*Microchera albocoronata*). Snowcaps are altitudinal migrants, moving down to lower altitudes after the breeding season. At either altitude, they frequent *Warszewiczia* trees and other flowers. Please bear in mind the activity of the volcano when considering whether to stay at the lodge. (tel 506-297-4134, US/Canada tel 888-246-8513; www.costaricagateway.com)

Talamanca Range

Tapantí National Park

This small 5,091ha/12,577ac reserve is a popular birding hotspot, opening at 6 AM. The reserve has just been extended to incorporate the Rio Macho forest reserve, making it an important biological corridor. The park now reaches all the way to Chirripó National Park, and from there to La Amistad and Panama. In the future, the goal is to extend the corridor north to Mexico and south to South America so that

Páramo

The temperature of the subalpine páramo (left) fluctuates 20°C/80°F within 24 hours. Plants are effectively living in a nutrient desert, because bacteria cannot break down debris under these conditions. The red leaves and leathery surfaces are a common sunlight defense found in the scrubby shrubs of Ericaceae, Poaceae, and Hypericaceae of the páramo. Dwarf bamboo (*Swallenochloa* sp.), shown on the opposite page, provides cover above the timberline of the páramo. Cushion plants grow dense clusters of small leaves that raise the temperature of their microclimate by a few degrees under the sheltering clump.

Below: Making the pilgrimage across Cerro del la Muerte for the Virgin of Los Angeles
Right below: Home-sweet-home on the páramo foothills

Snake Charmers

The feared *terciopelo,* or fer-de-lance (*Bothrops asper,* below), accounts for seventy percent of Costa Rican snakebites. Fortunately, the mussurana snake, or *zopilota* (*Clelia clelia*), can kill the fer-de-lance. The mussurana catches the fer-de-lance, injects venom, and constricts it to death. The mussurana carries anti-venom agents in its own blood that counteracts the fer-de-lance's blood-curdling, edema-inducing, and flesh-eating poisons. The mussurana is bright orange when young and can therefore be confused with a coral snake, but grows to be large and blackish. The mussurana is often seen slithering across roads. If you see one, leave it alone: it is protected by CITES and serves an important function in keeping fer-de-lances at bay. CITES is the Convention on International Trade in Endangered Speicies of Wild Fauna and Flora.

animals can continue to migrate along the entire stretch as they used to do.

The 1,525m/5,000ft elevation rainforest is a good site to look or listen for the 211 bird species in the area, including black-faced solitaires, three-wattled bellbirds, tinamous, collared trogons, red-headed and prong-billed barbets, emerald toucanets, azure-hooded jays, and various antbirds.

To reach Tapantí, drive from San José to Cartago, then on to Paraiso and Orosi. From there follow the signs to Tapantí. By bus, go from San José or Cartago to Orosi, and then take a taxi.

Several businesses in the area specialize in trout farming associated with the Río Grande de Orosi, including the Kiri Lodge and reserve (506-533-3040), which is a good site for birding.

Cerro de la Muerte

Oak forest covers the Talamanca Mountains to the treeline at around 2,898m/9,500ft. Above it, treeless páramo with shrubby reddish vegetation has adapted to withstand intense ultraviolet light and extreme weather. "Páramo" means "bleak plateau," and its vegetation is a unique mix of arid and tropical species. The páramo is a wind-swept, mossy landscape on the fringes of life. Páramo surrounds the Interamerican Highway pass at Cerro de la Muerte or "Death Mountain." The high pass earned its name before the highway was built, when exposure claimed people's lives as they climbed over the pass. The pass is located in Los Sautos Forest Reserve.

There is a field station on Cerro de la Muerte that focuses on the páramo. Cushion plants, named for their domed shape, are scattered across the landscape underneath dwarf bamboo (*Swallenochloa* sp.). Cushion plants have clustered small leaves and branches that provide microhabitats for insect communities. The cushions increase the temperature from that of the environment by a few degrees by providing shelter from the desiccating, cooling wind. In return, the insects concentrate nitrogen and scarce phosphorous around the roots of the plants. To make sure that no scarce minerals blow or wash away, the cushion plants have lateral roots that grow up into the cushion to capture breakdown products from decaying leaves.

You can stop to look at the páramo at marker 89 at Las Torres restaurant, or stay at several lodges in the area to experience this wilderness landscape. A trail leads from the restaurant to the antenna patch, from which you can see a plunging vista. Several farms have signposts offering ecotravellers

A colorful, simple home in hill country

Zamia

The caterpillars of a variety of blue hairstreak butterflies, (*Eumaeus minyas*, below right) are bright red. This signals that they are filled with the azoxyglycosides from their host plant, the zamia cycad. These substances paralyze and even kill mammals, but these caterpillars have adapted to use the poison as a defense against predators.

Zamias are cone-bearing cycads that evolved before flowering plants. Some produce sago starch, which is used for desserts, after the toxin has been removed. Talamanca Indians of the Bri-Brí and the Cabécar groups treat snake bites with a Zamia extract. *Zamia fairchildiana* (right and below) grows on the Pacific side of Costa Rica, and *Zamia skinneri* grows in the Atlantic rainforest.

forest access, where resplendent quetzals may be spotted.

Today, young men and women make a special annual pilgrimage from their homes all over Costa Rica to Cartago. These pilgrims include residents of the Valle del General who walk over Cerro de la Muerte on their way to Cartago. They make the multi-day walk to arrive on August 2 to honor La Negrita, the Virgin of Los Angeles, with only a towel or two to keep themselves warm at night. Each of the pilgrims comes to give thanks for individual miracles experienced in their family. La Negrita is thought to have appeared to a peasant girl in 1635, and is now Costa Rica's patron saint.

Genesis II Cloud Forest Lodge and Reserve

In this reserve, you'll find tropical white oaks (*Quercus* sp.) and graceful chusquea

Pre-evolved

Evolution has a way of appearing to anticipate the future. Cycads (opposite page) lived with ferns (this page) and evolved before flowering plants, palm trees, and conifers. Cycads and beetles probably originated the first animal–plant pollination system, using cycad scent. This may have prepared the way for flowering plants later on. Some cycads evolved to the point where they produced nectar, providing food for the scaly-winged ancestors to butterflies. These scaly insects evolved *before* flowering plants, 208–245 million years ago. Once flowers evolved, the scaly-winged insects rapidly evolved into butterflies, prepared by the cycad connection. There was a subsequent boom in flowers, coevolved with their insect pollinators.

bamboos that are filled with 153 species of birds, including resplendent quetzals, flame-throated warblers, band-tailed pigeons, collared redstarts, and mountain robins. The frogs of the area have not been infected with the diseases or polluted by the pesticide that have collectively wiped out species in other areas all over the world. The strict quarantine on boots put in place by the reserve owners helps to maintain optimum wilderness conditions (boots are supplied at the reserve). Guests and day visitors can take two-hour guided walks to explore this particular cloudforest and take the zip-line adventures through the canopy. Volunteers can participate in a month-long program doing reforestation and trail work and park activities.

This 38ha/96ac private reserve is on the west side of the Talamanca Mountains at 2,300m/7,500ft in altitude. It is adjacent to the Tapantí National Park, which protects the watershed of one-third of San José's water supply.

Coffee Family

The coffee relative *Cosmibuena valerii* (below) is common on the ridges of the most exposed peaks of cloud forests, where it is often part of elfin forests, dwarfed by wind and rain. You can identify coffee relatives by looking for the large white pinwheel flowers and opposite leaves. There are 154 coffee family species in the Monteverde understory and 430 in Costa Rica. You can tell this one apart from the others because it is the only scarlet-tipped pinwheel found in this habitat. Its nectar-laden flowers produce a heavy perfume that attracts hawk moths and other trapliners for pollination from great distances.

To reach the lodge, take the Interamerican Highway south from San José, then at 58km turn east for 4km to the lodge. (506-381-0739)

Talari Mountain Lodge

This small lodge is located near San Isidro del General and specializes in birdwatching and trekking, with dedicated expert guides. From here you can trek to Chirripó or Paraguas Peak. During high season, the lodge offers 5:30 AM guided birdwatching hikes, plus half-day tours to lowland, middle- and high-elevation regions. The lodge also organizes a week-long endemic birdwatching tour, exploring many regions. You should also consider a visit to Los Cosingos, the farm of noted bird expert and author Alexander Skutch. Talari Mountain Lodge is in premontane wet forest at 854m/2,800ft. Slaty spinetail, red-legged honeycreeper, and orchids are found nearby. (tel 506-771-0341, www.talari.co.cr)

Savegre Mountain Hotel

This 400ha/990ac reserve and lodge are located at an altitude of about 2,200m/ 7,200ft, among oaks and laurels where orchids and bromeliads thrive. Resplendent quetzals, black-faced solitaires, long-tailed silky flycatchers, and black guans are among the birds that may be seen in season. The lodge

Fooling for Keeps
Gonzalagunia rosea (left) is a coffee relative common in secondary growth forest, including in Monteverde road banks. The pink and white flowers develop into sprays of plump white currants. The plant puffs up these fruit with air using a styrofoam-like pith. This makes them appear more appetizing and substantial, although they are dry and tasteless. Black guans and prong-billed barbets snap them up, perhaps fooled by appearances. So are we: the attractive plant is planted in ornamental gardens.

runs the Quetzal Education Research Center, in association with an American university, where research scientists work on mushroom, epiphyte, and forest ecology projects.

To reach the lodge, turn onto the San Gerardo de Dota road at the 80km marker on the Interamerican Highway, and find the lodge at around 9km/5.6mi. (tel 506-771-1732, 506-390-5096, fax 506-771-2003; US tel 800-593-3305. www.savegre.co.cr)

Toucanet Lodge

This lodge is in the valley of the Los Santos Forest Reserve, home also to Cerro de la Muerte, and is close to a 2,200m/7,200ft cloud forest filled with 160 bird species. Páramo Las Vueltas is nearby. (tel 506-771-4582, fax 506-771-8841, selvamar@racsa.co.cr)

Mirador de Quetzales

As the name indicates, this lodge's specialty is quetzals. It is located just south of the

Glass Frogs

The heart and internal organs of the glass frog (*Hyalinobatrachium fleischmanni*, above) are visible through their transparent skin. The frogs' pigmented eggs are stuck on overhanging leaves, where their gel expands as the young develop. The males guard the eggs to ward off predatory *Drosophila* flies. The eggs usually hatch when it rains, dropping into the rainwater as tadpoles. They then prepare for self-burial by growing a network of capillaries at their skin surface, turning bright red. This allows them to breathe underground, away from predators, as they change into adults.

70km marker on the Interamerican Highway, about an hour and a half south of San José: turn west at the lodge sign. Guides are available. (tel 506-771-4582, fax 506-771-8841, www.exploringcostarica. com/mirador/quetzales.html)

Chirripó National Park

At 3,820m/12,533ft, Chirripó is the highest, coldest region of Costa Rica. It is regarded as sacred by indigenous peoples and is still a revered site for Ticos. The páramo habitat of tussocks and dwarf bamboo with a few goats and rabbits rises above the oaks, Poás magnolias, and cypresses of the lower slopes. Glacial moraines and lakes are scattered over the park, left from the ice age that ended 10,000–30,000 years ago.

Only forty people are allowed in this nationally popular park at any one time, so you'll need to book ahead (506-233-4160). The mountain should only be scaled by those prepared for several days of very cold, wet weather over rough terrain. There are hiking cabins located at 2,380m/7,800ft and 3,020m/9,900ft, spaced a few hours' walk apart, the first being about five hours' hike from the park entrance. Base camp is at 3,110m/10,200ft, another hour and a half up. From here, one can reach the peak in about two hours—the ideal time to summit is during the early morning before fog closes in. There are several trails leading to interesting areas and bird-filled river valleys below.

The park is 25km/16mi northeast of San Isidro de El General, 152km/95mi southeast of San José.

La Amistad International Biosphere Reserve

La Amistad has one of the wildest and richest ecologies in all of Central America, containing 80% of Costa Rica's plant and animal species. The Biosphere Reserve stretches across the Talamanca range and encompasses eight life zones of distinct habitats.

La Amistad is a UNESCO-protected World Heritage site of outstanding value. One-third of it is in Costa Rica, and two-

Trek Chirripó
Costa Rica Trekking Adventures organizes backpacking treks to Chimpo, Tapanti, and Corcovado (tel 506-771-4582, www.chimpo.com)

Costa Rican bamboo palm (Chamaedorea costaricana), around a buttress rainforest tree (left), is also used as an ornamental palm worldwide. Look for the orange fruiting branches that signal ripeness.

Bananas in Wilson Botanical Garden

Wilson Botanical Garden (opposite page) is one of five world repositories for the Heliconia Society International, so you'll find nearly all of Costa Rica's forty Heliconia species at Las Cruces, where the garden is located. Bananas are related to Heliconias and are also researched at the garden. New varieties such as this ornamental miniature banana (above) are being bred at the garden. The several varieties of commercial bananas are hybrids of just two Asian species, *Musa auminata* and *M. balbisiana*.

thirds are in Panama, yet even Costa Rica's share is an enormous 192,067ha/474,240ac. The park is large enough for jaguars to thrive, as they require large territories, and wild enough to hide many still-uncataloged species in its midst. A few lodges on the outer buffer zones offer the best way to experience the outer reaches of the reserve; La Amistad has few trails. Several indigenous people's reservations are found within the reserve and can be visited by arrangement through some ecolodges. The Bri-Brí and the Cabécar communities are the largest, and together amount to nearly 12,000 people in the Talamanca Mountains and Caribbean lowlands.

Dúrika Biological Reserve

Dúrika Biological Reserve is 17km/11mi east of Buenos Aires, a 1.5-hour drive. This is a cloud-forest paradise plunging across several life zones on the edge of La Amistad. The ecolodge has stunning views and is part of a self-sufficient community and bakery. The 800ha/1,606ac reserve is a buffer zone for La Amistad and shelters 301 bird species, including eagles, bellbirds, and toucans. Experienced birders may see up to 80 species in one day. Exquisite orchid habitats are accessible among the epiphytes, which are drip-fed by the clouds. Rainfall is a huge 3.5m/138in a year. Short or deep hikes into and across La Amistad can be arranged with the English-speaking resident guides, including a hike to Ujarras, a Cabécar Indian community (one to two days), a Cerro Dúrika camping hike (four days), and a difficult hike to the Atlantic coast (at least six days). The last option cuts across La Amistad International Biosphere Reserve, is offered only during May and October, and involves additional fees. (tel 506-730-0657, fax 506-730-0003, www.durika.org, durika@racsa.co.cr)

Ornamentals

Lycaste dowiniana (below right) is a wild species that is also cultivated in ornamental garden collections. The genus has both epiphytic and terrestrial forms, with pseudobulbs and pleated leaves.

Albergue Monte Amuo

Albergue Monte Amuo is an hour's drive from Portero Grande on the edge of La Amistad and offers 7km/4.3mi of trails and an ecolodge. (506-265-6149)

La Amistad Lodge and Reserve

La Amistad Lodge and Reserve is in the Las Tablas region of La Amistad and is associated with the Coto Brus area near La Melitzas on the Panamanian border. In addition to the three-story main lodge, the reserve is establishing more rustic staging lodges in remote areas, to act as exploration posts, reached by 4WD. From here, you can arrange for a visit to Las Cruces and the Wilson Botanical Gardens. Lance-tailed manakins are seen here (they look like long-trailed manakins but without the long tail). Both species have a "cartwheel" dance, in which two males swap places in a fluttering, vertical dance, vying for the female's attention. The two species do not overlap.

There are 400 species of birds to see here, including twenty hummingbird species. The 15,000ha/37,000ac pristine reserve and a small organic coffee plantation offers 60km/37mi of trails, which pass pre-Columbian petroglyphs.

The reserve is 26km/16mi north east of San Vito. (La Amistad San José office tel 506-228-8761, fax 506-289-7858; lodge tel 506-200-5037, www.laamistad.com)

San Vito

The Las Cruces Field Station and Wilson Botanical Gardens are managed by the world-renowned Organization for Tropical Studies (OET in Spanish) which also runs La Selva. Las Cruces and the botanical gardens are located in premontane rainforest at 1,190m/3,900ft. The field station has exceptionally high-quality lodgings for visitors in new seismic-stable rooms overlooking steep forest. The atmosphere is one of a small college campus rather than an ecolodge, with groups of

Leaf Tanks
Water-filled leaf tanks (above and below) provide all the nutrients that some bromeliads need. Bromeliads use the decaying debris that the umbrella-shaped leaves catch as their hydroponic food source.

students and young researchers coming and going, and everyone except local staff sharing meals in the communal dining hall. The advantage of this is that visitors, scientists, students, and ecotravellers alike can share their knowledge and discoveries at meal times. The ecolodge is isolated, so only the most dedicated birders, tropical ecologists, and heliconia-lovers tend to make their way here—but they come with plenty of enthusiasm.

Birdwatching is wonderful. Exquisite tanagers may be spotted in the fruit-filled Wilson Botanical Gardens and surroundings. According to Gary Stiles and Alexander Skutch in their authoritative *Guide to the Birds of Costa Rica,* "no other family contributes so much color to tropical American bird life, and the largest genus, *Tangara,* seems to exhaust the color patterns possible on sparrow-sized birds."

The station's professional guides and manager offer a variety of excellent walks into the garden and forest. These should be planned with the office in advance. The garden has a special collection of heliconias and bananas. There are clear walkways and

carefully tended beds of well-marked species. A map is available at the office.

Below the gardens are blankets of rainforest, through which paths and streams run. Glass frogs chirp there at night, and monkeys swing across the paths by day. (tel 506-773-4004. OTS office in San José: tel 506-524-0607, fax 506-524-0608, US tel 919-684-5774, www.ots.ac.cr, lascruces@ hortus.ots.oc.cr)

Focus on Wildlife: From Thermophiles to Orchids

Most travellers do not realize that Costa Rica's mountains are bioprospecting havens. Several companies, including Diversa, a US biotechnology company partnering with Costa Rica's INBio, are exploring enzymes from thermophiles, which are heat-tolerant bacteria from hot-spring vents. Enzymes from these bacteria are already used to

An unidentified orchid provides shelter for insects (above)

A single rainforest tree in the tropics can support 10,000 beetle species. Above, from top: shining leaf beetle, moth-mimic beetle, stag beetle, and sap-sucking bug. Top right: large leaf beetle.

stone-wash jeans, identify DNA sequences in crime cases, whiten paper without using polluting bleach, sterilize hospital equipment at room temperature, and help keep oil wells functioning. In the future, these bacterial enzymes could be used to help treat oil spills, create new fabrics, and generate antitumor drugs (see also sidebar, page 129).

Better known is that Costa Rica's moist mountainous rainforests and volcanic flanks are the places to go for orchids, or *guarias*. This small country hides an amazing 1,416 species of orchid, of which 88% are epiphytic. Some Costa Rican species are now found in homes worldwide.

Due to deforestation, many orchids have virtually disappeared from Costa Rican forests, including its national flower, *Cattleya skinneri*, one of four *Cattleya* species of the region. *Cattleya skinneri* used to be common on western slopes between 1,000–4,000m/ 3,280–13,120ft. A relative, *C. dowiniana*, is found on the Caribbean slopes and the Talamanca Mountains near the Panamanian border, having evolved in geographic isolation. *C. skinneri* flowers during the dry season from January to April and has pseudobulbs that enable it to be an epiphyte in drier conditions. This makes it ideal for growing in homes—which is fortunate, as *C. skinneri*'s habitat has been largely deforested in recent decades, so it is rarely found in the wild.

So, look for *Cattleya* planted around your ecolodge or when you return from vacation: it'll be found nodding in the new geography of grocery store aisles. Some orchid specialists assert that humans are the plants' newest recruits, since we tend and pollinate the flowers for our own needs. The multi-million–dollar orchid industry depends on the orchids' beauty and its ability to evoke love from its new caretakers and hybridizers.

Researcher Eric Janzen believes that many temperate zone biologists are intimidated by the variety of bizarre repro-ductive approaches found in tropical orchids, and so often choose to research species other than orchids in Costa Rica.

Careful study of orchids leaves some specialists to conclude that instead of being images of beauty, they are masters of deceit. Their game has been to get pollinated while living in a nutrient desert three hundred feet off the ground, their only food being from dissolved minerals drip-fed through the

Synchronized
Sobralia sp. (below) is a terrestrial orchid with huge delicate flowers that open simultaneously across an entire population of separate plants.

Dichaea muricata
(above) is an orchid that
flowers at the leaf axles.
The overall shape appears
similar to a fern.

canopy. Trade winds desiccate them one day; fog nurtures them the next; temperatures swing 15°C from dawn to dusk. This is quite different from the constancy of the warm, humid, darker forest floor. To survive these extremes, the plants employ all their resources: their strategy for pollination is to promise riches without spending a dime (see sidebar, page 127). Huge *Oncidium* (photo on page 121) are as showy as a store-bought bouquet. *Oncidium* are mimics of large flowering vines that have oil glands to attract bees. The bees mistake the orchid for these food-bearing flowers, and pollinate both species.

Some dramatic flowers that offer no rewards include *Cleistes*, *Cattleya*, and *Phragmipedium* species. Orchid bees get wise to their ruse: older orchid bees avoid *Colchleanthes lipsocombiae*. This appears to mimic a leguminous vine, and as bees grow older, they learn that the vine but not the orchid offers the rewards.

Many orchids' petals are covered with extra waxes to endure days or weeks of extreme desiccation while they sit and wait for a pollinator to visit. This cling-film factor is one reason why orchids provide such luminous boutonnieres that appeal to us for weddings and formal parties—flowers that can last with minimal water for days.

Most wild orchid blooms in Costa Rica are not much more than the size of a match-head, are pale green or off-white, and have exquisitely small pollination mechanisms. If you get used to looking for this Lilliputian world, you will soon spot them perched on the side of tree trunks, poking from mossy fallen tree limbs, and cascading down maidenhair fern and liverwort-covered roadside banks on the continental divide.

Take binoculars to get a better look. The little fairy caps, open books, clapper bells, or petal showers of these minute orchids are all uniquely designed for low-resource pollination. Wet and moist forest species include *Aspasia*, *Brassia*, *Cochleanthes*, *Kefersteinia*, and *Kegeliella*, many of which have evolved weird ways to survive. Dracula orchid flowers (shown on page

Twisty

Pictured above is *Epidendrum* after supination, a process orchids undergo in which the flower twists upside down as it matures. Note how the flower stem above is visibly twisted.

The lily (left) is among the plant collection of Las Cruces' Wilson Botanical Gardens

*Las Cruces' Wilson
Botanical Gardens*

126) have spotted, furry insides that mimic fungi. Fungus gnats creep into these down-ward-facing petals looking for a place to deposit their eggs, pollinating the orchids.

Some sit-and-wait orchids like *Lepanthes* sp. (shown on page 126) bloom below the leaf, which provides an umbrella shelter. As a storm approaches, which usually occurs in the afternoon, the light dims and rain starts pattering down. Flies, which are nonsocial and so have no communal nest (unlike bees, ants, and termites) seek the shelter that the little tents provide, out of the way of wind and rain. The yellow and pale green of the orchid blossoms is the only color that can be discerned under low light. Crawling up to the colored point at the apex, the flies pollinate the bright orchid blossom. For this benefit, the orchid need only provide its carefully constructed, long-lasting flower umbrella.

Sometimes you will find a bank studded with huge, luminous orchids, translucent with freshness and fading by the minute. These are the synchronous flowers of *Sobralia* (shown on page 157), *Palmorchis*, *Psilochilus*, or *Triphora* species—the entire population is coordinated to flower during one day. The glade of orchid blooms is, however, short-lived. This festival of blossoms attracts all the local pollinators to celebrate their good fortune at once, resulting in a successful fertilization party and also ensuring that some of the excessive volume of seeds will survive. The trigger for synchronization is a sudden rainfall and associated drop in temperature, which starts the budding process. This type of synchronized reproduction is found in corals, Cortez trees, olive ridley turtles, and marine bristleworms, pointing to a connectivity within nature at which we can only marvel.

Orchid bees and their orchids have coevolved a remarkable, energy-efficient, intricate relationship. Euglossine bees look like bumble bees, some with tongues so long that they trail behind them untidily in flight. The orchids do not reward their visitors with nectar, but instead exude perfumed oils that are collected by the bees in special leg buckets. The bees produce their own "carrier oil" that they smear on the orchid to absorb the more fragrant perfume of the "high notes"—just as a French perfumier does by using one of only

Orchid Flavors

Vanilla (below) is one of two orchid species grown throughout Costa Rica for culinary flavorings. The seedcase (upper image) has shed millions of minute seeds from the vanilla pod (lower image).

Groomers

Phorid flies (*Megaselina scalaris*) lay their eggs on the eggs of glass frogs. However, unlike some *Drosophila* flies that cannibalize the developing glass frog embryos, these phorid larvae only eat inviable eggs. The relationship benefits both: the fly cleans egg debris from viable embryos in exchange for food.

These fly species also have another function: When tropical rain torrents fall, the flies seek shelter. Some species of orchids have adapted their flowers so they are placed under the leaves (above), which are dome-shaped to shed the rain. Flies crawl under the "tarp" and, in exchange for shelter, pollinate the orchid.

six aromas in human perfume to act as the "base" carrier into which are added a variety of perfume sources. These become the "high notes" and give character to the scent. For the orchid, an oil is a more energy-efficient solution than nectar, because a few molecules of oil can diffuse through a large area as a long-lasting aromatic signal, whereas a huge number of sugar molecules are needed to sweeten a sip of nectar. Euglossine males collect a variety of scents from different orchid species and then fly to a lek, which is a parade area where many males fly, looking to attract females. Females are drawn to the perfume wafting from the legs of the many gathered males. When the perfume mixture is exactly right, the pheromonal effect kicks in and each female becomes interested in a mate. Tropical American orchids pollinated by euglossine bees include *Catasetum*, *Stanhopea*, *Trichopilia*, *Notylia*, *Trichocentrum*, *Dichaea*, *Lockhartia*, *Lycaste*, *Macredenia*, and *Macroclinium*. Oil glands are found in Costa Rica's *Ornitho-cephalus*, *Sigmatostalix*, and some *Oncidium* orchid species. Some of these fragrances include the oil of wintergreen, and are among the most primitive scents of the Jurassic rainforest.

Costa Ricans are a nation of orchid lovers and have deep knowledge of the species found in their country. Your visit to Costa Rica will be made much more fascinating if, as you meet new guides and lodge hosts, you stop for a moment to ask them about their favorite orchids in the wild, in gardens, and on rooftops.

5
Caribbean

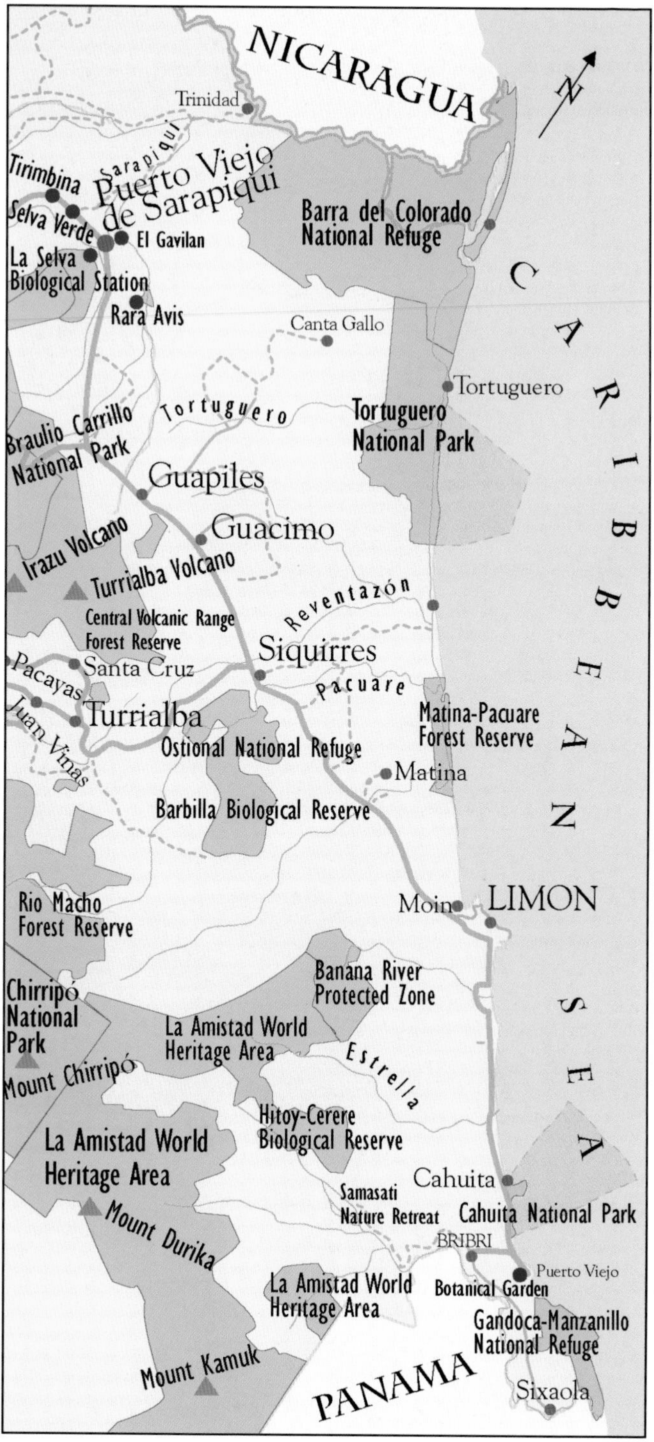

NICARAGUA

Trinidad

Tirimbina
Selva Verde
Sarapiqui
Puerto Viejo
de Sarapiqui
El Gavilan
La Selva
Biological Station
Rara Avis

Barra del Colorado
National Refuge

CARIBBEAN

Canta Gallo

Tortuguero

Braulio Carrillo
National Park
Tortuguero
Tortuguero
National Park

Guapiles

Guacimo

Irazu Volcano
Turrialba Volcano

Central Volcanic Range
Forest Reserve
Santa Cruz
Reventazón
Siquirres
Pacuare
Matina-Pacuare
Forest Reserve

Pacayas
Juan Viñas
Turrialba
Ostional National Refuge
Matina

Barbilla Biological Reserve

Rio Macho
Forest Reserve
Moin
LIMON

Banana River
Protected Zone

Chirripó
National
Park
La Amistad World
Heritage Area
Estrella
Mount Chirripó
Hitoy-Cerere
Biological Reserve

La Amistad World
Heritage Area
Cahuita
Samasati
Nature Retreat
Cahuita National Park
Mount Durika
BRIBRI
Puerto Viejo
La Amistad World
Heritage Area
Botanical Garden
Gandoca-Manzanillo
National Refuge
Mount Kamuk
PANAMA
Sixaola

SEA

Pinecone ginger
In Costa Rica, you'll find several colorful pinecone gingers (*Zingiber*, left and page 163). Their bract cones create moats through which the nectar-laden flowers can display pollen without being robbed by ants.
Pinecone gingers include shampoo ginger or awapuhi (*Z. zerumbet*), introduced to Hawaii from Polynesia and used for its milky juice to shampoo hair.

The green turtle drops perfect spheres in twos and threes, laying her eggs into the nest she has dug in the dark Caribbean beach. After each bout, she lets out her breath with the sound of a whale breaching. The pale eggs glisten with an antifungal coating and soon fill the deep cylindrical well, glowing in the dim red flashlight shone by the licensed guide. After laying, the turtle scoops torrents of sand over her eggs, then tamps the nest down delicately with fanned flippers. Later the same night, she'll swim away, leaving only parallel tracks leading back to the ocean. If she escapes the dangers currently threatening this turtle population, she'll return to nest two years later on the same beach where she, too, had hatched.

A turtle-filled beach is one of the highlights found in a few locations along Costa Rica's Caribbean side including Tortuergo National Park (pages 166–178). To the west, vast yet declining lowland Caribbean rainforests vie for existence against major banana plantations. The options for ecotravel are expanding, centered around conservation and research hubs. La Selva, one of the world's premier tropical research stations, is located here, and opens its doors and bunkhouses equally to researchers and

Plan for hot humid weather in the Caribbean. In Tortuguero, canals built to carry timber and bananas swell with wet-season rains.

ecotravellers. Day visits can be arranged for those preferring to stay in luxury ecolodges in the Sarapiquí River area nearby (pages 182–202). La Selva's deep primary and secondary rainforests shelter some of the most diverse and accessible communities of lowland tropical wildlife in Costa Rica. Travellers often comment that they see more rainforest life in one day at La Selva than anywhere else.

Limón is a cruise-boat port with charming old quarters. It has been a major coffee and banana port for over a hundred years. Travellers drawn to the distinct colors, fascinating cultures, and appealing music of the Caribbean and its indigenous peoples may also encounter Limón's higher crime rates. To the south, coral reefs have been devastated by a recent earthquake, and communities live with endemic malaria.

Ecolodges are opening up south of Limón along the coast and on the edge of the Talamanca Mountains (pages 206–221). These offer the newest ideas in ecotravel destinations and integrate their activities with the local indigenous peoples.

Any visitor to Costa Rica's eastern half should be prepared for humid heat and plenty of rain, for it is from the Caribbean that the prevailing warm, wet winds blow.

Barra del Colorado

Barra del Colorado is a huge rainforest park located in the lowlands to the north of Tortuguero along the Nicaraguan border. The ecolodges here were built for sport fishing rather than conservation visitors, but provide an opportunity to experience some of the remaining deep Caribbean wilderness without the cram of people focused around Tortuguero village. Several companies offer road and riverboat tours from San José or Sarapiquí to the Panamanian border and then down to Tortuguero via Barra del Colorado. Watch out for the pesky mosquitoes, and note that malaria levels tend to increase towards the border.

Laguna del Lagarto Lodge is in a good location to try to see the very rare and endangered great green macaws (*Ara ambigua*). (tel 506-289-8163, fax 506-289-5295, www.lagarto-lodge-costa-rica.com, info@lagarto-lodge-costa-rica.com)

Tortuguero National Park

Tortuguero village lies on a sand spit a stone's throw from the 20km/12mi ribbon of black sand where female green turtles

Bromeliad flower

Great Green Macaw

You may see the great green macaw (*Ara ambigua*) in Tortuguero and along the Nicaraguan border of the Caribbean lowlands. It ranges far across the area, dependent on dwindling clusters of the legume *Dipteryx panamensis*, incorrectly called swamp almond, for food and a diminishing level of nesting cavities. There are only about thirty-five pairs in this area, so wild sightings are scarce. Remaining birds are threatened by illegal trapping for the pet trade. Formation of the proposed new Maquenque National Park may provide an essential refuge for this endangered species.

(*Chelonia mydas*) land along this coastline to lay their eggs July to mid-October. Watching a female build her nest with precision and care under the cover of darkness is a once-in-a-lifetime experience that draws many ecotravellers to this wilderness.

Don't miss taking a small-craft boat cruise or two by day along the canals and backwaters that were built to serve as the timber and banana transportation system paralleling the coast. Or go it alone in a *cayuca* (dugout), which is easy to rent from the village. You may see endangered manatees, river otters, freshwater turtles, crocodiles, anhingas, and kingfishers around the canals. Three-toed sloths, spider monkeys, howler monkeys, oropendolas, macaws, tiger herons, and 308 other bird species hide among the canal-side trees. Large fronds of water-tolerant raphia palms or *yolillo* (*Raphia taedigera*) reach from the sky to the water's edge and are interspersed with vine-clad rainforest trees, spilling with fruit and aromatic blossoms. Their perfume becomes more potent at night to attract nocturnal pollinators.

Tortuguero Beach is a significant nesting

beach for green turtles, plus a scattered number of hawksbill (*Eretmochelys imbricata*), leatherback (*Dermochelys coriacea*), and loggerhead turtles (*Caretta caretta*), which nest March through May. Hawskbill turtle shells are still offered in poached tortoiseshell ornaments sold in San José, although these endangered species are now heavily protected. Don't contribute to this trade.

Tortuguero village was originally a major site for turtle hunters, who collected the animals and their eggs for ship's supplies and *bocas* (snacks), from the mid-sixteenth century until the 1970s. This included the use of the cartilaginous calipee, located inside the lower shell, for turtle soup, a delicacy fueled by demand from Victorian England. Turtles were kept alive on ships, negating the need for ice coolers. Prior to the Spanish cacao plantations that started the boom, the active harvesting of turtles by indigenous people was at a sustainable level.

The illegal tradition of digging up turtle eggs for *bocas* still continues more or less openly except on heavily guarded beaches. Perhaps 80 percent of turtle eggs laid are still poached. However, research activities, park service policing, and income generated by

Macaw Trees

Dipteryx panamensis is an emergent canopy tree that is easy to spot. It stands high above the Caribbean treetops with a broccoli-like froth of pink flowers. Great green macaws, monkeys, and people love the fruit of this legume. Macaws make their nests in these trees. Locate the tree by looking for fallen leaves (above) in which the midvein is closer to one side than the other. It fruits twice a year, at the start of the dry season and the start of the rainy season.

Horses provide a major means of transportation and fun

Strange Bedfellows

Watch for bold chestnut-headed oropendolas, a bird that is related to orioles. Chestnut-headed oropendolas create colonies of dew-drop-shaped, elongated basket nests. These crow-sized black and chestnut birds protect their young from killer parasitic botflies in amazing ways. Some colonies are built near wasp and bee nests. Bees and wasps are able to sense the presence of incoming botflies by their scent and sound, and deter the botflies. Colonies not associated with bees or wasps are protected by cowbird chicks. Oropendolas have learned to accept cowbirds among them. Cowbirds are parasites that lay eggs in other species' nests. In this case, however, the cowbird chicks preen the botflies off the oropendola chicks. What is amazing is that oropendolas with nests near bees and wasps, who have no need for cowbirds, remove cowbird eggs and are hostile to female cowbirds, a behavior that has been found to be learned.

legitimate Tortuguero turtle activities are helping to reverse these long-held practices.

All of Tortuguero beach is off-limits after 10:00 PM during nesting season to anyone who is not a researcher or a part of a guided turtle-watching expedition. Turtle guides are easy to book through your Tortuguero ecolodge or accommodations during the season. A short 2km trail from the park headquarters leads through *cativo* forest dominated by *Prioria copaifera* trees to the narrow 20km Tortuguero Beach, where one can see by day the signs of nocturnally created turtle nests. Tortuguero Beach is black with volcanic sand, but don't swim: the ocean has too many sharks.

Turtle research is conducted by the Caribbean Conservation Corporation. This is based in Florida and was founded expressly to protect the green turtles of Tortuguero at a time when their use was unsustainable. The corp's regional green turtle research station is located near Tortuguero Village. With prior arrangement, you can volunteer as a turtle-tagger and nest monitoring assistant, or even adopt a turtle: check the excellent CCC website (www.cccturtle.org) for details.

The CCC runs a small Natural History Visitors' Center in Tortuguero village, which offers video sessions on turtle conservation in addition to museum exhibits on local wildlife. There is also an information kiosk near the playground.

Balancing conservation and food use has never been easy. At the present, ideas for sustainable solutions include studying how to domesticate sea turtles for food while making sure they are conserved in the wild at sustainable levels. So far, the turtles have proved to be unsuitable for farming, but sustainable solutions seem to be slowly emerging. Unfortunately, turtle populations continue to plummet.

Tortuguero Ecolodges

Several ecolodges perch on the edge of the canals around Tortuguero village. There are several inexpensive hotels in the village itself that are not detailed here, and a tent camp with netted hammocks run by Boca del Rio Lodge and Campground (506-385-4676). Check with your accommodation about payment options; many do not take credit cards and there is no bank.

Tortuga Lodge is expertly run by Costa Rica Expeditions, with luxury cabins on 309ha/125ac of rainforest reserve and a central dining hall overlooking the river. An infinity swimming pool seems to blend with the river. The canal tour boat is a versatile electric-powered launch that makes little noise nosing around while the guide seeks out wildlife. The grounds have many rainforest flowers that attract butterflies and humming-birds, and there is a trail into the rainforest behind the lodge where poison-dart frogs can be spotted. (tel 506-257-0766, fax 506-222-0333, www.expeditions.co.cr)

When to Go

Green turtles can be spotted at Tortuguero Beach during nesting season on walks leaving at 8 PM and 10 PM. Trained local guides lead these from July 1 to October 15; book a guide as soon as you arrive at your accommodations.

Tortuguero canals are lined with king palms, raffia palms, and fruit-laden trees

Blue-Jeans Frog

The blue-jeans poison-dart frog is also called the strawberry poison-dart frog, (*Dendrobates pumilio*), as it comes in varying amounts of red tinged with blue (right). They eat ants and can often be seen during the daytime, stalking around the loose, damp leaf litter. Males chirp like insects to seek females. Interested females lay their eggs on a curled leaf that the male fertilizes. Once the tadpoles hatch, she (and sometimes he) carries the eggs up high into the canopy and deposits them one by one into a bromeliad cistern to develop. She then returns every nine days or so to feed her offspring with infertile eggs—these frogs provided the first documented case of a vertebrate feeding its young this way.

Laguna Lodge has a pool and jacuzzi, and is located near Tortuguero Village. (tel 506-225-3740, fax 506-283-8031, www.lagunalodgetortuguero.com)

Pachira Lodge is a newer ecolodge with an appealing Caribbean style. (tel 506-256-7080, fax 506-223-1119, www.pachiralodge.com)

Mawamba Lodge is close to Tortuguero Village and has a swimming pool and waterfalls. (tel 506-293-8181, fax 506-223-2421, www.grupomawamba.com).

El Manati offers simple cabins and rooms. Guests have the option to participate in manatee conservation activities organized by the owners (tel 506-383-0330, fax 506-239-0911).

Focus on Wildlife: Canal Life

Rare manatees (*Trichechus manatus*) browse on the buoyant water hyacinths of the canals, and it is here among the purple flowers that the crocodiles lurk, their two eyes almost invisible as they break the surface. Specialist manatee-spotting expeditions can be booked with Modesto and Fran Watson (506-226-0986, www.tortuguerocanals.com, fvwatson@racsa.co.cr). The Watsons also offer early morning tours and cruises on Riverboat Francesca from Moín.

Three-toed sloths (*Bradypus varie-*

Non-toxic frogs (below) are camouflaged

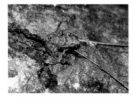

gatus) can also be spotted along canal sides. Sloths carry an additional ecosystem on their backs: their fur supports 900 insects.

If you take a night boat expedition, you may even catch a fleeting glance of the eye-shine from a margay or a jaguar receding into the forest. Behind the waterways are extensive blackwater swamps, colored dark with the bitter tannins that the trees produce to deter insects. Rare species include the green-and-rufous kingfishers and the great green macaw, which is on the brink of extinction in the wild. During the spring and fall, look for migrating Swainson's hawks, orioles, and warblers on their way to and from South America.

During June and July, gar fish (*Atractosteus tropicus*) move into shallower waters and locals fish for them. Gar fish evolved 410 million years ago, not long after large complex animals were first found in the fossil record; this genus evolved about 180 million years ago. It remains relatively unchanged, with platelike bony scales and a crocodile-like snout, its length reaching to 2m/39in. The gar is celebrated as one of Costa Rica's "living fossils."

Behind the waterfront, several ecolodges offer brief rainforest trails that you can explore after your turtle watching. From these, you can spot some really toxic

Heart Savers

Pumiliotoxin, advertised by the day-glow coloration of the green and black poison-dart frog (*Dendrobates auratus*, below) and blue-jeans frog, is an alkaloid poison that causes convulsions. Touching either of these frogs when you have a cut or scratch can cause serious poisoning. However, it has been found that pumiliotoxin initially stimulates the heart muscle. Researchers are investigating whether the green and black poison-dart frog's toxin might be used to boost the heart's function after a heart attack. The National Institute of Health has identified over 300 alkaloids from poison-dart frogs. Derivatives of these compounds are already being used for anesthesia. The green and black poison-dart frog is found in the lowland rainforests of northeast and southwest Costa Rica and can live to four years on a diet of ants.

Waterbirds

Bittern-like bare-throated tiger-herons (*Tigrisoma mexicanum*, left, as juveniles), green-backed herons (*Butorides virescens*, center), little blue herons (*Egretta caerulea*, right) during mid-molt from the white juvenile form, and anhingas (*Anhinga anhinga*, opposite page) are among the many waterbirds easily seen along Tortuguero canals. The anhinga's feathers are designed to absorb water, keeping the bird semi-submerged as it seeks its fish prey, with only its head and neck above the waterline.

creatures: the poison-dart frogs. As you watch them crawling over the leaf litter of the forest floor on matchstick-sized legs, their delicacy contrasts with their bright, menacing coloration. These poster children of the rainforest make good mothers. The strawberry poison-dart frog (*Dendrobates pumilio*) feeds her tadpoles by laying infertile eggs in the water-filled leaf whorls of bromeliads in which they swim, high up in the canopy. She does this every few days. The juveniles communicate with their mother, signaling their location to her by wagging their tails in a special circular motion. She responds by going down to the waterline and laying the eggs to feed them. Even more amazing, her eggs were originally laid right on the forest floor, in a little leaf puddle: the male and the female carry the hatched tadpoles on their backs for several hundred feet into the canopy and deposit the tadpoles into several bromeliad reservoirs. The male guards his territory of bromeliads ferociously, butting other males out.

The toxic compounds of the poison-dart frogs are being used as the basis for novel pharmaceuticals. A major new pain-killer has been derived from a skin compound found in an Ecuadorean poison-dart frog, closely related to the frogs found

in Tortuguero. This painkiller is fifty to two hundred times more effective than morphine at stopping pain, but does not appear to have morphine's hallucinogenic effects or addictive properties. This nontoxic derivative of the frog's poisonous natural form epibatidine has been synthesized by Abbott Laboratories. Carefully researched over decades, doctors feel it is likely to revolutionize pain treatment if released as planned in the near future, controlling both acute and chronic pain through separate neurological actions.

There is a fascinating connection between ants and poison-dart frogs. Research has found that if you remove poison-dart frogs from the rainforest environment and keep them in a terrarium, feeding them laboratory food, the toxic and pharmaceutical effects of their skin disappear. The chemical structure of epibatidine, the painkiller/toxin from poison-dart frogs, is extremely similar to that of plant-based nicotine. Somehow, the frogs are able to synthesize the painkiller, possibly by upgrading nicotine-like substances derived from ants, perhaps passed along the food chain from plants. In this and other ways, the rainforest's organisms are interdependent. Nicotine's insecticidal

Instinct

Herons (left) and motmots inherit an instinctive avoidance of coral snakes. They appear to use pattern and color recognition to avoid harm. The toxic Central American coral snake (*Micrurus nigrocinctus*) has a similar sequence of colors to the poisonous North American species: red-yellow-black-yellow-red. But not all of the four Costa Rican coral snake species have this sequence. One is bicolored, and there is a lot of variation within species. Yet these birds avoid them. The harlequin snake (*Scolecophis atrocinctus*) is one of ten snake genera and one butterfly caterpillar species that mimic coral snakes, thereby gaining protection from birds.

Bird Health

Half of the trees in the Caribbean lowland forests depend on birds for seed dispersal and ultimately for survival. The seasonal mobility of birds between tropical lowlands and highlands is essential to maintain this relationship. As the forests are cut up into farmland, Costa Rica has recognized the need to secure national parks in strategic locations that provide linking corridors. In some areas, agricultural land is being restored to rainforest to reconnect pockets of forest. In other places, isolation is causing species impoverishment.

properties are so significant that it was used by the Egyptians for crop protection.

The best wildlife viewing is generally on the waterways inland from Tortuguero or north of there, even though the main park is to the south. Further to the south, deforestation has severely limited the level of wildlife around the canal banks, although a corridor of green remains.

Caño Chiquero, Caño Mora, and Caño Harold (canals) lead back into thick primary and secondary rainforest. These can be reached by navigating southeast of Tortuguero village to the inland waterways. Caño Tortuguero runs parallel to the swift currents of Tortuguero River a quarter of a kilometer inland to the west. This cuts northwest to southeast, with a few navigational oddities. Rent a *cayuca* with an outboard motor (rather than paddles) from Tortuguero village, preferably with a guide, to look for the fairly abundant wildlife and birds on these stretches of the waterways. The park office and information kiosk in Tortuguero village have details about renting boats.

8km north of Tortuguero is Cerro Tortuguero, the remains of a volcanic cone that has eroded to stand at only 119m/390ft. Caño Palma Biological Station (506-381-4116) is nearby on the north side of Caño Palma, but is only accessible by

boat. Caño Palma is a rainforest conservation area open to visitors, with a research station run by the Canadian Organization for Tropical Education (Canadian tel 905-831-8809, fax 905-831-4203, www.coterc.org). You can volunteer to work at this station for a minimum of two weeks, guiding, assisting in field work, and running the station.

The pool at Tortuga Lodge (opposite) borders Tortuguero River (above)

Access

The best way to reach Tortugero village in the park is by plane: it is surrounded by vast stretches of lowland rainforest and swampland, cut off from roads. The plane lands on the narrow sand spit on which Tortuguero village is squeezed. Tortuguero River leads north from the village into the Caribbean Sea nearby. This is part of a series of canals built in the 1930s and expanded in the 1970s, that join the backwaters and run inland up the coast for 100km. The canals were originally built to transport timber, and now link Moín near Limón in the south to Tortugero village. To

Croc Bouquets

The eyes of American crocodiles (*Crocodylus acutus*, below right) and spectacled caiman (*Caiman crocodilus*) can sometimes be seen peeking above water hyacinths (above).

the north, the canal system reaches Barra del Colorado along the Nicaraguan border. You can take a privately rented boat from either end or traverse the canals on your own. Tropical Wind II (tel 506-758-4297, fax 506-790-3059) and Riverboat Francesca (tel 506-226-0986, www.tortuguerocanals. com, fvwatson@racsa.co.cr) run from Tortuguero to Moín.

You can also reach Tortuguero by bus and boat from San José via Limón and Moín. If you want to experience local life, take the public bus from San José to Cairiari near Guapiles. If you change buses at Cairiari and get onto the El Geest bus, you can get the Bananero boat from El Geest at noon (506-382-6941) and travel on the waterways to Tortuguero. Oasis tours offers visitors to the La Selva area the option of traveling to Tortuguero after a cruise of the San Juan River along the Nicaraguan

border, starting at Puerto Viejo de Sarapiquí. The trip takes two days. (tel 506-766-6108, fax 506-380-9493, www.tourism.com, oasis@ tourism.com). Otherwise, book a tour to Tortuguero from San José and your bus and canal arrangements will be prearranged.

Maquenque National Park

This proposed park is intended to provide a last-ditch sanctuary for great green macaws (*Ara ambigua*) in Costa Rica. The impending extinction in the wild of these feathered friends has drawn a great deal of attention,

Night Bells

The intense tinny sound of the tink frog (*Eleutherodactylus diastema*) is heard all night in the lowland rainforest and around the canals (above). You'll hear 'em but you won't see 'em—they hide behind bromeliads and leaves. They lay their eggs in bromeliads, and the eggs hatch directly into frogs, not tadpoles.

Ornamentals

Canna, or Indian shot, (*Canna indica*, right) is now cultivated in warm-weather gardens worldwide. It is native to the New World tropics on the Caribbean side.
Butterfly lily *(Hedychium coronarium,* top) is a true ginger that has spread across the Neotropics from the Old World.

although the macaws are not alone: many other species have suffered a similarly rapid demise, but not all are as charismatic as these birds and so their tragedy has gone unnoticed.

During the last one hundred years, 90% of the nesting ranges of great green macaws have disappeared. Outside Costa Rica the macaw is only found in a few similarly limited lowland ranges from the Honduras to northern Columbia. This endangered bird is rapidly dwindling because it is dependent on one tree, *Dipteryx panamensis,* for both nest holes and food. These trees are used for wood floors and are prized timber trees. To protect the macaws, tree removal is now restricted, in theory at least, to one half the standing trees. Other pressures remain: illegal logging and poaching continue. Fledglings are easily poached, raising up to $300 a bird.

The situation is grave. The Tropical Science Center that manages Monteverde also coordinates much research under the Great Green Macaw Research and Conservation Project associated with George V. N.

Powell. Radio tagging funded by the British Embassy has shown that there are fewer than 35 breeding pairs of wild birds left in Costa Rica, fifteen less than necessary for a biologically viable population. Fortunately, another population is relatively close by, across the Nicaraguan border.

The few remaining Costa Rican pairs are located north of the Sarapiquí River, where they spend time during non-breeding season, and southeast of the San Juan and the San Carlos rivers, where they nest.

The proposed new conservation area is in the current breeding area to the west of Barro Colorado National Park. If funded, the new park should extend the La Selva biological corridor to San Juan. However, the Costa Rican government needs to raise funds to purchase the property or find a way to reward prospective future private reserve owners for protecting this endangered species.

Pacuare Reserve

Leatherback turtles nest on the Pacuare beach at night. A successful turtle conservation program has reversed significant poaching levels and saved the decimation of this species here. Volunteers have the opportunity to join tagging, nest monitoring, and hatching research (leatherbacks@aol.com).

Pacuare Lodge

This is a dazzling ecolodge on the banks of the Pacuare River within the protected zone. Arrive by land or by rafting the rapids. This is an adventure spot with wonderful visits offered to indigenous Cabécar communities. (tel 506-225-3939, US tel 800-514-0411, UK tel 800-773-4202; www.junglelodge. costarica.com)

Food Bundles

Pejibaye palm fruits were a Costa Rican staple for centuries, and you can buy them, boiled, on street corners everywhere. The palm has an interesting pollinator: a minute beetle. 10,000 *Derelomus palmarum* beetles swarm over one flower spray in a single night; the palm signals them to come by releasing a special beetle-attracting aroma when its male flowers are mature. The beetles are covered in bristles ideal for pollination. The palm entices the beetle to walk all over the female flowers by placing trichomes, or food bundles, at strategic places. In this way, the flower is pollinated and the beetles are satisfied.

Feeding the Defense

Wild ginger (*Costus laevis*) is found in the forest's light gaps. You can tell these gingers by their spiral leaf arrangement. The large cone from which the flowers open contains extrafloral nectarines. These feed an army of 26 species of ants that are very effective in protecting the flower from some predatory fly species whose larvae eat its seeds.

Pacuare and Reventazón Rivers

The demand for hydroelectric power competes with the rafters and kayakers who shoot the rapids of the Pacuare River. 80% of Costa Rica's electricity comes from hydroelectric plants, primarily driven by Lake Arenal. The level of electricity generated by private companies is capped, so the government needs to build large new projects to increase electric supply. One of the projects planned is the Siquirres dam across the Pacuare River, at the beautiful Dos Montanas Ravine. This would flood two Cabecar Indian families, destroy the Class II, III, IV, and V whitewater rapids on the Pacuare River, and drown out habitat in pristine areas. The construction of the dam has been scheduled; whether it will go ahead remains unclear. All parties appear focused on resolving how to create new electricity sources with less impact on the environ-ment.

The Reventazón River is the second major whitewater river in Costa Rica, and there are plans in progress for a dam at its ravine as well. The Fundación Ríos Tropicales is a nonprofit organization dedicated to the conservation of these rivers (tel 506-233-6455, www.riostropicales.com). The foundation arranges river kayaking adventures as part of its mission.

CATIE Lagoon and Center

Purple-crested gallinets and other water birds can be seen on the lagoon at the Centro Agronómico Tropical de Investigación y Enseñanza (CATIE) in Turrialba, a world-class tropical research center that houses experimental orchards, seed collections, an herbarium, and agricultural projects for researchers and students. A trail heads from here towards the Reventazón River. A guided tour of the facilities and plantations can be arranged in advance by calling 506-556-2700.

Sarapiquí River Region and Puerto Viejo de Sarapiquí

Red torch ginger (Etlingera eliator, top) and varieties of red ginger (Alpinia purpurata, bottom two flowers) can be found scattered through the rainforest.

The northern lowland Caribbean rainforest around the Sarapiquí River and Puerto Viejo de Sarapiquí is fascinating for committed ecotravellers. Prime ecolodges vie with expanding banana plantations for land use in this low-income rural region. For Costa Rica as a whole, bananas and ecotourism generate two of the top four

Ghost Bats

Honduran white tent bats (*Ectophylla alba,* above) create tent roosts in *Heliconia* and *Calathea* leaves in which they stay for several weeks between feeding. Mothers raise their young inside, protected from rain and predators. The bats sever the lateral veins so that the leaf collapses on either side of the midrib. These roosts often are shoulder-height, so if you are quiet, you can crawl underneath and see the fluffy creatures within. This bat has been found in only thirteen locations within Costa Rica, including La Selva and Braulio Carrillo.

sources of foreign income, along with coffee and electronics.

Unfortunately, bananas have been grown as a monoculture in a way that causes major depletion of the soil, heavy pesticide and fertilizer runoff, and excess waste from unrecycled plastic bags. The bags are used to protect ripening clusters but end up in rivers and oceans, suffocating sea life. The banana plantations also remove the natural food needed by rainforest animals, which withdraw to the dwindling islands of virgin rainforest and restored secondary forest.

The Rainforest Alliance in New York has pioneered more sustainable approaches; bananas grown by these methods are labeled ECO-OK® to signal to consumers the desirability of supporting these crops. Some major banana producers are beginning to adopt these newer strategies in Central and South America. An integrated approach is to leave small patches of rainforest scattered across the banana plantations to provide remnant forest habitats, similar to hedgerows in European countries.

Standard Brands, the umbrella organ-

Bat Flowers

Nectar-feeding bats have co-evolved with the flowers from which they feed. The flowers are often pale yellow and stink, like *Mucuna urens* (left). The bats digest some of the high-nitrogen pollen by first dissolving the tough pollen coat in a soup made with their own urine (which they drink), plus lashings of nectar and copious stomach juices full of hydrochloric acid. The flowers use the bats for pollination, rewarding them with nectar spiked with the essential amino acids that these particular bats need. The flowers advertise their wares by opening at night during bat-time, and hanging their blossoms below the canopy where bats can easily find them. Bat flowers occur in various forms called cauliflory (bursting from branches), penduliflory (hanging from feet-long stems like this one, above left), and flagelliflory (displayed on whip-like stems).

ization for the Dole fruit brand, is a major banana producer in the Sarapiquí area. Standard Brands' farms are making efforts to increase their sustainability, but have caused major siltation and pollution problems in the area and are not currently certified as ECO-OK®. Fortunately, the program is rapidly expanding. Chiquita has committed to full certification, with the majority of its farms now complying to ECO-OK® standards.

Not far from the Sarapiquí area, one can visit an ECO-OK® banana plantation at the Agricultural College of the Humid Tropical Region (EARTH), east of Guacimo. Groups of ten or more can visit the rainforest reserve, banana processing plant, papermaking factory, and plastic recycling center. (tel 506-713-0000, fax 506-713-0001, www.earth.ac.cr)

Puerto Viejo de Sarapiquí was once the primary coffee port for Costa Rica. From the early 1800s to 1890, the inland port was used to export coffee to countries ringing the Atlantic, via Limón. Boats came inland to pick up their cargo along the San Juan River, which joins the Sarapiquí River. Later a railroad was built that diverted

Seed Predators

Green Amazonian parrots (*Amazona sp.*), including red-lored parrots (*A. autumnalis*), yellow-naped parrots (*A. auropalliata*), and mealy parrots (*A. farinosa*) flock to the fruiting and flowering trees of lowland rainforests. Mealy parrots are found on the Pacific side only. They are all seed predators, cracking every tiny seed inside figs and other fruits. Listen for their raucous squawking as they fly rapidly from one feeding station to another. The red-lored parrot does well in plantations and pasture, so numbers increase with deforestation, but the mealy parrot is dwindling. One third of Neotropical parrot species are threatened by the pet trade and deforestation. Ironically, a mixed flock of over two thousand Amazonian parrots is thriving in the wild near Pasadena, California, where pet-escapes are feasting on non-native palm fruit from trees planted along Pasadena and Hollywood streets.

goods to Limón directly, and Puerto Viejo de Sarapiquí was bypassed for regional development. It is only in the last few decades that bananas have become a bigger business in this area, although the Caribbean region as a whole has been a major producer for some time.

You can take one-day kayak trips on the Sarapiquí or local rivers with Kayak Jungle Tours at La Virgen, 12km south of Puerto Viejo. Aguas Bravas offers whitewater and guided float rafting on the Sarapiquí River, Toro River, and Peñas Blancas River (tel 506-292-2072, fax 506-229-4837). The Peñas Blancas is known for the best whitewater. You can hire cruise boats and dugouts with motors in Puerto Viejo in order to float along the Sarapiquí River from Transportes Aquatico Oasis.

Along parts of the river with slower water and trailing vegetation, look for the sungrebe (*Heliornis fulica*). Pairs of this coot-shaped, striped bird, with their long, thin necks and plump bodies, build nests in

Spiral heliconia (right)

established territory. When alarmed, the brooding male scoops up his chicks into special underwing pouches made of specially folded skin and feathers and swims away. This compensates for the unusually rapid incubation time (11 days); the chicks hatch in a very weak and immature state during the early wet season. If you watch carefully while along the river, you are likely to see anhingas, cormorants, and kingfishers sitting on tree snags over the water, the anhingas drying their wings.

Regular news can be found at www. sarapiquirainforest.com.

Access

From San José there are two routes to Puerto Viejo in the Sarapiquí region: over the good new Braulio Carillo Highway, (Highway 32), through the national park towards Guápiles, then turn left at Santa on the rough road (Highway 4), leading from Limón to Puerto Viejo de Sarapiquí. This can take half a day depending on the road conditions. La Selva and the Sarapiquí ecolodges are located near Puerto Viejo. Or drive via Heredia to Varablanca and on to Puerto Viejo; this route goes by Poás Volcano.

An OTS bus goes from San José to La Selva on Mondays at 7 AM, and there is a public bus from San José to Puerto Viejo.

Racket Tips

Central American and Mexican motmots are the most stunning of this tropical family, which seems to have originated in Central America. The rufous motmot (*Baryphthengus martii*, right) is easily found in the Caribbean rainforest and joins mixed flocks that move after army ants in search of fleeing prey. Like kingfishers, to which they are probably related, motmots eat berries and catch fish. Listen for the motmot's quiet owl-like hooting, which sounds a bit like tennis balls hitting the court, a sound that it projects with ventriloquistic ease. And check out its tail: the shaped tips are formed from feather shafts at the end of the tail when the shafts at mid-tail fall out naturally. A similarly plumaged motmot from South America has no racket-shaped tips and is probably a different race of the same species.

La Selva Biological Reserve

When L. R. Holdridge purchased Finca La Selva, with its fruit farm and primary forest, as a weekend getaway from San José, the study of ecology was in its infancy. But Holdridge changed that. His contribution as a leading systematic tropical ecologist has left its mark. From his experience in Haiti, Holdridge grouped the habitats of the world in Life Zones. To do this, he classified habitats according to humidity, altitude, and latitude, finding that these three factors were enough to predict similarity. His system is used extensively in Latin America. He also left the legacy of La Selva, now a household name in the research circles of tropical ecology. Work done at La Selva has significantly increased our understanding of tropical ecology worldwide, particularly of lowland rainforests and silviculture (the growing and cultivation of trees). Educational opportunities range from guided half-day rainforest tours to a major eight-week course in tropical ecology, attracting researchers and students from all over the world. The center also offers a course in tropical studies for nonscientists, attended by business and political leaders. The education and research opportunities have produced La Selva's own cadre of policy-makers and university professors. The biological reserve is run by the Organization for Tropical Studies (OTS in English, OET in Spanish), which continues to expand the role of this important research center in the world of academic institutions. OTS is a collaboration between fifty universities. Smaller sister OTS stations are found near San Vito in the south and Palo Verde in the north west.

The Audubon Society has recorded over 300 bird species in a single day at La Selva. There is a total of 436 bird species (nearly half of those found in Costa Rica) here, 120 mammal species, 56 snakes, 25 lizards, 49 amphibians, 400 ants, 500 butterflies, 350 trees, and 1,864 vascular plant species. Orchids and epiphytes are abundant but are even better at higher altitudes, in places where there is a mist of water droplets and not the extreme drenching found in the lowlands. The wettest months here are July, August,

Toucans

The chestnut-mandibled toucan (*Ramphastos swainsonii*) holds fruits in its beak, then throws them into the air to catch them in its throat. Toucans (above) select fruit in order of ripeness using color as their guide: they start with black, then maroon, then red berries. Males feed females fruit, and they boldly seek eggs, nestlings, and lizards. The large chestnut-mandibled toucan sometimes mixes with slightly smaller, keel-billed toucans. You are likely to see a succession of up to eight of one or both toucans swooping between fruiting trees, helping secure more than one tree for feeding. These similar toucan species differentiate themselves through their call: the keel-billed is a croaker and the chestnut-mandibled is a yelper. This croaker–yelper relationship is found in other cooperative-species pairs of similar toucans.

Episcia lilacina (below) grows in the wettest lowland Central American rainforests and is cultivated as a hot-house ornamental worldwide.

Hope Breeds Eternal

Many people think that rainforests are diverse because they have remained the same for so long, since before Jurassic times. But it turns out that tropical rainforests may be diverse because of their *instability*. Evidence for this dates from the last major ice age, when most of the New World including Costa Rica became dry and cool, contracting the tropical rainforest into a patchwork of small refuges. Each island became a center for evolution, which formed many new species. Later, these new species came together as rainforests expanded again, merging a profusion of similar tropical species. This is easily seen in pairs of different toucan species that live together. Although conservation remains critical, the data are hopeful for the future of the rainforests: on the east coast of Brazil, 88% of the forests have been cleared, but only eight resident animal species have become extinct, fewer than expected.

Zipliner passenger zooms over rainforest canopy (above)

November, and December, though rain occurs year round and totals over 4m/156in.

Visitors are likely to see a greater variety of tropical wildlife at La Selva over a period of a few days than in any other reserve in Costa Rica, primarily because the lowland Caribbean rainforest is so rich in species and also because trail access is so good. The reserve has 26 trails totaling 61km/38mi. These are in two sections: the central ecological reserve, which is easy to access due to its flatness, and the surrounding major Caribbean rainforest, which is further away and hillier. This forest is in easy reach of the main office. Boardwalks, a short cement path, and excellent trail maintenance open up all these habitats to exploration. Permission is required to traverse the more remote trails. The habitats are quite diverse, including secondary forest, riparian vegetation, regenerating orchards, experimental plots, an arboretum with 1,000 trees, and "pristine" rainforest, the latter of which forms two-thirds of the property of 1,516ha/3,746ac. The arboretum and experimental plots provide important long-term information on silviculture and forest growth rates by accurately counting tree age using data records and actual dates. The age of tropical forest trees is otherwise hard to determine; the traditional tree-ring method fails in the tropics, where the lack of summer–winter seasonality means that no tree rings are produced.

The research has revealed a major surprise about what we consider to be pristine rainforest. The presence of 2,430-year-old charcoal samples in one of the swampy lowland forests indicate that what was previously thought to be rainforest untouched by man is in fact just the opposite. It turns out that the hunters and farmers of the region have had a significant effect on what previously appeared to be pristine rainforest with a scattering of

Rainforest Resilience

Minerals and nutrients of the rainforest are held in the plants and few inches of root mat, not in the soil, unlike in temperate zones. It was thought that once the topsoil was removed, tropical rainforests would be doomed. However, new evidence now brings this into question. While regeneration is still impossible for some ancient areas, such as the Tepuis of Venezuela that are mineral deficient, the volcanic soils of Costa Rica appear rich enough to re-establish themselves eventually over time if carefully managed.

Location in La Selva where 2,430-year-old charcoal was discovered from man-made fires (left)

Royal Red

The new leaf of the royal palm (*Roystonia regia*) is red (right), hence its name. Research by Dr. Sharon Robinson shows that the red pigment is an anthocyanin sunscreen compound that protects the newly forming photosynthetic organs as they develop in the high-intensity tropical sun. The pigment turns purple or red according to the acidity of the leaf. The pigment remains until the leaf matures and starts photo-synthesizing with other pigments. During mature photosynthesis, chloroplasts absorb red light and store the energy as sugars. Other sunscreeners include wild tree poinsettias, with red leaves at the top where the sun is most potent. In this case, the red color also acts as a homing signal to pollinators. These are mature, native species of the poinsettias used in holiday decorations. *Welfia georgii* (above) is a another common and important fruit-bearing rainforest palm in the Serapiqui area whose young leaves are red.

recent orchards. Indigenous peoples have also helped select for some trees and against others. Thus people have lived with and influenced the rainforest from the time that they moved in.

It is only recently that this dynamic interaction has become so extreme that monocultures threaten the forest's existence. Deep history provides examples of ways in which man and wilderness have lived together sustainably. These and other discoveries have given support to the government's current policies of expanding critical rainforests into mosaics and corridors, in which key species in each sector will be in genetic communication with their neighbors.

La Selva is an important part of an altitudinal migratory corridor. The new Braulio Carrillo National Park boundaries were extended to meet the La Selva reserve in order to provide a continuous series of rainforests that reach from the lowlands to Barva volcano at 2,500m/1,550ft and provide the type of extensive habitat needed by jaguars and other wide-ranging species.

The Puerto Viejo and the Sarapiquí Rivers border the property and smaller streams dissect it, increasing the level of edge habitats and canopy visibility. You can get a feel for the wildlife around the Puerto Viejo River from the suspension bridge

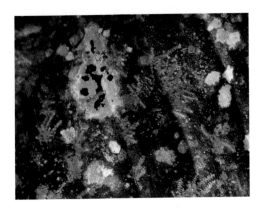

Sunspeck Species
Tropical leaf surfaces, damp
wood, and sharp spines are
often green with a complex
community of tiny organisms
(left). This community starts
with the colonization of the
surface—from leaves to
spines—by slime molds,
fungi, yeasts, and bacteria.
These provide a foothold for
lichens, mosses, and liverworts
that grow actively in this
epiphyllus community.
Tropical plant "sunspeck species" have dark green leaves
that "switch on"
photosynthesis as soon as a
sunspeck appears, and do not
switch off until a long time
after the light has moved on.
Many of these are now
common houseplants. Most
other rainforest species switch
on more slowly, and switch off
immediately when the light
goes, so they cannot survive on
the dim forest floor. The
characteristically glossy leaf
surfaces and "drip tips" found
on rainforest leaves help keep
surfaces drier and thereby freer
of the network of colonizing
lichens and algae that otherwise would compete for light.

close to the main offices. You may spot two-species flocks of toucans knocking back berries in the treetops, kingfishers as they observe from tree snags, and white-tipped sicklebills feeding on heliconias.

Look for the single 50cm/20in basket pouches of the scarlet-rumped cacique (*Cacicus uropygialis*) hanging low over the water from the boughs of *sotacaballo* trees (*Pithecellobium longifolium*). The nests are often situated near wasps' nests to give the chicks additional protection against predators, especially monkeys. The caciques are common but clever birds, related to red-winged blackbirds, who tend to form mixed flocks with oropendolas, black-faced gros-beaks, and fruit crows to rummage for insects. Such groups are very effective at flushing insects, finding edible berries, and detecting prey, and the richness of tropical food types allows each species to thrive by specializing cooperatively instead of competing.

The evergreen tropical wet forest has many buttress and stilt-rooted species; the buttresses help to aerate the trees and capture nutritious debris by making little dams during the flooding wet season. The open understory is given shape by dwarf palms and flowers bursting from the trunks of cauliflorous trees or on long pendulous stalks—both apparently in order to attract bat pollinators. Wide-leaved heliconias and

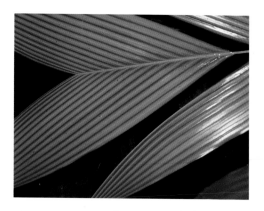

Fishtail Mimics
Fishtail palms (right) fruit only once before dying. The color of their fronds has been matched by several snake species.

Arboreal rear-fanged vine snake species catch lizards and are so thin as to disappear from view. Oxybelis fulgidus (above) is green and found in the Guanacaste region and Caribbean lowlands. Oxybelis aeneus, the grey vine snake found in the Pacific slope dry forest and southwest rainforests, freezes when threatened— but if further challenged, it opens its huge black-lined mouth in a startling threat display.

gingers capture the minimal light that penetrates the thick canopy, providing bright flowers and hinged roofs to shelter Honduran white tent bats—who are delightfully cuddly in appearance.

The signature tune of this lowland forest is the ringing call of the great tinamou, which sounds like a ringing wine glass, repeating with increasing tremulousness. The tinamou are related to flightless rhea of South America and are extremely primitive birds, resembling large, souped-up chickens. Their ventriloquistic abilities mean that they are extremely difficult to locate even when their call is loud, which has saved them from being wiped out, as their meat is much sought-after. Fortunately, this adaptable bird is doing well even in secondary forests, and you are likely to hear or see one in La Selva.

Another bird that can throw its voice is the rufous motmot (*Baryphthengus martii*). Its call may sound like distant tennis balls being thwacked by a racket, even though the bird may be only a few arms' lengths away. It sits quietly in the shade, wagging its racket-shaped tail feathers (see page 188). The motmot family has a unique place in Costa Rica because their population is centered in Central America. There are more motmot species in this region than elsewhere, which means they may have evolved here. The rufous motmot eats insects, *Heliconia* berries, and palm fruit with its heavily serrated bill. It will follow an army ant swarm to sally for flushed prey. Motmots nest like kingfishers, their relatives, in long tunnels in muddy banks, sometimes borrowed from mammals.

The white-whiskered puffbird (*Malacoptila panamensis*) is a fluffy cinnamon-striped bird that, like other puffbirds, perches for hours scanning for insects and frogs. The related, but much larger and less common, white-necked puffbird (*Bucco macrorhynchos*) can also be seen, sitting stationary on the edge of clearings, strikingly black and white. It can spot prey up to 18m/60ft away. Look for the arboreal nests they make in termite carton nests.

Small flocks of stunningly colored birds such as the golden-hooded tanager (*Tangara larvata*), bay-headed tanager (*Tangara gyrola*), and green honeycreepers (*Chlorophanes spiza*)—whose males are deep turquoise—may be spotted as they forage for melastome fruit, *Cecropia* berries, and figs in the upper canopy of the mature forest and in the secondary growth areas around La Selva. Each of these is an exquisite gem, particularly when directly illuminated by the sun.

Barred antshrikes are rarely seen, but your guide may be able to attract one by sounding its call. Their zebra stripes are perfect for camouflage in the dappled

Palm Ambushers

Watch for highly dangerous bushmaster snakes (*Lachesis stenophrys*, below left), which have learned to nestle close to *Welfia* palm trees, waiting for a dinner of the spiny rats, peccaries, coati, or agouti that seek out its seeds. Bushmasters protect their venom from light, which can break the poison down, by storing it in black-lined jaw sacs. Pit vipers like these have infrared heat sensors on their noses (the pits) that are sensitive to changes in temperature of 0.0003°C. Not only do they track warm-blooded mammals, but also lizards whose body temperatures are slightly above the ambient level as a result of sun basking. Salamanders, like the one in the hole above, remain protected by their cool body heat.

Sap Suckers

Imagine eating maple syrup, and nothing else, for a lifetime. Not only would you get tired of it, you'd probably die of dietary deficiencies. Sap suckers such as aphids live this way: they need tryptophan and leucine, essential amino acids that are rare in plant sap. Aphids solve this problem through symbiosis. *Buchnera* is a bacterium in aphids that synthesizes an excess of these amino acids from scratch. A 200-million-year-old union resulted in the first aphid, an insect that was a billion times more successful than its generalist parents, sisters, and brothers. Now, neither the aphid nor *Buchnera* can live alone. When the aphid's eggs are fertilized, the maternal colony of bacteria that are enclosed in a cellular home near the aphid's ovary forms an inoculating tube that pierces the aphid's early embryo and injects bacteria. These then form a new bacteria colony in the developing embryo, perpetuating the relationship.

shadows, and both sexes have a prominent crest for expression. Antshrikes are among the birds that follow army ants and seek out the beetles, spiders, and caterpillars that are flushed by the swarm.

La Selva's ecosystem continues to change: bird species never previously recorded are now appearing. Extensive deforestation on the Caribbean side may be causing a reduction in transpiration, shrinking the montane rainfall and changing the microclimates. It is possible that birds are adapting to new habitats in order to survive, and this may be translating into genetic evolution. Scientists have recorded evidence of evolution in similar instances, for instance in the changing structure and shape of beaks of Darwin's finch species on the Galapagos Islands. This occurred over a mere few years as a result of changes in seasonal patterns that meant different beak structures had different levels of success in food acquisition. This stunned biologists into realizing that some species will demonstrate genetic changes in their breeding populations over much shorter periods of time than previously imagined possible.

Guided tours through the primary and secondary rainforest leave in the morning at 8 AM and afternoon at 1:30 PM. Advance reservations are required (tel 506-766-6565, US tel 919-684-5774, www.ots.ac.cr/en/laselva, laselva@sloth.ots.ac.cr). A map of the reserve and 26 trails is available from the field station. For those staying at the

Figs (right) and other fruit provide major food resources

A Heliconius *mimic on hotlips (above)*

Tropical timbers raise travellers over the wetlands and rainforests of Selva Verde (left)

field station, food is served in a large mess hall, where ecotravellers mingle with researchers. However, non-research local workers are required to eat elsewhere, unlike in the Santa Rosa field station where park personnel eat together with visitors and researchers. You can order a bag lunch from the kitchen a day in advance.

Selva Verde Lodge and Reserve

Selva Verde is an excellent choice for travellers who want rainforest luxury combined with natural living near La Selva. The 192ha/475ac reserve is located in the vicinity of Puerto Viejo in secondary and virgin rainforest. A suspension bridge goes over the Sarapiquí River behind the lodge. The comfortable lodge is made of a series of luxury units on stilts, connected by raised, covered walkways of polished hardwoods. Resident guides offer early birdwatching tours and expeditions into the primary rainforest reserve, which has some steep muddy paths. Visitors can take self-guided walks through the secondary forest around the lodge and riverside, which attracts a large number of species of birds, stick insects, mammals, and poison-dart frogs. The species are similar to those in La Selva (previously discussed), which is a few minutes' drive south and more extensive. The lodge has a small butterfly garden that breeds local species. Conference

facilities are available. Next to the lodge is a learning center designed to improve educational opportunities for local families. (tel 506-766-6800, fax 506-766-6011, US tel 800-451-7111, www.holbrooktravel.com)

Tirimbina Reserve/Centro Neotrópico Sarapiquís Ecolodge

Tirimbina ecolodge is a good place to stay in comfort near La Selva and has stunning architecture inspired by indigenous art. The 300ha/740ac reserve is located across a suspension bridge over the Sarapiquí River. The trail includes a suspended walkway over a gorge in the rainforest. 2.5-hour guided hikes leave at 8 AM from the ecolodge. Recently, a tomb field with stone carvings and petroglyphs was also discovered on the grounds. (tel 506-

Giant lobster claw (Heliconia bihai) grows upward (left), and falls downward (H. stilesii, right)

761-1004, fax 506-761-1415, www.sarapiquis. org, magistra@racsa. co.cr)

El Gavilán Lodge and Reserve

El Gavilán is an easy eight minutes from La Selva and provides good accommodations. The 182ha/450ac reserve of primary rainforest is 2km from the lodge, which is located on the banks of the Sarapiquí River. Over a hundred species of birds can be spotted here, including green ibises, bronzy hermit hummingbirds, and tawny-chested flycatchers. (tel 506-234-9507, fax 506-253-6556, www.gavilan.lodge.com, gavilan@ racsa.co.cr)

Rara Avis Reserve and Lodge

This wilderness ecolodge is unique—it originally set the standard for in-the-wild rainforest adventure. The species richness is intense and filled with rarities. Travellers are completely immersed in wilderness and need an extra level of commitment to get here at all. The 1,280ha/3,163ac reserve is in plunging montane rainforest, and includes an orchid garden, several tree platforms, a waterfall, a butterfly farm, and extensive rainforest trails. There are several accommodation chalets, each offering a unique window onto a particular habitat, and visitors can spend the night on a tree platform. There are 390 recorded species of birds here, including snowcap hummingbirds.

Access needs to be arranged with Rara Avis because the final 15km/9mi from Las Horquetas is inaccessible to 4WD. Instead, transfer at Las Horquetas to Rara Avis' own tractor-trailer for a 3-hour ride. Las Horquetas is located by Highway 4 south of Puerto Viejo. Rara Avis recently changed ownership, so check for current details. (tel 506-764-1111, fax 506-764-1114, www.rara-avis.com, raraavis@sol.racsa.co.cr)

Fungi Fuel

Without a type of fungi called mycorrhizal fungi, the rainforest would die out. You can spot this fungi by finding thin veils of fungal filament around root areas. These fungi are vital because of the way they trap phosphorous. Phosphorus is unavailable in lowland tropical rainforest soils. Non-tropical plants get essential phosphorus from a mat of feeder roots and root hairs extending into leaf litter, which works well for trees in light gaps with high nutrient levels. Unlike in temperate forests, however, these mats are rare in the tropics. Instead, most tropical rainforest plants get phosphorus through a symbiotic association with mycorrhizal fungi. These are specialist fungi linked to plants, sponging up minerals that they exchange with the plants for sugars. Tropical forests on old infertile soils depend on tree species with strong mycorrhizal interactions set up to support even mature trees.

Battle Flags

Anole lizards (*Norops* sp., above and right), are very common, particularly at the ground level visible to ecotravellers walking through the understory. The intensely colored throat dewlap of the male (above) is used for display to alert other males to territorial boundaries, which they defend from high perches. The male bites and chases away intruding males to defend his rights to the approximately three females that live within his territory. There are twenty-five anole lizard species in Costa Rica, each with a different colored dewlap that stands out from a distance like medieval battlefield colors.

Oro Verde

Oro Verde guest accommodations are in the Duarte house, surrounded by a reserve of 2,500ha/6,180ac. Birdwatching is a focus, with many activities offered, including Oro Verde rainforest hiking, morning and afternoon guided bird-watching, and snorkeling at Balena Marine Park, which is 3.5km/2mi away. The lodge is 18km/10mi south of Dominical. (tel 506-743-8072 or 506-843-8833, www.costarica-birding-oroverde.com)

La Danta Salvaje Reserve & Lodge

This 405ha/1,000ac primary forest lowland reserve is on the edge of the Braullio Carrillo highlands. You can see a 150m/492ft waterfall on one of the trails. Crested guan, silky anteaters, and signs of jaguars may be spotted on the four-day excursions based at the lodge. These leave about every two months. Check with the lodge for updates on excursion offerings.

The reserve is located just south of Guapiles off Highway 4 (tel 506-750-0012, ladanta@racsa.co.cr).

Caño Negro Wildlife Refuge

This wetland is located in the north of Costa Rica and has been a prime birdwatching haven, although check for current details as siltation is changing the nature of the lake. The wetland is fed by runoff from the Frío River and covers 9,972ha/24,623ac at its maximum. The shallow freshwater lake is right in the middle of the central flyway for 200 species of North American migrating birds, many of which overwinter here. Waterbirds cluster as the lake dries up during the brief dry season from November to April. Huge waterbirds include stately jabiru (*Jabiru mycteria*), which breed in the Tempisque river basin; wood storks, (*Mycteria americana*), which come at the end of the dry season; and abundant olivaceous cormorants (*Phalacrocorax olivaceus*). The jabiru may be starting to breed in this refuge.

At night, the eyeshine of spectacled caimans (*Caiman crocodylus*) and, on rare occasions, ocelots (*Leopardus pardalis*) may be seen from your dugout canoe if you venture out on your own. By day, watch small clusters of gorgeous roseate spoonbills (*Ajaia ajaja*) sweep the river for food, silhouetted by the plunging fronds of royal palm (*Scheelia rostrate*), holillo (*Raphia taedigera*), and corozo palm (*Elais oleifera*). Quiet tour boats are ideal ways to try to spot howler monkeys (*Alouatta palliata*), spider monkeys (*Ateles geoffroyi*), white-faced capuchin monkeys (*Cebus capucinus*), and the three-toed sloth (*Bradipus variegatus*) as

Pollinators

Trigona sp. stingless bees (by banana flower, below) store their colonies in subterranean tree hollows. Their teapot-spout nest hole pokes from the base of their home tree as a type of bridge defense from army ants. Workers stick marauding ants with glue. Nests can last the lifetime of their sheltering tree. These bees collect pollen and nectar from up to twenty local species each day. When a bee finds a particularly rich and abundant food source, it marks leaves in the area with a pheromone and returns to the nest to gather recruits.

Some stingless bees, however, are parasites. *Leistrimella* sp. releases citral, a lemony pheromone, to jam the defense communication signals of *Trigona* bees that it attacks. *Leistrimella* bees steal huge amounts of pollen and honey before they depart.

Elevation Clearwings

The family of Satyrid butterflies have only four walking legs and include the gossamer-winged beauty *Citherias menander* (right). They sip rotting fruits and sap. This species is a clearwing. Colored clearwings habitually fly at a specific height in the rainforest; one color is favored at each level. The color is perfectly adapted to make the insect invisible to predators at that particular vertical position. From our unusual position on the ground, they stand out, but most predators are in the canopy.

they browse in the trees. Black-necked stilts (*Himantopus mexicanus*), black-bellied whistling ducks (*Dendrocygna autumnalis*), and anhingas (*Anhinga anhinga*) are more common. Anhingas, wood storks, and vultures soar together high in the air above the wetlands. Northern jacanas (*Jacana spinosa*) skip on the water vegetation using their long toes to distribute weight over a large area. Nicaraguan grackles (*Quiscalus nicaraguensis*), an endemic species associated with Lake Nicaragua just over the border, are found from here north on wetlands.

Fish include the prehistoric gar (*Atractosteus tropicus*) and snook (*Centropomus undecimalis*). The most interesting of the water species, at least until recently, were the bull sharks (*Carcharhinus leucas*) that used to come to Caño Negro, up the San Juan river floodwaters from the ocean, until silting-up bocked their passage. Lake Nicaragua, close to the north, has its own population of so-called freshwater sharks.

Several ecotravel tours go to Caño Negro, which is 291km/180mi north of San José. Day tours leave from La Fortuna hotels. They are the best way to get to the lake and include guided boat cruises to see mammals, reptiles, and birds. Individual travel to the lake is difficult. If you go on your own, take a good 4WD vehicle and drive to Los Chiles or San Rafael. Request a boatman to take you to Caño Negro on the Río Frío (five hours from Los Chiles). To drive all the way, you need to be prepared for flooded roads and no services during the wet season. Annual rainfall is over 3m/117in.

Braulio Carrillo National Park

Braulio Carrillo National Park is the newest major park in Costa Rica. It spans the 2,906m/9,500ft Barva Volcano and plunges through rainforest to the diverse Caribbean lowlands at 150m/500ft in altitude, enveloping 47,500ha/117,300ac. This park was specially expanded to allow altitudinal migrants, such as the bare-necked umbrellabird, to move upwards seasonally to breed and then return to the lowlands. This area is rich in species: 6,000 plant species, 400 bird species, and 135 mammal species. The purchase of land for this national park involved a major contribution from the United States as part of a land-for-debt swap.

Trails are virtually nonexistent or are too wild and dangerous for regular eco-tourists to use, except for several short trails

Owl Butterfly

The owl butterfly (*Caligo* sp., below left) has six Costa Rican species with blue and brown upper sides and huge eye spots underneath. These eye spots are a startle strategy: birds attack the eyespots, but the butterfly's wings are large enough to survive shredding and allow them to fly away. *Caligo* caterpillars eat large amounts of banana leaves where they hide themselves by lining up with the leaf vein.

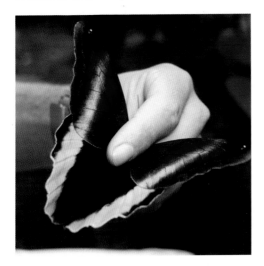

Stick Defenses

Thorny, spiny plants use a coating of bacteria, fungi, and yeast for germ warfare. A pricked mammal often gets an infection from the bacteria-laced arsenal and learns not to touch the plant. Warree palms (*Acrocomia vinifera*) and similar plants (below right) use this epiphyllus defense strategy, as you'll see from their dirty-looking 2-inch spines splayed at odd angles from the young trunk. Warree palms were probably introduced by pre-Columbian Indians; they are found only in disturbed areas. The palm seeds are rich in oil and protein, and the sap was used for a fermented drink.

Stick insects (below right) fit right in among these thorny plants

just inside the northeast entrance, the Carillo Ranger Station, on the Siquirres Highway (Route 32). The best option is to take the canopy tram. However, the location means that visitors from San José have to drive all the way through the park before they can get out and explore. Route 32 is an excellent road, but during heavy rain it is subject to dangerous landslides and should be avoided.

The Atlantic Rainforest Aerial Tram and Bungalows (tel 506-257-5961, fax 506-257-6053, www.rainforesttram.com) explores the canopy of a 475ha/1,173ac private reserve, taking about ninety minutes to complete. This reserve is safer than the area outside it. There are guide-led trails through secondary and primary forest. You can also swim in the river pools and watch hummingbirds around the waterfalls. Accommodations are available for those wanting to stay longer or to experience the nocturnal life during a night hike. For birders interested in diversity, it is usually possible to

Flower Mimic

This bromeliad and orchid look-alike is in fact unrelated to either pineapples or orchids. However, *Cochliostema odoratissimum* (above, left) does have a tank and an umbrella-whorl of narrow leaves (with a clear midrib) that traps moisture and nitrogen-rich debris to increase the longevity of the species. The showy flowers are appealing to us, and it does well as a potted plant in Costa Rica. In the wild, the blue form is found on the Caribbean lowlands and white form on central and southern Pacific slopes.

spot between 70 and 140 species of birds on a single route in a day. An Audubon bird count in 2003 recorded 400 bird species in one day, including the commonly found chestnut-sided warbler (*Dendroica pensylvanica*), the rarer black-and-white hawk-eagle (*Spizastur melanoleucus*), great green macaw (*Ara ambigua*), red-rumped woodpecker (*Veniliornis kirkii*), the strong-billed wood-creeper (*Xiphocolaptes promero-pirhynchus*), gray-headed manakin (*Piprites griseiceps*), black-and-white becard (*Pachyramphus albogriseus*), sharpbill (*Oxyruncus cristatus*), and rufous-winged tanager (*Tangara lavinia*). This is a good place to come to spot the seasonal bare-necked umbrellabird and solitary eagle. The tram is located roughly 50 minutes away from San José on the Braulio Carrillo Highway, (Route 32), 5km/3mi after the Río Sucio Bridge.

My guide warned me that there may still be risk of armed robbery or other trouble from a few remaining Contra rebels in various areas, including on the most

Cyanide Shooters

The forest-floor millipede *Nyssodesmus python* (above) is found in rainforests on the Caribbean slope. These millipedes consume leaf debris. When threatened, they spray a toxic stream of hydrogen cyanide mixed with benzaldehyde that can reach one foot away. These millipedes are the only land arthropods that carry a high level of calcium in their exoskeleton, providing an important recycling function. Calcium is generally in low supply in the rainforest, so millipedes concentrate the calcium before it gets washed away, thus keeping the calcium level higher than it otherwise would be.

In this species only, males usually ride on the backs of females long after copulation is complete in order to ward off competing males.

remote trails and the Puerto Viejo side, such as the Botarama trail that leads to Río Sucio. Therefore it is may be unwise to take the extremely rough and remote 40km/25mi Transect trail from the Barva Ranger Station (by Barva Volcano) to the Magsasay Ranger Station near the Magsasay prison colony. This virtually unused trail takes about four days with a guide and there are shelters along the route. Check for the current conditions. Magsasay Ranger Station is 4.5km/2.8mi from La Selva Biological Station. If you continue to La Selva, both permission and a La Selva guide are required.

The Carillo Ranger Station offers a new, steep nature trail, the 3km Sendero Natural. However, this is not said to be in a safe area.

Orchids load the banks on either side of the highway just outside the southwest entrance on the San José side, near the Zurqui Ranger Station, where the major road climbs over the fog-laden central cordillera cloud forest. However, the road is a busy and dangerous one for walkers, with trucks carrying enormous loads of logs and supplies, so don't stop your car to explore along the road. Botanists and birders should find it interesting to stay at Villa Zurqui (tel 506-268-5084, fax 506-268-8856, hvzurqui@racsa.co.cr) for a night and venture forth from there. The manager of this comfortable, fireplace-filled hotel can direct you to a nearby quiet and sunny side road across private farmland just to the west of the central divide, where orchids, bromeliads, heliconia butterflies, and toucanets can easily be seen in the trees and on the mossy banks. The villa is not set up as an ecolodge; however, many birding guides bring visitors here.

Barva Volcano

You can reach Barva Volcano from the Barva

Ranger Station in southwest Braulio Carrillo National Park. You may want to leave your car where the road gets too rough above San José de la Montana and Paso Llano and walk to the ranger station—the 2,900m/9,510ft crater is an hour's walk from there. Hikers have gone missing, presumed lost, from the area. Jungle Trails (Los Caminos de la Selva) can take you on a guided hike to the volcano (tel 506-255-3486, fax 506-255-2782). The oak woodland and cloud forest is interspersed with pasture. You may see or hear scintillating hummingbirds, nesting resplendent quetzals, or black-faced solitaires. Lago Barva is an acidic pond formed in the extinct volcanic crater. Trees around it have been dated as 2,000 years old. The volcano seems to be becoming more active, so check for details before you go.

Talamanca Region: Limón, Puerto Viejo, and Cahuita

Afro-Caribbean, Latin, and indigenous Bri-Brí communities in the Talamanca region provide a wide diversity of activities for

Non-competitive
The thoas swallowtail (*Papilio thoas*) is a swallowtail butterfly that you may see visiting *Lantana*, hotlips *Psychotria* (here), and *Stachytarpheta*. Its larvae eat piper leaves and look like bird droppings. The male butterflies sip salt, which they need to mature properly, from damp sand banks. The host plant of the similar-looking giant swallowtail (*Papilio cresphontes*) is a different species, so they look the same without competing for the same food source.

A romantic city park in Limón
Photograph by Michelle Worth

ecotravellers: from a serene walk in cinnamon gardens to rappelling up a kapok tree, dancing to Caribbean music at the beach, or delighting in the indigenous masks and handicrafts in local markets. More ecolodges and tent camps are opening up, particularly in the southern Talamanca region that promises hilly forests, gorgeous beaches, dolphins, and reefs. However, the

Talamanca flatlands have a lower density of prime ecotravel sites than the northern area of the Caribbean side of Costa Rica, partly due to the level of deforestation that made way for banana plantations in the Estrella Valley, and partly due to the lack of roads, which has only recently been amended. The slash-and-burn agriculture practiced by Bri-Brí peoples has resulted in a significant area

Queen's wreath (Petrea volubilis) is a purple-and-green Neotropical vine cultivated in gardens and found native in rainforest from sea level to 900m/ 2,950ft. Its calyx lobes become wings and little floats when the seed is ripe.

of secondary forest around the rivers as well, with a depletion of large mammals and raptors. The indigenous populations expanded their cultivation activities in the 1950s after the banana plantations of the Talamanca Valley were abandoned due to disease.

However appealing they may seem, Limón, Cahuita, and nearby Puerto Viejo have a higher level of drug-related violent crime, so ecotravellers should not travel alone. Take theft-deterrent precautions and avoid locations and nightlife where muggings may occur.

Ecolodge and private reserve owners are increasing communication with the banana plantation managers and headquarter companies about the advantage of sustainable practices. Without changes in plantation approaches, major erosion will continue. The associated deforestation is already changing the rainfall and hydrology of the area, increasing the likelihood of severe flooding from untamed runoff. The increased sedimentation, exacerbated by a major recent earthquake, is killing coastal coral reefs and affecting fish stocks. Significant deforestation along the entire Caribbean side is reducing air moisture levels and may be drying out the weather patterns on the far western side of Costa Rica, causing smaller clouds to fly higher from the prevailing east wind.

The Talamanca Mountains offer rugged terrain, difficult for the cultivation of dessert crops like bananas, pineapples, and coffee. However, deforestation occurs here too. The foothills are home to three-quarters of Costa Rica's indigenous peoples. Bri-Brí, Cabécar, and many other indigenous communities are located in reservations. Some ecolodges help visitors learn more about the medicinal plants used by these communities and introduce you to a few of the ways of indigenous peoples by visiting reservations where tours are offered.

Costa Rica, in contrast to other Central American countries, is known for

Mall Aroids

Anthurium upalaense (above) is an aroid common on the Caribbean lowlands. Its rosette-whorled leaves sprout as an epiphyte, with the red fruit trailing like a beacon from a long stem. Other aroids are known as candle plants (below left). The related prayer plant (*Calathea leucostachys*) has handsome striped leaves and white flowers. It loves shade, which makes it perfect for growing in malls in developed countries. It originates in Central American Caribbean rainforests and is grown in cacao plantations.

its safety and its good public health system. However, some areas are more difficult for international ecotravellers to manage. Here in Limón, water, ice, and fresh fruit and vegetables may be contaminated as a result of a breakdown in water systems after a major 1991 earthquake hit this region. Therefore many Talamanca visitors go to their destination without stopping at Limón. Malaria is found in some parts of the region, associated with banana plantation workers, who move in and out of Costa Rica from malaria-prone countries. The *Anopheles* sp. mosquitoes catch malaria from human carriers and pass it to other humans, so mosquito nets can go far in preventing infection. Malaria is also found in the indigenous population. For these reasons, particular caution should be taken when planning to visit the Talamanca region.

Selva Bananito Reserve and Lodge

This 850ha/2,000ac private reserve is by the Bananito River and borders La Amistad Biosphere Reserve near Limón. This is one of the handful of places in Costa Rica where you can experience being near La Amistad without having to get completely wild and wooly. Eleven comfortable cabins form the lodge. The lodge is solar-powered and is located on a family farm of 416ha/1,000ac devoted to sustainable agriculture, where you can see these worthwhile farming practices at work. The ecolodge was launched in 1995. The reserve is about a ten minutes' walk away. Guided rainforest hiking is combined with the option of climbing 200ft up a kapok tree or rapelling down waterfalls. Over 300 hundred bird species can be seen here; La Amistad extends into Panama and forms one of the three most important bird migration corridors in the world. Raptors migrate starting in mid-March and mid-October.

The reserve contributes financially to the Limón Watershed Foundation, which focuses on the Banana and Bananito Rivers. The owners, the Stein family, work to protect the conservation areas from poachers and illegal logging and to educate the local government and people about the value of sustainable rainforest and agriculture in the area. Logging abuses have been videotaped and this has resulted in the suspension of two logging companies in the area for illegal practices.

The Limón Watershed Foundation is also part of a commission looking into the excessive flooding caused by deforestation, the recent earthquake, and banana plantations. Members of this commission

Root Exchange

Aerial roots growing from epiphytes (opposite page) appear to benefit their host. In return for light and rootspace given by the host tree, the epiphyte captures prized phosphorus, calcium, and potassium from dust and rainwater and feeds these rare nutrients to special aerial roots grown by the host tree. These roots grow directly from the host into the epiphyte root-mat high on tree branches. Nutrient uptake is significantly increased by mycorrhizal fungi that cover epiphyte roots and extend their reach and efficiency. Epiphyte loads can become so high that they can bring the host tree down. However, studies have found that many tropical trees are designed so that they first sacrifice individual branches that are overweight. The trees actually cut sap flow to speed up the weakening process and dump the limb before the entire tree falls over.

Bird Migrants

Five to ten billion birds, one half of all North American migrant birds, return to their evolutionary cradle in the Neotropics to winter, some reclaiming the exact territories that they occupied the year before. The birds include Kentucky warblers (*Oporornis formosus*), which pick caterpillars and ants from understory leaf undersides; ovenbirds (*Seiurus aurocapillus*), which glean for insects on the forest floor; gray catbirds (*Dumetalla carolinensis*), which relish tropical fruit and make mewing calls; and fruit-loving wood thrushes (*Hylocichla mustelina*). To learn more, see John Kricher and William E. Davis' recommended *A Neotropical Companion*.

include several government agencies and also the Standard Brands company, a major banana grower in the area associated with the Dole brand. In addition, two US schools are paired with the impoverished Bananito schools, which is proving a positive relationship. The foundation depends on contributions from individuals.

The lodge also offers a rainforest study program and Spanish immersion course for college and high school students.

To reach Selva Bananito, drive from San José to Limón and continue towards Sixaola on Route 36 until 20km south of Limón, which takes about 30 minutes, then turn west at Bananito for 15 km (river fording required). You can also take the bus to Limón and a taxi to Bananito and arrange to be picked up there. (tel 506-253-8118 for the San José office, 506-284-4278 for the cell phone at the lodge, www.selvabananito.com)

Rancho Naturalista

This lodge is located in the Caribbean foothills near Turrialba at about 3,200ft. Look for sunbitterns, black guans, and hummingbirds. (San José tel 506-433-8278, US tel 888-246-8513, tel at the lodge 506-554-8101; fax 506-267-7138, www. ranchonaturalista.net, crgateway@racsa. co.cr)

Grasshoppers appear in their usual laterally compressed form and also and in X-shaped flattened prototypes (right)

Estrella River Delta

314 bird species have been recorded on a private reserve right in the middle of the Estrella River delta flyway. Carrol L. Henderson notes that one observer counted over one million raptors migrating across the area in October of 2000. The wetland has navigable waterways ideal for quiet birdwatching from rented dugouts. The Aviarios del Caribe Lodge (tel/fax 506-382-1335, aviarios@costarica.net) has been instrumental in conserving the delta. The owners also run a sloth rehabilitation center. Tours for day visitors depart at 6 AM and 2 PM. Access: 10km/6mi north of Cahuita.

Cahuita National Park

Coral reefs are scattered along both of Costa Rica's coasts, and Cahuita National Park protects what was the country's largest reef. However, the major upheaval associated with the 1991 earthquake marooned much of the reef above the waterline. The remaining reef is repairing itself slowly. Its long-term future is still in the balance due to the high levels of sedimentation caused by deforestation in the Talamanca mountains and lowlands, mainly from banana plantations, as previously discussed.

Blue parrotfish (*Scarus coerulens*), the incredible black-and-gold-scaled French angelfish (*Pomacanthus paru*), queen angelfish (*Holacanthus ciliais*), and barracuda (*Sphyraena barracuda*) are among the 123 fish species that flit among the intricate domes of brain coral (*Diploria crivosa*). Some of the domes of brain coral reach the entire span of a diver's arms.

Among the other 35 coral species that survived the quake are elkhorn corals that come in two varieties: deer's horn coral (*Acropora cervicornis*) and flatter reddish moose horn coral (*Acropora palmata*).

Boa Constrictor

Look up in trees and you may see boas (*Boa constrictor*) sleeping from their last meal. Juveniles can be arboreal, and occasionally a huge boa moves upwards from its more regular territory lower down on the ground. Boas hunt rats, bats, ocelots, and anteaters. They plan each move, settling in burrows and on blossoming trees waiting for prey. They use thermal imaging plus chemical senses that are actively wafted into their mouth sensors by their forked, directionally acute tongues. Even though they are nonvenomous, mature boas can inflict deep bite wounds.

Sustainable Tourism

Sustainable beach hotels in Puerto Viejo by Cahuita include Cariblue hotel (tel 506-750-0035, www.cariblue.com) and Casa Camarona (tel 506-283-6711, lodge tel 506-750-0151), both by Cocles Beach.

Gorgonian fans are found in deeper waters, their fronds spanning currents to sieve foods. 140 mollusk species and 44 crustaceans add to the colors of the reef. The wreck of two ships, possibly slave or pirate ships, are located at the edge of the reef. Plan ahead for scuba equipment—San José may be the nearest rental location if other alternatives are not found prior to departure. While diving, beware of the black sea urchin spines, which can cause secondary infections if they are not removed and the wound cleaned immediately.

Cahuita is also under the major flyway for migrating birds, including thousands of North American raptors. On the drive down, look for collared aracaris and blue-headed parrots. Cahuita Point is mostly swampland graced by delicate palm trees, lianas, and *Pterocarpus* trees, which have large buttresses. Look for three-toed sloths, coatis, and white-faced capuchin monkeys in the trees. Yellow-crowned night herons, northern boat-billed herons, rufescent tiger-herons, green-and-rufous kingfishers, and green ibises are among the birds to spot around the wetlands.

Buses to Cahuita leave from San José and from Limón. From Cahuita village, there is a 4km/2.5mi trail to Puerto Vargas Ranger Station, which takes a couple of easy hours in the Caribbean climate. You can snorkel at several locations at the white beaches under palm trees on the way. Snorkeling equipment is available from Cahuita, a colorful, buzzing Caribbean village. There is only one phone for the entire village's switchboard, 506-758-1515; each accommodation in the village has an extension number. Violent crime has been reported in the area, unfortunately, and two tourists disappeared in 2000.

Hitoy-Cerere Biological Reserve

The 9,154ha/22,610ac conservation area is right in the middle of three indigenous people's reservations: Tayni Reservation to the north, Telire Reservation to the southwest, and Talamanca Reservation to the south. Set in the foothills of the Talamancas to the west of Cahuita, above huge banana plantations, this heavily forested reserve is not often explored. However, it has a lot to offer for day visitors. It is loaded with epiphytes, or *hitoy* in the local language. There are many edge zones because of the many rivers, or *cerere*, which dissect the canopy and open it up to a greater variety of Caribbean species than pure rainforest. These streams are one way for visitors to get into the reserve to watch the numerous birds in addition to the primary trail, Sendero Espavel, 9km/5.6mi. Some terrain is precipitous, with high heat and humidity adding to the challenge. The 1991 earthquake caused significant havoc to the reserve, which is still recovering.

4WD taxis can reach the reserve from Cahuita and vicinity and pick you up at a prearranged time.

Samasati Nature Retreat

The 100ha/250ac reserve in the rainforest foothills is one of the many focuses of this luxurious but simple yoga, mediation, and get-away-from-it-all retreat. You'll enjoy

Cooperators

The groove-billed ani is a cooperative bird that often builds a single nest holding four pairs. Anis raise their young communally, which sociobiologist Sandra Vehrencamp has studied carefully. Vehrencamp has shown that females can sometimes throw out eggs of other females, but that the whole group is nevertheless more successful than single pairs would be. Cooperative breeding more usually involves a community of birds that band together to raise their young from separate nests. In some types of cooperative breeders, non-breeding helpers assist in defending territories, raising chicks, and feeding young. Helpers may never breed. This challenged our understanding of Darwinian evolutionary theory; it was originally thought that no genes could be passed down to confer the non-breeding helper traits. However, it is now accepted that because helpers at the nest are relatives of breeding birds, some of the genes and altruistic traits are passed down through their parents and siblings.

Juicy sub-canopy berries (left)

Swiss Cheese

The familiar Swiss cheese houseplant is a member of the *Monstera* genus that evolved within Central America. The weird thing about these plants is that they grow towards the dark. This is in order connect with tree trunks, which they can then grow up. As they do this, the leaves change shape from disks into the lobed or holey form that we know. The holes imitate insect damage, signaling to predators that the plant is already eaten, so they will avoid it. You'll spot the juvenile moon-shaped disks of a close relative, *Monstera tenuis* (right), growing flat against tree trunks. When it switches into a huge, deeply pinnate leaf to take advantage as the light levels increase higher up the tree, its growth continues upwards. It is triggered to change form as it gains or loses contact with the tree surface. If its weight pulls it from the tree, it becomes a slender leafless shoot and seeks out another tree to colonize.

the excellent vegetarian fare. A ten-day package takes you to the locality's highlights, including dolphin watching, kayaking, snorkeling, and rainforest exploring. The retreat is close enough to Hitoy-Cerere to arrange a visit.

Samasati retreat is located southwest of Cahuita along a 4WD road. Pickups can be arranged. (tel 506-224-1870, US tel 800-563-9643; fax 506-224-5032, www.samasati.com, samasati@samasati.com)

Puerto Viejo Tropical Botanical Garden

Puerto Viejo (not to be confused with Puerto Viejo de Sarapiquí) and the coastline to its south is very pretty, with white beaches, coral reefs, and coconut-palm beaches. As a result, it has become popular. However, violent crime rates are higher than desired, possibly associated with the drug trade.

Its botanical garden provides a small but excellent look at the interface between use of the wilderness and the need for conservation. An associated steep loop trail extends the botanical garden and explores an adjacent 8ha/20ac rainforest reserve. This trail takes about an hour and passes through rainforest, cacao orchards that are regenerating into secondary forest, and pastureland where native species are being reintroduced by hand. This cacao was used to make chocolate; many area farmers grew it until the crops were destroyed by cacao blight in the 1980s. Vanilla, ginger, pepper, and cinnamon are some of the crops grown for research in the experimental garden. The garden is building a collection of tropical fruit species and you can see bromeliads, heliconias, orchids, and ornamental gingers, which are found in gardens all over the world but many of which originated in Costa Rica's rainforests. The 4ha/10ac garden is bordered by the Kekoldi Reservation and Chumuri Reservation.

Gandoca-Manzanillo Wildlife Refuge

This 300ha/740ac reserve in beautiful, palm-tree-laden wetlands attracts a significant amount of wildlife. The primary purpose of the refuge is to protect Manzanillo Beach, where turtle nesting can be observed. Four species of turtles clamber onto the beach from March through July along its 9km/5.6mi expanse. The refuge also stretches across 4,000ha/9,880ac of protected coral reefs, so there is ample opportunity for snorkeling, diving, and kayaking among the dolphins that frequent the area. The 500 species of fish who reside here include angelfish, parrotfish, jack, and snapper. There are 40 species of coral, including unusual lettuce coral and intricate brain coral domes. However, runoff from deforestation tends to increase sediment

Chicle
Manilkara zapota is a latex-producing tree that was used to make chewing gum. The latex oozes after damage to the bark (above). Now gum is produced synthetically. Many rainforest plants produce latex, which is so sticky that it renders browsers immobile. One caterpillar species that eats gum-producing papaya leaves avoids being glued together by nicking the leaf artery and retreating as the sticky sap gushes in a rivulet across the leaf. The caterpillar then has a full meal on the rest of the leaf before the plant can synthesize more latex.

Ant Seekers

Tiger-stripe patterned army ant butterfly females *Melinaea ethra* (above) are found mainly on the Caribbean side. They follow army ants, seeking the white spots of nitrogen-containing uric acid from antbird droppings. They also seek amino acids in the droppings, plus nectar in flowers. Other female heliconius butterflies get essential nitrogen by mushing nectar with pollen on their proboscis in order to release amino acids. These various nitrogen sources extend the lives of the Heliconius butterflies to about six months and significantly boost the number of viable eggs produced.

levels and reduce visibility. Additional reefs and feeding areas for dolphins outside the refuge have been identified by the Talamanca Dolphin Foundation for possible addition to the refuge. This nonprofit was founded by the owners of Aquamor, which offers snorkeling and kayaking equipment along with expert, low-impact dolphin-watching and PADI dive expeditions. Dives leave from the beach or from small *pangas* (dugouts), kayaks, or boats. (tel 506-759-0612, fax 506-759-0611, www. greencoast.com, aquamor@racsa.co.cr)

Gandoca lagoon and river provide good birdwatching for 380 species. Tarpon spawn in the shallows, and as you glide along in your *panga*, you can also spot snook, basilisk lizards, and otters. Basilisks can scamper across the surface of the water by spreading their weight across elongated toes. Crocodiles may be present, and unusual oyster mangrove systems are also found in the area.

If you wish to learn about green pharmaceuticals, watch birds, or look for dolphins, you can coordinate with community leader Florentino Grenald (tel 506-750-0398, 506-750-0191).

To volunteer with turtle research here, contact ANAI (Talamanca Ecotourism and Conservation Association, tel 506-224-6090, fax 506-253-7524, www.anaicr. org, anaicr@racsa.co.cr). This organization offers a variety of opportunities (not only with turtles), including the chance to stay with a local family and speak Spanish, to go on "field adventures," or to test food plants from other parts in the world to see which ones can grow well in the locality.

Almonds and Corals Lodge

The Almonds and Corals Lodge offers luxury tent cabins on stilts right in the middle of the Gandoca-Manzanillo Refuge, with a full restaurant (San José office 506-272-2024, lodge 506-759-9057, www.almondsandcorals.com). The camp's name comes from the wild almond trees that line the beach with coconut palms, and the reefs that dot the waters of white Manzanillo Bay, from Point Uva to Monkey Point. A day visit to the Sixaola River area and Panama can be arranged. Cultural tours are also available that visit indigenous reservations.

The refuge is 25km/16mi south of Cahuita, 2km from Manzanillo fishing village, about four hours from San José by road via Limón.

ASACODE Reserve and Lodge

Ecotravellers interested in learning more about sustainable silviculture and reforestation at the community level can explore the work at the ASACODE farmer's association. Farmers here are planting native trees in experimental plots, and felling rainforest hardwoods selectively using water buffalo instead of heavy trucks for haulage. The farmers offer basic accommodation at the lodge, with tours of their

Ant Mimics

Some beetles and spiders (top and center above) have evolved the narrow-waisted look of ants to signal they have the venom of ant stings. Velvet wasps (third from top) are ants that mimic the cautionary coloration of wasps. One beetle has the blunt-headed look of the painful Caribbean bullet ant (*Paraponera clavata*, below), but when the beetle flies, it mimics a wasp. (Avoid placing hands on railings and tree trunks to avoid the searing pain "bullet" inflicted by this ant.)

Papayas are grown as a dessert crop throughout Costa Rica

activities and the rainforest reserve. Contact ANAI in San José for more information (tel 506-224-6090, fax 506-253-7524, www.anaicr.org, anaicr@racsa.co.cr). Access is from the Bribri Sixaola road.

Bastimientos National Marine Park, Panama

A brief trip into Panama from Sixaola is worthwhile if you are interested in exploring the excellent diving in this marine park and archipelago. This vibrant ecoadventure destination is abundant in coral reefs and turtles. Kayaks and dugouts are available for rent, with or without a guide. The tourist town of Bocas del Toro on Isla Colon has dive shops and offers tours. (www.bocas.com/btisturi.htm)

6
Osa Peninsula and
Golfo Dulce

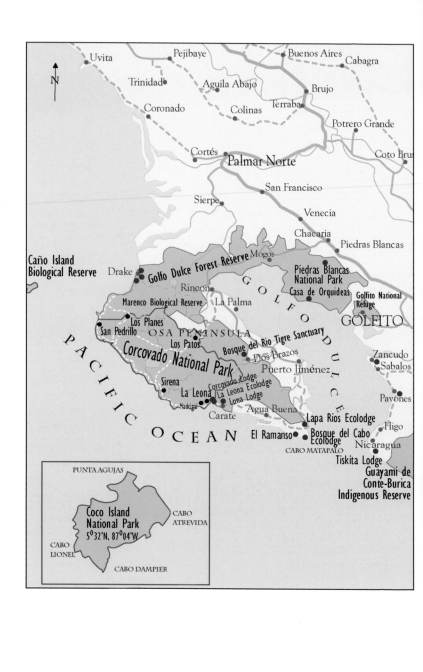

Two red-lored parrots perch quizzically in the treetops above my hammock, then make way for three scarlet macaws whose rainbow-colored feathers accentuate their name. You can tell that the three macaws are a family, the grown chick a fraction smaller than its doting parents. In surrounding trees there are dozens of raucous macaws, but only two chicks in all. I soon become surrounded by a quick-moving troop of red-backed squirrel monkeys, their ginger fur glowing in the dappled canopy sunlight. By the end of the day, I have seen four monkey species in the rainforest above

Rare scarlet macaws (Ara macao) flock around the Osa Peninsula (above)

Matapalo Beach (page 223) is known for surfing

Macaws

There are only three viable breeding flocks of the eye-popping scarlet macaws (*Ara macao*) in Costa Rica (previous page), all now on the Pacific side after Caribbean populations were wiped out by deforestation. Families of twos and a few threes can be spotted along the Osa beaches and forests. Look for the rounded leaves and chewed husks of beach almond trees (*Terminalia catappa*, below), which are among the wide variety of seeds and nuts these macaws consume as predators, not seed dispersers. Communal roosts are often in mangroves. They also cluster at clay licks (a natural form of Kaopectate) to detoxify their diet and obtain scarce minerals. Charles Munn has assessed that each wild Peruvian macaw is so attractive that it brings in $750–$4,700 in ecotourism dollars a year.

Lapa Rios

Matapalo Beach, a place with probably the highest monkey diversity and density of all of Costa Rica. The beach is also a cool, remote place to surf.

The Osa Peninsula is a rainforest refuge of immeasurable gifts. It holds the largest Pacific rainforest in Central America and the greatest variety of wildlife, but it is truly wild, wet, and steamy. The region is so wet that nearby Caño Island is said to receive more lightning strikes than anywhere else in the world. The entire area has a conservation office dedicated to the Osa region: ACOSA (Area de Conservación Osa, tel 506-735-5036).

Ecotravellers brave it to the Sirena Field Station in Corcovado National Park, or seek out luxury ecolodges in private reserves surrounding the park around Golfo Dulce and Drake Bay. The best Golfo Dulce lodges rest high on forested sea cliffs, so they have fantastic views and are cooled by tropical breezes. These factors also keep the mosquitoes away, an advantage not found inside Corcovado.

One reason for the Osa's diversity is that the peninsula is probably the only region in Costa Rica that has remained a rainforest the entire time the Central American land bridge has existed. During the most recent ice age, the prevailing tropical rainforest dried out and was largely replaced by savanna, reducing the entire American rainforest to a dozen patches here and in Amazonia. This tropical isolation spurred the evolution of similar species on each rainforest "island." As a result, the Osa Peninsula has evolved several endemic species, including 23 plants, 9 fish, and 20 bird species, while retaining the deep and broad genetic lineages of the ancient rainforests that seeded it as it rose from the ocean 2.5 million years ago. This habitat is home to 375 bird species, 140 mammals, 117 amphibians and reptiles, 3,100 species of plants, including 500 trees, and upwards of 6,000 species of insects.

Sometimes when rainforests are labeled "diverse," visiting ecotravellers have a hard time figuring out why, because the animals are hiding and the trees are so similar-looking it is difficult to distinguish them apart. The Osa Peninsula is different. The variety of life here is visibly overwhelming; the trees are a magnificent range of shapes and sizes; and you can find true ecolodges and the best guides. Exciting new lodges are opening too, including the stunning Playa Nicuesa Rainforest Lodge on the northeast edge of Golfo Dulce,

Turtles

You can volunteer to help turtle hatchlings reach the ocean safely. Community turtle conservation programs are run at Playa Carate, Playa Platanares, Playa Piro, Playa Río Oro, and Playa Tamales. More information can be obtained from the TUVA Foundation in Puerto Jiménez. The most common nester and the focus of help is the small olive ridley or Tortuga *lora* (*Lepidochelys olivacea*). On the Osa Peninsula, this turtle comes singly rather than in *arribadas* (see chapter one). They eat shrimp and tend to get caught in shrimp nets. A local subspecies of Pacific green turtle or *la negra* (*Chelonia mydas agassizii*) also uses these beaches. Green turtles eat sea grass. Both species come onto the beaches to nest more actively from May to December but can be found year-round. Leatherbacks (*Dermochelys coriacea*) are huge, jellyfish-eating turtles that occasionally nest along these shores from November to March. Sponge-eating hawksbills (*Eretmochelys imbricata*) also come ashore in scattered locations.

Restoration Rainforest: the Human Story

"People often say they like nature," says Stephen Kaplan, a medical researcher, "yet they often fail to realize that they need it." A line of dramatic research studies by E. O. Moore, R. S. Ulrich, and S. Verderber suggest that access to even a window view of nature (as opposed to a view of a brick wall) can significantly reduce the incidence of illness among healthy people, or shorten hospital stays and improve the results of surgery among the sick. About this, Kaplan says: "Nature is not merely 'nice.' It is not just a matter of improving one's mood; rather it is a vital ingredient in healthy human functioning." Kaplan has developed a theory called "directed attention" to explain some of these measurable restorative effects.

So, for a boost to your physical and mental fitness, take a walk on the wild side while you are in the rainforest. Take a moment to focus intently on what you see, hear, smell, and touch in these natural surroundings, and taste some of the tropical rainforest fruit cultivated for the markets of Costa Rica.

When you return from your vacation and during times of stress, you can switch into a restorative mode by savoring the memory of the most inspiring moment in nature that you experienced. Photographs of your trip and calming music help too.

A small nerve connecting the brain and the heart has been recently discovered that may account for this relaxing result. A relaxed, healthy heart communicates to the brain via the nerve directly, as well as using adrenaline and hormonal communicators that signal the heart's state. When calm, we may be more likely to think of creative solutions that don't occur to us when under stress. Calmness may also be associated with immune-boosting mechanisms, although none of this is clearly understood.

For some, being in nature may be a stressful experience associated with danger, rather than a place to unwind. Make sure that you are wise about the ways you seek renewal. Look where you put your feet and hands. Go with a guide. And take plenty of water, a hat, and sunscreen.

Corridors

The Meso-American Corridor is a major conservation plan that has evolved from the smaller Paseo Pantera program and now aims to create continuous rainforest from Columbia to southern Mexico. The view (right) shows forest stretching north to Corcovado National Park and includes private reserves dedicated to conservation as well as forests owned by active logging companies. In the future, conservationists hope to make the expanse a protected migratory corridor connected with the Talamanca Mountains. Illegal deforestation and poaching are currently major concerns. Inside Corcovado park are collared peccaries (*Tayassu tajacu*), Baird's tapirs (*Tapirus bairdii*), agoutis (*Dasyprocta punctata*), red brocket deer (*Mazama americana*), and pacas (*Agouti paca*). The Corvocado Foundation, Cecropia Foundation, Neotropical Foundation, and TUVA Foundation are working with the Nature Conservancy to achieve the area's conservation goals.

The Isthmus of Panama was formed 2.5 million years ago. This isthmus connected the north with what was left of the Gondwanaland south. Gondwanaland animals and plants evolved over a period of 40 million years in the connected supercontinent that now has split into Australia, South America, Africa, India, and Antarctica. After the isthmus formed, armadillos, ground sloths, porcupines, and a flightless bird species moved north. Moving south were humans and other species including bears, tree squirrels, skunks, horses, dogs, cats, rabbits, tapirs, deer, and other mammals now extinct. Monkeys appear to have rafted from Africa, which was mcuh closer at that time. About half of the genera of Central and South America appear to have came from the north.

which is made of recycled materials and is accessible by boat. (tel 506-735-5237, US tel 866-348-7610, 512-342-7160; www.playanicuesa.com)

Corcovado National Park

Corcovado National Park is the jewel in Costa Rica's rainforest crown. It is incredibly wild and hard to reach, but it probably crams more diversity per unit area than anywhere. 5% of the world's birds are found here, and it has more tree species than those in all temperate countries combined. About one-half of the Osa Peninsula is protected in this park as a result of a land purchase in 1977 made by the Nature Conservancy. Corcovado

National Park stretches across 41,787ha/ 103,259ac of tropical wet lowland rainforest rising to the montane forest of Cerro Rincón (745m/2,444ft). The park itself has many lofty rainforest trees, including the giant silk cotton tree (*Ceiba pentandra*), 77m/253 ft tall, the largest tree in Central America. At the center of the park is the *yolillo* palm swamp of the Laguna Corcovado, home to crocodiles, caimans, jabiru, and tapirs that wallow at dawn and dusk, and even the occasional jaguar on a fishing trip. White-lipped peccaries roam through the forest. This tropical wet forest experiences an incredible rainfall of at least 5m/195in, with a short "dry" season mid-December to mid-April, during which it rains occasionally. The unprotected land surrounding the park is still largely primary forest owned by logging companies, with many illegal logging trucks hauling their hardwood loads away at night. Fortunately there are many small private reserves in this area as well, some owned by ecolodges.

The main Sirena Field Station is in the center of the park near the coast and the mouth of the Sirena River, which flows through the lagoon. This is the central ranger station; the others include Los Patos, San Pedrillo, La Leona, and El Tigre (Dos Brasos). There are several long-distance trails cutting through the park connecting the ranger stations, except for El Tigre, which has hardly any trails.

It is essential to take plenty of bottled water, a hat, sunscreen, mosquito repellant, and sulfur powder to dust your socks with to avoid chiggers. Ticks and sand-based "no-see-ums" are common in some areas. Water is available from the field stations but bring plenty of your own.

Corcovado is difficult to access unless you can afford to fly to Sirena. There is a small landing strip at Sirena that is 10

Hyperdiversity

Heliconia butterflies (above) evolved on the huge linked continent of Gondwanaland. Their distribution shows that one of the major rainforest refuges after Gondwana split up was in Costa Rica on the Osa Peninsula. This became an "island" of rainforest when the surrounding habitat dried out during climate changes associated with an ice age. By acting as an isolated rainforest refuge, the peninsula spurred evolution of a hyperdiverse community. This now provides an exceptional destination for ecotravellers.

Final Refuge

Central American squirrel monkeys or *titi* (*Saimiri oerstedii*, below) sing a dawn chorus of male–female duets. They can only be found within Costa Rica around two small areas centered on Manuel Antonio National Park and on the Osa Peninsula. There are only 4,000 of these charming, ginger-colored animals left, and they are extinct in Panama. The scattered distribution of the squirrel monkey, which is unlike the other Neotropical monkey species, puzzles ecologists. It is possible that the squirrel monkeys were brought with humans. At this point, the future of the squirrel monkey is under the most severe threat of any monkey in the country due to deforestation of its habitat. The Osa Peninsula may be its final holdout.

minutes from Golfito (VEASA air charters 506-232-1010), or from Puerto Jiménez (Alfa Romeo Aero Taxi 506-735-5178). Sansa and Travelair fly to Golfito daily from each San José airport. There is also service directly to Sirena from San José that can be chartered with private air services (VEASA 506-232-1010). You can rent a boat to reach Sirena or hike into it from the outside along trails from Los Patos Field Station in the east (18km/11mi), La Leona Field Station in the south (11km/6.8mi, needing 5 hours), or San Pedrillo Field Station in the north (20.5km/33mi, seven hours, closed during the wet season).

Getting to these entrances is an expedition in its own right. It takes six to nine hours of challenging walking to reach Sirena from any entrance and additional time to reach the entrances themselves. Corcovado trails are across slick clay or hot sandy beaches and can be very slippery when wet. The beaches are lovely, but there are sharks, so swimming is not advised. Fortunately, there are some nice freshwater swimming holes around waterfalls and streams on some trails. Night walking can be the best way to cover the distance under cooler conditions if you are prepared for the

Motmots

Listen for the quiet, ventriloquistic "whoop whoop" of the blue-crowned motmot (*Momotus momota*, left). The call of this iridescent species probably gave the "mot mot" its name. Unlike other birds, motmots are often seen sitting still quite close to observers. Similar to their kingfisher relatives, motmots sit on a perch watching for prey. The blue-crowned motmot snatches insects and snakes before returning to its lookout to stun them and can also be found associated with army ants, which flush out its prey. Motmots can also hover and snip off palm nuts and other fruit. Motmots are a widely distributed Costa Rican rainforest gem easily missed by ecotravelers: look for the pendulum swing of their racket-tipped tail around low to head-height branches.

potential dangers—watch where you place your feet and hands. The rainforest comes alive at night and some guides prefer it this way. You may also spot sea turtles nesting on the way, or jaguars checking them out on the beaches.

Ecotravellers flying in from other countries should acclimate themselves for a few days before hiking extensively in Corcovado; the hikes are long and the weather hot and humid. If you have little extra time, fly in and stay at Sirena to take the shorter trails or get a feel for the Osa Peninsula by staying at a good ecolodge outside the park and walking their trails.

Activities and Places to Stay in Corcovado

You can stay within the park or at several dedicated and excellent ecolodges just outside its periphery that also offer guided park visits. Within the park, you can join others at the main Sirena bunk house or camp at San Pedrillo, Los Patos, or La Leona Ranger Stations. However, food is no longer

Scarce Cats

Television documentarians
seeking to feature jaguars
(*Panthera onca*) in the wild
have a hard time finding
them. Some stage their
footage using captive animals
in surroundings that appear to
be rainforest, but are planted
by hand. However, it is still
possible to see jaguars in the
wild, especially on the Osa
peninsula. A mother and her
cub walked past the astounded
cooking staff at Bosque del
Cabo, Osa peninsula, late one
evening. Perhaps she was on
the way to a large troop of
coatis that had roosted in a
tree. Jaguars have huge
territories, which need to be
intact for them to thrive. The
presence of jaguars indicates a
healthy rainforest. In
Corcovado, they love
swimming in rivers and
roaming the beaches, where
they occasionally kill sea
turtles, perhaps as a form of
play. Jaguars came from North
America across the Isthmus of
Panama landbridge about 2.5
million years ago.

How the Jaguar Got Its Spots

How jaguar (and leopard) spots are formed is a
major talking point among scientists. These
researchers include complexity theorists, nonlinear
mathematicians, and biologists. These scientists have
formed the surprising idea that the complex,
gorgeous pattern of graded spots on a leopard's coat
can be explained by a series of simple repeating steps.

The mathematics to explain this has been
developed from a specialty called "cellular
automata." Simple cellular automata programs can
be used to reproduce the development of a leopard's
spotted coat on a computer screen; the computer
program replicates the biological chain of events.

Biologically, a leopard's skin is peppered with
pigmented cells called melanocytes that produce fur
color. As the pattern on the coat forms on the pale
leopard fetus, these cells can be turned on or off by
two competing chemicals. One chemical activates
the melanocyte to produce color, while the other
inhibits it. Once activated, a melanocyte not only
produces color, it also produces more of the activator
chemical. This activator spreads out and turns on
the surrounding melanocytes, which become dark,
making this area into a leopard spot over time.
However, the spot is in a moat of the deactivator
chemical that is busy turning off surrounding
melanocytes, which remain pale. The two chemicals
compete as they diffuse across the coat, turning on
and off color formation over and over until the
system gains equilibrium. Finally, the coat matures
and becomes a record of the two-dimensional
chessboard contest between activated color splotches,
the sea of deactivated honey-colored cells, and
gradations in between.

The process of forming complex patterns out
of only a few inputs that are repeated or "iterated"
over and over is called self-organization. In this case
there were only four inputs: melanocyte-on,
melanocyte-off, activator, and inhibitor. In this way,
the leopard's coat is an example of how simple a
complex system can really be. By understanding this
natural system, complexity scientists hope to better
understand the simple underpinnings of other
complex systems, natural and man-made.

provided by the park service, so you need to bring your own. To reserve a bed or get a camping permit in the park, contact the Puerto Jiménez office of Corcovado National Park. (tel 506-735-5036 or 506-735-5580, corcovado@minae.go.cr, www.costarica-nationalparks.com/corcovadonationalpark.html)

Local naturalist guides are available to guide you within the park. Osa Aventura is the recommended Corcovado National Park guide service for most ecotravel needs. Owner Mike Boston is both a biologist and a guide, and has earned an international reputation for finding and explaining the wildlife. (tel 506-735-5670, fax 506-735-5717, www.osaaventura.com)

Los Patos Ranger Station

The main trail from Los Patos to Sirena (18km/11mi) is a shadier, undulating route

A Pacific beach reached from Bosque del Cabo

that tends to offer more wildlife than other ways into Corcovado. The trail crosses Río Rincón 26 times. Los Patos is 12km/7.2mi from the old gold-mining village of La Palma, north of Puerto Jiménez.

To reach Los Patos, you can take a bus to La Palma, either from Puerto Jiménez or San José. From La Palma, take a taxi to the park entrance—there will be plenty of hiking within the park.

La Leona Ranger Station

La Leona is a 3.4km/2.1mi walk along the beach from Carate. The larger rivers here are home to crocodiles. Most of the trail from La Leona to Sirena (16km/10mi) is up the hot sandy beach, so blister- and sun-proofing is essential. Listen for monkeys and scarlet macaws. There are several bat caves and interesting waterfalls along the coast.

Several Golfo Dulce ecolodges offer guides that take the La Leona route into the park from Carate, returning within one day. This is not ideal—the pace tends to be too fast to see much—but it does provide a taste of the park.

Carate is a small village accessible by plane, car, or taxi from Puerto Jiménez

(24km/15mi). Turtles nest on Carate Beach, and caiman and crocodiles swim in the bay. You can also fly direct to Carate from San José. A cooperative taxi truck leaves each day except Sunday from Puerto Jiménez at 6 AM for Carate and returns in the evening, acting as an affordable public bus for locals and ecotravellers. Check with your ecolodge for more information.

San Pedrillo Ranger Station

For those starting from the north side, you can take a boat from Sierpe or Drake Bay to San Pedrillo, through the mangroves, or walk to San Pedrillo from Drake Bay along the beach (22km/14mi). Plan to do this during low tide. The trail is open from December to April, due to river flooding the rest of the year. The route involves significant beach walking.

Sirena Research Station

At the Sirena research station travellers blend in with tropical researchers. Accommodations include bunk houses, showers, and a covered, raised-floor camping area for wet weather.

Sirena trails provide the most varied

Snake Eaters

Snakes are the primary food of the common laughing falcon (*Herpetotheres cachinnans*, below). Look for them perched at the edge of forest clearings and paths. You are likely to hear their laughing call before spotting them.

Matapalo Beach

experience of Corcovado. Eight fascinating trails lie relatively close to the field station. Sendero Claro follows the Claro River after navigating a ridge and is one of the best short walks in the area. Trail distances are: Guanacaste (1.4km/0.8mi), Espaveles (1.6km/1mi), Río Pavo (0.7km/0.4mi), Ollas (3.6km/2.2mi), Corcovado (2.5km/1.6mi), Naranjos (1.2km/0.7mi), Sirena (0.7km/0.4mi), and Claro (3.7km/2.3mi).

The Sirena office in Puerto Jiménez can provide park accommodations and booking information for the 48-bed Sirena bunkhouse and campground (tel 506-735-5036). You can also volunteer to assist in conservation programs through MINAE (506-257-2239).

The Claro River made ecological history when a researcher captured the first ever documented mass movement of snails, watching as thousands of freshwater snails (*Neritina latissima*) migrated up the Claro.

Therefore you may witness long bands of counter-current snail traffic, as the snails avoid being flushed out to sea where they otherwise would die. Walking along the river bank is an ideal way of experiencing a range of habitats, and the sand is a good tracking site. Kingfishers abound. If you decide to go upstream instead of following the trail downstream, check with park rangers to make sure there are no gold-mining *precaristas*, or squatters, in the area, which may present a safety issue.

Corcovado Lodge Tent Camp

Costa Rica Expedition's well-managed Corcovado Lodge Tent Camp is located just outside the southern border of Corcovado National Park near Carate, overlooking the Pacific. Although it sounds like you'll be camping, it is really a luxury camping setup with tropical tents on platforms equipped with beds and chairs. There is a separate dining hall. The lodge is a 45-minute walk from the Carate landing strip and village. Boats also ferry visitors from the camp to the national park or to Caño Island, or bring you in from Puerto Jiménez and Golfito. The resident guide has in-depth knowledge of the area. There are high platforms in rainforest trees for canopy observation, and you can camp on the

Frog Toxins
Batrachotoxin is the worst poison-dart toxin of all. It occurs in the rare Golfodulcean poison-dart frog *Phyllobates vittatus*, (below) and the lovely poison-dart frog *P. lugubris* of the Caribbean slope. Batrachotoxin prevents nerve transmission and neuromuscular contraction, resulting in paralysis. The frog-eating snake *Leimadophis epinephalus* can eat *P. terribilis* (which carries the highest level of batrachotoxin known) without dying; it may have adapted to do this by developing especially large adrenal glands. Interestingly, adrenaline, which is produced by the adrenal glands, is a treatment for some nerve gases. Possibly the mecahanism that *Leimadophis* uses is the same as the process that adrenaline goes through as it helps a nerve gas victim. Therefore, the more we know about how nature deals with toxins, the better we can deal with our own.

Termite Mounds

Nitrogen-rich termite mounds (opposite page) are high-quality nutrient "sinks" that concentrate scarce nutrients and fertilize the soil when the termite waste, stashed to avoid attracting attention, breaks down. This is dependent on a 230 million year-old symbiotic association between cellulose-digesting gut microorganisms and their termite hosts. Termites have to live in a community in order to repopulate the micro-organisms from one termite to another after every molt, a caste system that has lasted twice as long as that of ants, probably the oldest animal society in the world.

Beach almonds, palms, and scarlet macaws

platform for a nocturnal immersion. Costa Rica Expeditions offers combination packages with discounted prices to the tent camp and its other prime Costa Rican destinations. (tel 506-257-0766, US tel 800-886-2609, fax 506-257-1665, www.costaricaexpeditions.com)

La Leona Ecolodge Tent Camp

La Leona Ecolodge Tent Camp is located near La Leona Ranger Station, just outside the south edge of Corcovado National Park. It includes a 30ha/75ac primary reserve and nine acres of beachfront. (tel 506-735-5704 or 506-735-5705, www.laleonalodge.com, info@laleonalodge.com)

Luna Lodge Reserve

Luna Reserve, 12ha/30ac, surrounds Luna Lodge, which overlooks the Carate River at the southern border of Corcovado National

Park. A harpy eagle was spotted in the area in 1997, 1999, and 2002. (tel 506-380-5036, US tel 888-409-8448, www.lunalodge.com, information@lunalodge.com)

Bosque del Río Tigre Sanctuary

Bosque del Río Tigre Sanctuary and Lodge is near Dos Brazos, a village northeast of the Corcovado National Park border that is turning from gold mining to ecotourism now that the squatters have been turned out of the park. This occurs as a difficult chapter in recent Costa Rican history seems to be closing. Some squatters were attracted to the park for gold mining, and several violent confrontations ensued, gaining international attention. Now the squatters have been evicted and people seem to be moving on. The 13ha/31ac primary and secondary reserve is filled with birds and mammals. You may see a weasel relative called a tarya (*Eira barbara*), coatis (*Nasua narica*), and several monkey species. On a morning walk you could spot 40–100 bird

Termite Snacks

Nasutermes termite soldiers (above) taste like carrots— try one. Anteaters (which eat termites too) don't like this taste, so they avoid the soldiers and eat the unarmed workers far from the nest. The aromatic component comes from the volatile mono- terpenes contained in the soldiers' nasal glands. These oils smell similar to turpentine and are chemically related to the oil of lemon zest. The nasute soldiers squirt these defense substances from their bulbous "noses" ("nasute" is Latin for nose) when the nest is damaged. These soldiers have no jaws and are fed by blind workers, whose only way of knowing what to do is through pheromone-laced scent trails and drumming sounds heard through their knees.

Look for slaty-tailed trogon nests inside the carton of termite nests (left), hermit hummingbird nests in heliconia, and toucan, tityra, parrot, and arracari nests in tree holes

Coral Chemistry

Coral growing in shallow seas resists excess ultraviolet by creating sunscreen. Special pigments in the coral's zooxanthellae convert UV-light to less damaging light of a different color. Zooxanthellae are brown algae that can photosynthesize. These are dinoflagellates of various colors crammed into the coral polyps. The algae give the coral polyps UV-protecting color, oxygen, and 95% of the sugars they produce in exchange for the protection of a calcium carbonate skeleton, valuable nitrogen and phosphate waste-products from prey captured by coral stingers, and carbon dioxide. However, the coral does not wait for the sugars: it uses special enzymes to make the algae "leak" nutrients. Coral also produces acetate waste, which is transformed into waxes by the zooxanthellae. These waxes return to the coral and are packed into coral eggs, providing a packet of compact energy for the coral larvae's colonization journey.

Cup coral Tubastraea coccinea *is a non-reef-building coral found in these tropical Pacific waters. The color is not produced by zooxanthellae (an algae), as in most corals, but by pigments. One of its threats is the toxic red tides of the dinoflagellate* Cochlodinium catenatum, *which smother this coral in a gooey, poisonous slime.*

species. A night walk and medicinal plant walk are also options; other hikes offered include those along the Río Tigre, Río Pizote (*pizote* is the name for a coati), to Carate via Piedras Blancas, and to Corcovado National Park (with drop-off and pickup service). The resident guide is well respected. (Puerto Jiménez office tel 506-735-5062, cell 506-383-3905, US tel 888-875-9453; Post Office fax 506-735-5045, www.osadventures.com, info@osadventures.com)

Drake Bay

Drake Bay (named after Sir Frances Drake, who landed here in 1579) is a diving, surfing, kayaking, whale watching, and rainforest hiking haven on the Pacific coast north of Corcovado National Park. The bay is difficult to get to. You'll arrive via the Drake Bay airstrip from San José or Palmar Norte, or disembark from a small-craft boat trip along the mangrove-lined River Sierpe, from Sierpe near Palmar Norte (75 minutes). There is also a new, rough road that is best avoided. In addition to Drake Bay activities, ecotravellers can navigate to the north entrance of Corcovado National Park either by walking along the coast (3km/8mi) or taking one of the scheduled lodge boats that ferry ecotravellers to and from the reserve. Monkeys, scarlet macaws, toucans, and humpback whales abound. Caño Island is 16km/10mi due west, expanding the superb diving options offered by the lodges. The best diving, though, surrounds Cocos Island 480km/300mi south, whose plunging rainforests swathed the opening scenes of the movie *Jurassic Park* (see the Cocos Island entry, page 252).

Humpback whales are a highlight of Drake Bay because you can see two different populations each year. The Antarctic group comes to these tropical waters to calve June through November, and the Arctic whales calve November through April. Researchers identify each individual by the shark bites out of the flukes, or fins. Other whales you may see include orcas, pilot whales, sperm whales, sei whales, and false killer whales. Literally thousands of dolphins swim in the bay, including pantropical spotted dolphins, spinner dolphins, bottlenose dolphins, rough-toothed dolphins, and common dolphins. At night, you may see the waters sparkle with phosphorescence as microorganisms are oxygenated in waves or by propellers.

These coral-like anemones grace a rock pool at the south end of the Osa peninsula, guarded by rock fish

Coral Groomers

Reef fish are found in colorful clusters comprised of several types of fish. One of these is the butterflyfish. The beaked coral fish *Chelmon rostratus* (above) is a butterflyfish that plucks at coral polyps using its tweezer-tipped snout. It strongly defends its coral patch and is found in pairs near the coralline seabed. It has a false "eye" spot near its dorsal fin that distracts predators from its more vulnerable head. At night and during high stress, some butterflyfish turn black.

Activities and Places to Stay at Drake Bay

Marenco Beach and Rainforest Lodge is one of the first Costa Rican ecolodges and attracts researchers as well as ecotravellers to its 500ha/1,235ac reserve (tel 506-258-1919, US tel 800-278-6223; fax 506-255-1346, www.marencolodge.com, info@ marencolodge.com). Nearby is the newer tropical beach and ranforest getwaway Punta Marenco Lodge, which offers seasonal free travel from San José (tel 506-841-9329, www.puntamarenco.com).

Drake Bay Wilderness Resort has excellent snorkeling, scuba diving, kayaking, and river canoeing, with a full range of hikes, mountain biking, and marine and rainforest excursions (tel 506-284-4107, tel/fax 506-770-8012, US tel 561-762-1763, www.drakebay.com). Elderhostel, the educational travel organization for older adults (www.elderhostel.org) runs whale research expeditions from this resort. The resort is associated with Gulf Islands Kayaking (office in Canada: 604-539-2442).

La Paloma Lodge offers PADI-certified scuba instruction, snorkeling, and tours from their catamarans (tel 506-293-7502, www.lapalomalodge.com). Aquila de Osa Inn offers great snorkeling and scuba diving around Caño Island, expeditions to Corcovado, classic

Watch out for the spines of toxic firefish (right). To avoid another ocean hazard, do not touch or pick up cone shells. Cone shells can use a harpoon to lance poison a hand's breadth from the edge of the shell. This can inject a lethal dose for humans.

Many anthias or fairy basslets (above) are beautifully colorful reef fish. They're found among Indo-Pacific and Caribbean reefs.

Sand Spewers

Listen for parrotfish chomping when you are diving among reefs. Parrotfish are the number one creator of sand in the tropics, making even more sand here than erosion alone. They do this by grinding algae, coral, and rocks in their mouth (a pharyngeal mill) and sucking nutrients from the debris before spewing out the sand sediment. These herbivores have fused teeth with incredible power, creating bite grooves in the chalky surfaces. Parrotfish hide in mucus cocoons at night, like some of the wrasses from which they evolved. Parrotfish species can change sex, from a drab female or a hermaphrodite to a male that is usually brightly colored blue or green. Parrotfish's looks are very variable; they share 120 color patterns for different occasions. Some lone parrotfish have an unpatterned color that changes to a striped "school uniform" when they join a group. They change their looks by controlling chromatophore pigment cells that adjust white, yellow, orange, and red.

hardwood lodges and delicious meals (tel 506-296-2190, toll-free US/Canada tel 866-924-8452, www.aquiladeosa.com).

Casa Corcovado Jungle Lodge includes trips to Corcovado and Caño Island in its three-night package and is located close to the national park. (tel 506-256-3181, fax 506-256-7409, www.casacorcovado.com, corcovado@racsa.co.cr)

There are less expensive options than these resorts that still offer great eco-explorations. Río Sierpe Lodge is owned by a birding specialist, and is in an ideal spot to see mangroves, river life, and primary forest by hiking or on kayaks. The lodge offers extensive trips, including to Panama's cloud forests, Corcovado, and Caño Island (tel 506-253-5203, fax 506-253-4582, www.riosierpelodge.com). Poor Man's Paradise offers charming cabins and tent platforms, a coral reef, horseback riding, and in-depth knowledge offered by a local family (tel 506-771-9686, www.poormansparadiseresort.com). Cabinas Jade Mar is run by a nature guide and offers lagoon swimming and diving trips to Corcovado and Caño Island

(tel 506-384-6681). Cocalito Lodge is wonderful for birders and botanists. (tel 506-284-6369, Canada office 519-782-3978, www.costaricanet.net/cocalito, berrybend@aol.com)

Delfin Amor Ecolodge is tent-based and offers dolphin encounters, dolphin research, and dolphin conservation. (US tel 831-345-8484, www.divinedolphin.com, delfinamor@divinedolphin.com)

Proyecto Campanario is a reserve and tent camp field station offering rainforest courses for individuals, teachers, and groups (tel 506-258-5778, www.campanario.org, info@campanario.com). Mirador Lodge is run by organic gardeners and offers excellent vegetarian food (tel 506-214-2711, US tel 877-769-8747, www.mirador.co.cr). Albergue Jinetes de Osa offers scuba and specializes in dives to Caño Island. The lodge offers cabin or camping accommodations. (tel 506-371-1598, US tel 800-317-0333, crventur@costaricadiving.com)

While in Drake Bay, take a night hike with Tracy Stice, "the Bug Lady," to see nocturnal animals. Your accomodations manager can arrange this.

Caño Island Biological Preserve

Drake Bay offers many great ways to experience sea life, including Caño Island, known for its schooling pelagics. Five coral platforms provide a gorgeous way to view the pristine marine life around the island. The corals are a wonderful example of plant–animal symbioses. The animal corals contain zooxanthellae, which are photosynthetic algae. These zooanthellae produce sugars for the coal host, which in return catches small prey and necessary minerals for both animal host and algae hitchhikers. Pacific coral reefs are relatively small and less diverse than the healthier, hard-to-find reefs on the Caribbean side.

Yet because of its pristine waters and intact reef, the tropical island is one of the best dive sites in Costa Rica. The reefs of Caño Island, Corcovado, Guanacaste, and San Antonio National Parks are now the only sources of coral larvae and juveniles for Pacific Costa Rica reefs, seeding many decimated reefs affected by deforestation, which has caused damage by increasing runoff. The silt clogs the coral and blocks light, which kills coral.

Choose where you go carefully. The north and east coral flats of the island are shallower and more sensitive to warming during the cyclic El Niño seasons that occur roughly every three to seven years. During these times, coral bleaching occurs and the particularly heat-sensitive species *Pocillopora* sp., *Gardinerosis planulata*, and *Porites panamensis* go into a suspended bleached state. They expel their colorful zooxanthellae, which become toxic at high temperatures, and a percentage of corals die. More heat-tolerant coral species have been found to date to have low mortality. All of these species usually recover and regenerate as the temperature cools.

Most coral polyps only come out at night, so a night dive can reveal wonderful colors invisible to daytime divers. Twenty-

Blue Jewels

Blue-clawed crayfish (below) are among the jewels that brim in freshwater pools in the rainforest. This one's tail is on a net-veined *Melastome* leaf. *Melastome* species are among the heaviest and sweetest fruit producers of the rainforest.

The orange cup fungus (Cookeina speciosa, opposite) is widely distributed

Organized Ameivas

Three species of ameiva lizard (this page) are found on the Osa, yet they do not compete. The delicate ameiva (*Ameiva leptophrys*) basks in the sun on trail sides and in forest clearings, especially mid-morning. The four-lined ameiva (*Ameiva quadrilineata*, right) basks on the beach and colonizes forest clearings sandier than those its relatives seek out. The festiva lizard (*Ameiva festiva*, top) is widely distributed. It has a pale yellow or white dorsal stripe and white blotches. It is found in leaf litter at the forest's edge, sunning in sun flecks just like the delicate ameiva. However, they do not compete because the festiva lizard eats during the second meal shift, later in the morning after the other species is finished.

Minute Rock is the place to go for a nocturnal dive; as the corals open and become full of color, one is surrounded by beautiful coral "flowers." This is also an excellent site for octopus and lobster.

One major coral form found around Caño Island is branched or finger coral, created by coral polyps budding into branches. Look for the pink of lace coral (*Pocillopora elegans*) dotted around the reef surface at the dive site called Coral Gardens. *Pocillopora damicornis*, *P. elegans*, and *P. eydouxi* are finger corals that dominate these reefs, although they are rare in other parts of Costa Rica. *Pavona clavus* is a finger coral widespread around the world and also found here. During the 1990s, much of the shallower *Pocillopora* reefs were decimated by a cyclical El Niño warming event and by a major attack by crown-of-thorns starfish. The starfish eats the coral and can kill entire reef systems

The second major form of coral includes boulder, brain, and stone corals, which are created by polyps splitting into

Fragile Emotions

Spider monkeys (*Ateles geoffroyi*, left) are particularly shy because they have been hunted as food by people for thousands of years. Spider monkeys are the largest and fastest of the four species of monkeys in Costa Rica. A troop of about twenty monkeys tends to split up into foraging units, seeking ripe figs and other food. They are the only Costa Rican monkey to brachiate, to move by swinging from one forelimb to another. Its long tail is used like a limb. A patch of bare skin acts like a fingertip where the tail wraps the branch and increases the sensitivity of the monkey's tail hold.

If you see a captive monkey, don't pay attention to it and do not reward the owners. Juvenile monkeys are taken from their mothers, who are killed. Separated from their natural teachers and playmates, the monkeys often become violent, aggressive, and emotionally disturbed as they mature.

two over and over again, expanding exponentially. The Wreck, or El Barco, displays many of the fifteen species of stony coral (the type of coral that forms a reef) found around Caño Island, including lobed coral (*Porites lobata*), another of the commonest corals in the area. Lobed coral builds atolls by spreading over dead *Pocillopora* platforms. These formations are cemented by dull-looking encrusting corals that help keep the reef together. Corrugated coral (*Pavona varians*) is extremely elegant, its inner skeleton made of pleats that radiate from each wrinkle. *Oulangia bradleyi* is a coral found in the Galapagos as well as here, and does not have any zooxanthellae or symbiotic photosynthetic organisms. It forms very small colonies. Planulate coral *Gardineroseris planulata* is an intricate false brain coral with gorgeous crenulated formations.

Look for triggerfish *Pseudobalistes naufragium*, which are responsible for lobed coral's success story. This triggerfish disperses mature, viable chunks of lobed

Hummers

Long-tailed hermit hummingbirds (*Phaethornis superciliosus*) depend on passion flowers (*Passiflora vitifolia*) for nectar during the dry season. Stingless bees fend off the hummingbirds about one third of the time, then rob the passion flowers of nectar by chewing a hole in the flower base. Ants also use these holes to reach nectar. These bees and ants bypass the intricate evolution that the passion flower has undergone to assure pollination: its flowers are shaped to dust hummingbirds with pollen and shield from other visitors.

Bosque del Cabo cabins (this and opposite page), with veranda chaise longue (above) and outdoor shower (below left), surrounded with orchids and ginger.

coral: it nips off pieces of coral to eat, and in the process some coral floats away and reestablishes itself in new areas. Triggerfish have a toothpick-like vertical caudal fin that can be locked in place at right angles to their body.

One favorite destination is Devil's Rock, or Bajo del Diablo, which is visited by manta rays (also known as devil rays) February through April. A huge variety of reef species and pinnacle formations make this one of the best dive sites in Costa Rica. Four eel species hide in rock holes. Moorish idols, king idols, surgeonfish, and puffers flit around the rocks, surrounded by huge cubera snappers, groupers, and amber jacks. Schools of tuna, white-tipped reef sharks, and barracuda may whirl around divers, while large schools of spotted eagle rays float over the bottom, giving the rock its name.

Another fun dive is under the arches of the Arc near the Cave of the Sharks. The Arc houses white-tipped reef sharks among the butterflyfish, angelfish, and colorful parrotfish that flit around the coral. Reef sharks are the least aggressive of sharks, and are active at night after mostly sleeping by day.

Caño Island was named for its waterfalls by Juan de Castañada, a Spanish explorer who visited the island in 1519. Indigenous peoples appear to have lived on the island until 500 years ago, and it was also possibly used as a pre-Columbian cemetery. Artifacts found there include huge stone spheres, gold offerings, and polychrome pottery, as well as tombs guarded by stone statues.

You can coordinate snorkeling and scuba dives from Drake Bay through your lodge. The Caño Island National Park office can provide more information (tel 506-735-5282). For those staying near the central Pacific coast of Costa Rica, the Mystic Dive Center in Ventanas near Palmar Sur offers several dive excursions to Caño Island and Ballena National Park. (tel 506-788-8636, www.mysticdivecenter.com, info@mystic-divecenter.com)

Tapirs

The variety of Baird's tapirs (*Tapirus bairdii*) found on the Osa Peninsula have a very thick mane. This coincides with the high density of jaguars and is thought to be an effective defense against attacks. Maneless tapirs are found in South American mountain populations where the altitude is too high for jaguars. Baird's tapirs are found in Mexico, Central America, and Colombia and are the largest American tapirs. It is reported that they may be easier to see around mineral licks, but otherwise they are hard to find. Tapirs migrated to South America across the land bridge 2–3 million years ago. They are relatives of early horses and rhinos. They live to be about 30 years old.

Canyons of Light

One reason the tropics are more diverse than temperate forests are the varieties in light. Witness a tropical rainforest clearing in a storm, and you'll be blasted by wind and rain that comes and goes with stunning extremes. Landslides, tree-fall, and limb-fall are much more frequent in the tropics than in temperate forests. This creates more light gaps, a greater frequency of rapid change in light, and a huge diversity of light levels and humidity in every microhabitat. As each light gap opens, this creates new canyons of light in the forest. Sun angles, land slope, nooks and crannies all combine to increase the richness in light variety. The diversity of microhabitats increases species richness of both plants and animals. Yet the constant change means that no one competitor can get an advantage for long over another, and succession never stabilizes. So one effect of dynamic change, even destruction, in the luxuriant tropics is, paradoxically, not extinction but greater diversity.

Cocos Island National Park

Cocos Island, with its plunging waterfalls and intense rainforest, is an extension of the Galapagos, and offers many world-class dive sites that are truly pristine. There is no aircraft landing site, so any access is by boat. Live-aboard dive boats usually run expeditions from a week to ten days' duration. Cocos Island has an unusually high level of pelagics, with schooling hammerheads, whale sharks, humpback and orca whales, dolphins, and many white-tip sharks. The rocks hide many moray eels under the schooling fish. Several endemic bird species are unique to the island: the Cocos finch, Cocos cuckoo, and Cocos flycatcher.

Cocos Island is 300 miles from Puntarenas; Puntarenas is about three hours' drive north of San José. Aggressor Fleet has a charter luxury dive boat that leaves for Cocos

Island from Puntarenas, with pick up in San José for six-day dive trips. (US/Canada tel 800-348-2628 or 985-385-2628, fax 985-384-0817, www.aggressor.com)

Hunter Fleet offers two dive boats with ten-day dive expeditions of up to three dives a day and one night dive, plus visits to Cocos Island, its waterfalls, and Malpelo Island. Nitrox training is offered. (US tel 800-203-2120, tel 506-222-6613, fax 506-289-7334, www.underseahunter.com)

Spicing it Up

In the wet season, rainforest trails are decorated by the intense scarlet aril that covers the seed of wild nutmeg (*Virola* sp., above and below). Birds are attracted to the red and toss the whole seed back. They digest the aril and regurgitate the intact seed, dispersing it effectively. Culinary nutmeg comes from the seed of the related *Myristica fragrans*, and the spice of mace from the *M. fragrans* aril. Nutmeg species are common rainforest trees. The inner bark of some of the 65 *Virola* species is used as a "nightmarish" hallucinogen by several Amazonian and Orinoco Indians, and contains indole alkaloids.

Focus on Wildlife: Underwater Photography Tips

Water visibility increases significantly as you get away from the mainland. The lowest tides in daylight will coincide with the new and full moons. Water increases the magnification of the camera lens by one-third, so macro lenses focus farther away. Water is 1,000 times less transparent than air, so flash should be used in nearly all underwater situations except just below the surface. However, don't use a flash for whales, dolphins, or turtles. For non-digital cameras, red filters counteract the absence of red light that kicks in about a meter below the surface. For digital cameras, color-correct once you capture the image by increasing the magenta setting. For photos of rock pools above the waterline, place a cut PVC pipe section or other large open ring on the surface to still ripples. Disposable cameras are good budget solutions for wet work.

Golfo Dulce

Prime luxury ecolodges and adventure tent camps overlook Golfo Dulce's aquamarine waters and forested hills. "Luxury" in these cases means ultra-comfort, jungle style: No phones; airy screens and shutters; romantic

Tent Bats

The tent-making bat (*Uroderma bilobatum*, right) roosts under palm and Heliconia leaves. The bat nips the veins to collapse the leaf blades into a shelter. Each roost functions as either a maternity colony or day or night shelter. This bat eats figs and other fruit, and some insects. Look for them under Caribbean and Pacific lowland rainforest trees. Insectivorous sac-wing bats (*Saccopteryx bilineata*) roost on the trunks of strangler figs and kapok trees, or on rock overhangs. You can spot the male (below) on a beach rock overhang, guarding his harem of up to nine females. Scent glands under each of his wings are so large they form the "sac" of this bat's name. He fans his scent towards the females while fluttering in front of them.

cabin designs with palm frond roofs and loft vents open to the ocean breezes; hammocks and outdoor showers among orchids; swimming pools with views and jungle swimming holes.

Osa Peninsula lodges on the west side of Golfo Dulce are located along a 4WD road south of the airstrip at Puerto Jiménez. New lodges are opening to the north and the east side of the gulf, closer to Golfito. A couple of ecolodges are located in the hills to the west near the erstwhile gold-mining villages of Dos Brazos and Los Patos, where birdwatching is prime. The Puerto Jiménez and Golfito airstrips are an easy hop from San José, avoiding the treacherous roads on the way.

Activites and Places to Stay on Golfo Dulce

Surfing, diving, fishing, guided rainforest hiking, zip-lining, waterfall climbing, and a visit to a botanical garden are activity options offered by these conservation-oriented ecolodges. Or you can book activities directly: Go kayaking with Escondido Trex, found inside La Carolina Restaurant (tel 506-735-5210, www.escondidotrex.com) or volunteer with the TUVA (www.tuva.org) and Neotropical Foundations (www.neotropica.org) in Puerto Jiménez to help in conservation efforts.

The gulf provides limited local diving. Fortunately, all ecolodges on the gulf offer dive trips to reefs outside its deep waters for greater variety. The Punta Islotes Reef on the north shore of Golfo Dulce was a 5,500-year-old shallow fringing reef that was decimated in the 1980s by sedimentation from deforestation, slash-and-burn agriculture, and road building. The crisis was topped off by two severe El Niño warming seasons spaced about a decade apart, compounded by smothering red tides of toxic microorganisms. Punta Islotes Reef and nearby Punta Bejuco Reef now consist of a few living peripheral lobed coral formations (*Porites lobata*), but the major part of these reefs is dead and unlikely to recover soon. The only solution is major changes to the surrounding ecosystem in terms of reducing sedimentation, plus artificial restoration measures.

The only reefs surviving well in the gulf are the deeper ones on the outer Golfo Dulce including Sándalo (on the south shore) and Punta el Bajo (in the north), where you can still find several thriving coral and fish species.

The fish in the Golfo Dulce are sparser and less diverse than those just outside it because the gulf is extremely deep here, reducing the light levels, food, and oxygen concentrations. Shallow species are similar to those found along the coast. Deep gulf fish include *Cynoscion* and *Porichthys* species.

You can arrange for a guide to take you for a day visit within Corcovado National

Vulture Club

King vultures (*Sarcoramphus papa*) soar high in plumage fit for a coronation. They watch other vultures for signs of food because their sense of smell is limited. Turkey vultures (*Cathartes aura*) are among the only birds with a good sense of smell and can sniff out carcasses hidden from sight beneath the canopy. Black vultures (*Coragyps atratus*), which cannot smell at all, find food and garbage by sight, and by following turkey vultures. All three benefit from this interdependence: king vultures have big enough beaks to open large animals that light-bodied, smaller-billed turkey and black vultures cannot deal with. In the process, more is made available to each species, which feed in succession on different parts of the carcass. Black and turkey vultures migrate through Costa Rica. A resident turkey vulture subspecies is identified by a blue rather than red band at the back of the head.

Leaf Mimics

Walk along a rainforest trail and you'll notice the leaf litter moving out of the corner of your eye. This is the Brandsford's litter frog (*Eleutherodactylus bansfordii*, above), which comes in sizes from minute to about one inch long and is the commonest frog in Costa Rica, active in the daytime. There are thirty-five other litter frog species. If you check several Brandsfords out, you'll see that there are about three major color varieties in any one place: some rough-skinned, others smoother, all with pointy heads. Each one mimics a leaf fragment while searching for ants, larvae, and spiders.

Dip into a forest pool (above) for a refreshing break

Park. If you aren't booked inside the park but are planning on visiting, stay at a lodge close to the park—lodges on the east side of the gulf are too far for an easy day trip. If you are staying at an ecolodge between Matapalo and Carate, the private reserve surrounding you is joined to a continuous stretch of forest that connects with Corcovado, so you can see an enormous diversity of species from your hammock or on nearby trails if you are still, watching early and long enough. Therefore, with quiet attention and a few hours of exploration with a good resident guide, you may see more along paths from your private lodge than during a fast day trek through the clay-lined trails of Corcovado National Park.

Each ecolodge has distinctive aspects, so choose the one best for you. All offer at least one trail through their private reserve, some have resident guides, and a few offer yoga and relaxation platforms to complement the thrill of zip lines and treetop viewing.

The electricity grid does not extend across the peninsula, so any power must be generated locally using micro-hydroelectric or gas generators or solar power. Most of the ecolodges are foreign-owned and provide significant employment to local builders, trail-engineers, nature guides, cooks, and maids.

Bosque del Cabo

Bosque del Cabo is a highly recommended ecolodge for ecotravellers, with the best resident naturalists and birding guides found in Costa Rica. It offers extensive and well-planned trails through primary and secondary private rainforest (200ha/500ac). These reach down to Pacific and gulf beaches where you can surf, or you can walk all the way to Corcovado National Park.

The ecolodge is located on Matapalo Point, at the southernmost tip of the peninsula, south of Puerto Jiménez. The luxury lodge is solar powered, and offers a zip line, rainforest plunge pools, waterfalls,

Root Parasite
This fungus look-alike (below left) is in fact a bizarre, saprophytic (living on dead or decaying matter) flowering plant. *Heliosis cayennensis* is a rare member of the Balanophoraceae family, and has no chlorophyll. It steals all its energy from the roots of surrounding plants.

Skipping Dragons

The double-crested basilisk (*Basiliscus plumifrons*, below) is bright green and found in the Caribbean and southwest Costa Rica
Three basilisk lizard species are fairly common in the lowlands of Costa Rica, growing up to 3ft/1m long. Look for their trailing tails as they sleep on tree branches above water. Young basilisks can run over water for up to 20 meters by using their widely spread hind toes and skin flap paddles to bounce off the surface tension.

guided short walks and longer hikes, and chef-cooked meals shared *en famille* with other guests at dinnertime. Each bluff-top palm-thatched cabin has shimmering views across the Golfo Dulce or the Pacific, cooled by ocean breezes. Coatis wander the grounds.

In addition to the tropical cabins, the lodge includes two luxurious houses perched above the Pacific, with full kitchens and the option of joining the main dining room a couple of minutes' walk away. Ideal for honeymooners, families, and groups of friends seeking a special vacation.

Watch the sun rise over Matapalo Beach, the premier Osa surfing site, and spend the day among macaws and monkeys. Cool off in the outside shower, festooned with orchids and heliconias. Later, go for a fascinating night hike to watch a sloth awaken with her baby as the sun sets, find

bats roosting under palm leaves, or see what's hopping around the local pond. (tel/fax 506-735-5206, www.bosquedelcabo.com, phil@bosquedelcabo.com)

Lapa Rios

Lapa Rios has more of a resort feel than that of an ecolodge, and is located on a ridge just above the coastline south of Puerto Jiménez. The pool is unsurpassed for its view. The property's private reserve (over 405ha/1,000ac) has a limited set of trails on steep ground behind the lodge, so dedicated ecotourists may feel cramped for options unless they sign up with one of the guides to explore further afield. The guides do not live on the property. The lodge recently changed ownership and has become somewhat institutionalized after its promising beginnings and award-winning status. It offers a full suite of activities, meals, and luxury thatch-roofed open-air lodging with gorgeous hardwood floors. (tel 506-735-5130, fax 506-735-5179, www.laparios.com, info@laparios.com)

El Remanso

El Remanso was built using environmental principles and is smaller than Lapa Rios and Busque del Cabo, on a reserve of 57ha/140ac south of Puerto Jiménez and on the Pacific side of Osa Peninsula. It has

Booting out the Beast

Migrations of urania, the green page moth (*Urania fulgens*, left), occur every year between August and November. Urania is a common green day-flying moth that looks like a swallowtail butterfly. They head southeast, away from their host plants, *Omphalea diandra* lianas. The Osa Peninsula is a major site for Costa Rica urania. About every eight years the urania migration reaches a huge peak. This is probably a result of a buildup of toxic chemicals in the host plant as they respond to increased chomping by massing larvae. Female urania moths can sense when the plants become too toxic. If so, they migrate. The urania end up in areas where *Omphalea* vines have not yet built up their chemical defenses, and so continue to thrive while the original population regroups.

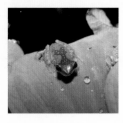

Egg Gulpers

The banana tree frog (*Hyla ebraccata*, top) is a tropical frog that lays its eggs on leaf tips above water. Listen in the evening for the male red-eyed treefrog (*Agalychnis callidryas*) "clucking" for females on vegetation near the water. Females lay eggs at leaf edges, like banana tree frogs, the male on her back fertilizing them. She wets the eggs with jellified pee that is made from water absorbed into her bladder. She filled her bladder through her skin earlier, when she and the male took a dip in the pool. Her eggs hatch as tadpoles in about five days, but often are swallowed up before that point by rear-fanged venomous cat-eyed snakes (*Leptodiera septentrionalis*, above and opposite page) before the tadpoles can fall into the water and swim away.

charming, rustic cabins and also a larger guest house, all with stunning Pacific views. El Remanso specializes in rappelling and tree-climbing adventures, in addition to offering a suite of local activities that include fishing, diving, and hiking through Corcovado. The canopy is opened up with tree platforms and zip lines, and you can scale waterfalls with safety ropes. The owners live on site, are actively involved in environmental work, and are founders the Cecropia Foundation, a conservation organization. The TUVA foundation, another important conservation organization, has a turtle nursery on the neighboring Piro River and you can arrange to watch the early morning turtle release of hatchlings. El Remanso has an office in Puerto Jiménez. (tel 506-735-5569, fax 506-735-5126, www.elremanso.com, info@elremanso.com)

Piro

Piro Forest Reserve encompasses 3,500ha/7,000ac of primary rainforest and associated ecolodges conserved for the direct benefit of local people who offer guided hikes, buffalo rides, and canopy views from tree platforms. The Piro Diversity Center organizes courses on forestry conservation and management. Piro accommodations can be arranged with the network of associated local families. This is an enterprise coordinated by the TUVA Foundation, which based in Puerto Jiménez. (tel/fax 506-735-5013, www.tuva.org)

Piedras Blancas National Park

The relatively new Piedras Blancas National Park, in the Esquinas Mountains on the northeast side of the Golfo Dulce, is also known as the "Rainforest of the Austrians," because of its funding source, and is now an extension of the Corcovado National Park. It forms an important part of the planned Interamerican Corridor linking the precious biology of the peninsula with the Talamanca Mountains and the Amistad International Biosphere Reserve. The forest is dryer and less diverse than Corcovado, but is nevertheless a tropical jewel. There is a field station in the village of La Gamba for biological education and research.

Playa Nicuesa Rainforest Lodge

This wonderful new lodge offers beachfront water adventures and rainforest immersion inside the Piedras Blancas National Park (tel 506-735-5237, US tel 866-348-7610 or 512-342-7160, www.playanicuesa.com). Access is by boat. Fly into Golfito.

Tree Food

It pays to learn about trees if you're a birdwatcher. Birds sip from the flowers of soft-wooded balsa trees, gorge themselves on melastome and cecropia fruits, feast on capulin species, and dig into the lemony pulp of the beans of the guaba tree. These fast-growing light gap trees attract euphonias, manakins, tanagers, and honeycreepers. Slower-growing canopy trees require shade to establish themselves. Food-producing canopy species that are easy to identify include fig trees (*matapalo*, *Ficus* sp.) and a type of mahogany called cedro (*Carapa guianensis*). Cedro is found in swampy areas and produces fruits like huge Brazil nuts (above) that are gnawed by a variety of mammals. *Ajo negro*, or black garlic (*Anthodiscus chocoensis*), and *ajo* (*Caryocar costaricense*) are huge trees with garlic (*ajo*)-scented flowers.

Transparent-winged cicada

Dengue

The day-flying *Aedes aegypti* mosquito carries dengue fever, a serious disease that can be fatal if caught more than once. This mosquito is currently found in densely populated areas, including all major Costa Rican cities and towns, although the disease tends to occur in major outbreaks. You can easily spot the mosquito's white banded legs. The mosquito was eradicated from Costa Rica and neighboring countries after an effective control program in 1970. But after the program stopped, the mosquito has spread to cover more areas than before and at a higher elevation than ever. To avoid this disease, keep an eye on newspaper headlines to adjust travel plans and wear mosquito repellent.

Esquinas Rainforest Lodge

The Esquinas Rainforest Lodge is located near Piedras Blancas reserve, and it is close enough to Golfo Dulce for kayak tours of the bay or of Río Coto mangroves. The lodge was created with funding from the Austrian government, which aimed to create a sustainable haven for ecotravel and rainforest research. Guests can sign up for the rainforest adventure week, which explores the rainforest while staying at the lodge. (Reservations office tel/fax 506-775-0140, lodge tel 506-775-0901, www.esquinaslodge.com)

Golfito

The former United Fruit Company town of Golfito is undergoing a colorful decline. There are several ecolodges around Golfito, but most are eclipsed by those on the Osa Peninsula. Golfito Forest Reserve can be reached directly or by taking a boat to Playa Cacao from Golfito.

Orchid Garden

International cruise boats and ecolodges include Casa de Orquídeas on their itineraries. This exquisite orchid garden at Playa San Josécito near Golfito can be reached by ferry from any of the Golfo Dulce towns. Guides are available Sunday through Thursday. (tel 506-775-0353)

Zancudo

Relaxing sport-fishing cabins are scattered along the sand spit of Zancudo beneath humid forest, accessible by boat pick-up from Golfito and Puerto Jiménez. Zancudo is south of Golfito on the east side of Golfo Dulce. It is worth taking a kayaking and birdwatching tour of the Coto River mangroves and bay with Zancudo Boat Tours. (tel 506-776-0012, loscocos@loscocos.com)

Chocolate Dependency

Dragonflies are bothered by no-see-ums, a diverse cross-section of microscopic biting flies. Most of the time no-see-ums leave people alone, but sometimes they cover us in welts that may or may not itch. All no-see-ums have important ecological roles. *Corethrella* sp. are midge relatives that use the call of male frogs to hone in on their next blood meal. This ecto-parasitic relationship dates back to Jurassic times. Female frogs, who are silent, do not get bitten. Cacao plants, which produce chocolate, are primarily pollinated by Forcipomyia no-see-ums which also need a "blood" meal from katydids and dragonflies (left) to raise viable young. The larvae of no-see-ums frequent bromeliad tanks as aquatic miniature worms, vacuuming up many noxious species.

Avon Skin-So-Soft Bath Oil is one of the only effective repellents for no-see-ums, the original formula containing carrot oil as its active ingredient. Birds are ahead of us: many birds line their nest with sprigs of insect-repellent vegetation, including carrot oil.

The aerodynamics of dragonfly flight are completely different from that of a fixed-wing aircraft. New fluid dynamic studies, computer modeling, and chaos theory have cracked the puzzle of how dragonflies hover so well. The secret is in the dynamic eddies that curl off the top of the moving, rough wings. These long-lasting vortexes create half the lift associated with each wing-beat, by shedding eddies in both clockwise and anti-clockwise directions in one beat. The shear between both is called an "unsteady effect," which creates velocity when the wing oscillates rapidly. An example of these eddies can be seen when a horizontal sheet of paper is left to fall, zig-zagging down. Dragonflies take care to keep their flight muscles at premium working temperatures because they need maximum power to lift off. When cold, some species can turn black to absorb more heat. When hot, dragonflies turn their tails towards the sun to minimize sun trapping.

Leaf-cutter ant workers and winged males (top) and large queen (bottom)

Pavones

Tiskita Reserve and Lodge is located 4.5km/2.8mi from the surfer crowds of Pavones beach, which offers the "longest wave in the world." This is about an hour and a half south of Golfito by car on the mainland and is close to the Panamanian border on the east side of Golfo Dulce.

The 162ha/400ac reserve is in secondary and primary premontane wet forest surrounded by a slightly drier ecosystem called "moist forest" and actively attracts four troops of Central American squirrel monkeys, two-toed sloths, two types of blue morpho butterflies (*Morpho peleides* and *M. cypris*), and 275 bird species. Look for chestnut-mandibled toucans, green and mealy blue parrots, scarlet-rumped and blue-gray tanagers, laughing hawks, violaceous trogons, and frigate birds. The lodge has

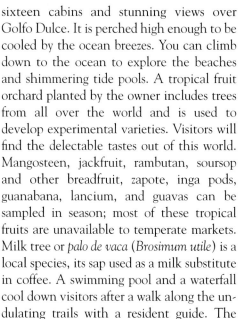

sixteen cabins and stunning views over Golfo Dulce. It is perched high enough to be cooled by the ocean breezes. You can climb down to the ocean to explore the beaches and shimmering tide pools. A tropical fruit orchard planted by the owner includes trees from all over the world and is used to develop experimental varieties. Visitors will find the delectable tastes out of this world. Mangosteen, jackfruit, rambutan, soursop and other breadfruit, zapote, inga pods, guanabana, lancium, and guavas can be sampled in season; most of these tropical fruits are unavailable to temperate markets. Milk tree or *palo de vaca* (*Brosimum utile*) is a local species, its sap used as a milk substitute in coffee. A swimming pool and a waterfall cool down visitors after a walk along the undulating trails with a resident guide. The

Leaf-cutter ants (top)
Minima ant on leaf (left)
carried by media worker
Leaf-cutter ants clear all
vegetation from around
nest tree (below right)

Ant Time

Army ants (*Eciton burchelli,*
right) eat themselves out of
house and home every 35
days. It takes the colony 14
days to move the queen and
brood to a new home, a
temporary bivouac. Then the
colony fans out in raids from
the bivouac for 21 days in a
highly cyclic rhythm that is
controlled by a pheromone
secreted according to the
larva's level of maturity. The
raiding cycle is triggered
when the larvae hatch, at
which point the pheromone
stimulates soldiers to march.
They eat half the crickets and
roaches in the surroundings,
and set back other nearby ant
species so much that it takes
them three months to recover.
Once the larvae spin cocoons,
the pheromone is stopped and
this stimulates a bivouac
formation, starting the cycle
over again, precisely timed.
If you find an advancing
front of army ants, follow
them back to the bivouac for
a look. Don't stamp your
feet—it enrages them and
their bites are painful.

owners have launched the Tiskita
Foundation to expand the amount of
conserved land in the area.

Access: fly to the Tiskita private airstrip
from San José (price included in packages).
Or drive to Pavones south of Golfito across
the Coto River ferry, then on to Tiskita. A
detailed route map is available from the lodge
office. (tel 506-7296-8125, fax 506-296-
8133, www.tiskita-lodge.co.cr)

Focus on Wildlife: Ants

Army ants, leaf-cutter ants, acacia ants, and
bullet ants are at home in different
microclimates of the Costa Rica tropics.
Before you dismiss them as pesky critters
with tiny brains, give them a second look.
For one thing, any community of organisms
that behaves as a complex self-organizing
system, as an ant community does, is receiv-
ing a lot of research attention at this time.
Scientists are digging into such complex
systems in an attempt to better understand
everything from stock market cycles to
global warming models to the origins of
human creativity. This is a "hot" research
topic at this point in time, and one that is
spawning its own set of business consultants
schooled in chaos and complexity theory.

For example, some ant species show us
that creativity (theirs and possibly ours) is
hatched on the fulcrum that exists between
chaos and order. To explore this in more
depth, scientists have identified key

Jungle Sutures

The bivouac of army ants (left) is made of living ants knitted together. Wave a stick gently through the community and it will part like a soufflé: somewhere inside is the queen.

The bivouac of the black-bodied, brown-headed army ant *Neivamyrmex pilosus* is infiltrated by the beetle *Diploeciton nevermanni*. This beetle wanders around enough inside the nest to pick up the ant pheromones essential to ant recognition. The ant believes the beetle to be another ant because it smells the same. The beetle is more red in color than the ant, and its hind legs are slightly longer, but otherwise it fits right in. The reward of this subterfuge is to feed off the highly nutritous brood from the nests of *other* ant species that *Neivamyrmex* attacks and brings home.

The mandibles of live army ants are so powerful that they have been used to close wounds, similar to sutures.

components: essential to these types of nonlinear systems is a feedback mechanism. Ants communicate by "tappings, stridulations, strokings, graspings, nudgings, antennations, tasting, and puffings and streakings of chemicals," according to Bert Hölldobler and Edward O. Wilson. Ants are not mini-machines, but exquisite expressions of living individuality. Wilson indicates that "personality differences are strongly marked even within single castes" for some ant species. In one species, each individual ant lives on the edge of "chaos," a mathematically definable state that is neither random nor completely repetitive, but appears to be a disordered state. This continues until this ant species colony density reaches a threshold level of intense communication. This is the point of creativity, the switch between chaos and order, where many options are possible. At the point where the density reaches the critical level, suddenly, the individually ants behave differently. The community changes dynamically, eventually settling down into the other extreme, that of an ordered, rhythmic "superorganism" where the community acts as one. This type of behavior is not unique to these ants and, when described mathematically, has similarities to other systems where sudden changes occur and new stable forms emerge, from stock markets to business organizations.

Army ants not only build their own communities, they attract other species

Some individuals of the Central American whiptail or festiva lizard (Ameiva festiva, above) have an intense blue tail that stands out against the leaf litter. Its body is thereby hidden from predators, which go for the tail in a non-lethal strike.

into their activities as well. This is another principle of complex systems: anything that one element does affects the entire community. This has been called the "butterfly effect," in which butterfly wings flapping in China could theoretically trigger a series of events that result in a hurricane in the Western Hemisphere.

You can sometimes see how this interrelation works by looking carefully at tropical ants. Look for the black haze of *Eciton burchelli* army ants as they blanket the forest, killing anything they can catch, and flushing the rest. Then wait for a scattering of antbirds and foragers that may appear, seeking insects fleeing the ants: spiders, scorpions, and moths. The birds leave the formic-acid-filled ants alone.

The antbirds coexist in mixed, territorial flocks of up to fifty species. In Amazonia these flocks are larger and more noticeable than in Costa Rica, where they tend to blend into the understory and are hard to find unless one is accompanied by a guide. At their best, tanagers, ovenbirds, motmots, vireos, flycatchers, woodcreepers, and cuckoos fill the ranks, each species foraging at a different height for different food. Antshrikes provide a lookout, shrieking a warning if predators hover near. The bicolor antbird, black-faced antthrush and spotted antbird are full-time "professional" ant followers whose behavior has closely evolved with that of the ants. Other antbirds and relatives are more occasional followers. Some antbird species can also be spotted away from army ants, moving quietly near the ground in thick understory.

Antbirds are not the only animals to follow army ants. Mites, millipedes, woodlice, flies, butterflies, spiders, springtails, bristletails, beetles, blind snakes, and even a mollusk have been found associated with army ant swarms, many following their pheromone trails. In this way, army ants show the interrelationships forged by a single tropical species. We are only beginning to grasp the significance of the new types of patterns inherent in the dynamics of these populations.

The sail-carrying leaf-cutter ant provides another example of species interrelationships. This ant clips as much foliage as all Costa Rican vertebrate herbivores combined—including paca, mice, porcupines, ctenosaurs, iguanas, sloths, and monkeys. These ants include Acromyrmex, with 24 species, and Atta, with 15 species.

Yet the attine ants (Atta sp.) don't actually consume a single leaf. Instead, they troop the leaves into their underground fungus gardens. The nests contain one of a handful species of cellulose-digesting Basidiomycete fungi that are only associated symbiotically with ants. Free-living fungal relatives exist as parasol mushrooms. In the fungus garden, the ants carefully clean the leaves to remove foreign fungi as they chew them up, then defecate rectal fluid on the pulp to add protein-digesting enzymes and all 21 essential amino acids needed by the

Bug Spray

If you choose to do without anti-malarials, avoid malaria-prone areas. Use mosquito repellent and sleep under mosquito nets treated with permethrin repellents; you can also purchase clothes with this repellent locked into the fabric. The activity of *Anopheles*, the vector for malaria, peaks at 1 AM. Humans are the other carrier. If you purchase your net, make sure you get the fine-net variety, as larger holes will not be effective. Most ecolodges offer beds with mosquito nets, but bunkhouses in ecolodges often do not. Avon Skin-So-Soft is good for the minute biting no-see-ums that occasionally swarm at night. Sulfur powder works well when dusted on socks and ankles to fend off chiggers.

Diquis Gold

Diquis gold was made actively from 500–1550 CE and was cast into animal effigies of jaguars, frogs, crayfish, llamas, and other images, indicating their South American influences. Diquis peoples chewed coca leaves with lime. The lime was carried in ceramic vials similar to those found in Colombia. The reach of these influences extends far: recently, traces of cocaine that could only originate from South America have apparently been found in an Egyptian mummy, hinting of a possible link. Diquis stone spheres of granite, andesite, and sedimentary rock appear to be hundreds or thousands of years old. Their origins puzzle archeologists. The spheres are nearly perfect and were hauled into linear alignments near burial sites, although some weighed up to 17,600kg/16tons.

fungus. Finally, they plant a little fungus sprout on top of the culture as a starter. Then they let the humidity and temperature grow a high-quality fungus diet that is entirely free of toxic plant defense compounds.

Despite the ideal tropical conditions for growing all things fuzzy, the nest only contains one type of fungus. This is carefully controlled: the ants are clothed with bacteria that symbiotically produce an antifungal agent. This prevents the ants' bodies from contaminating the garden. They also weed out leaf-borne foreign fungi from their garden culture. When they relocate, the huge queen ensures continued purity by taking a mouthful of fungus with her, like a bit of sourdough starter, when she is carted by her attendants to her new nest. In doing so, she ensures the ongoing success of the mutually dependent fungus species as well as of her own offspring.

The easily found stinking toe tree, or guapinol (*Hymenaea courbaril*), and a range of tropical trees fight back against the leaf-cutter ants. But not, as one might assume, by producing ant-repelling compounds in their leaves. Instead, they beef up their already established antifungal defenses and cram their leaves with turpenoids, steroids, and waxes (oily fungus killers), and phenols, flavonoids, and glycosides (water-soluble poisons). You can smell these compounds if you crush the leaves and detect turpentine or acrid aromas mixed into the "green cud" scent. This systematic defense appears to be associated with the plant's need to repel fungus attack directly, because the level fluctuates with the degree of humidity. The value of this defense is that attine ants avoid these leaves.

This is proving a useful observation for agriculture; leaf-cutter ants destroy a significant level of Neotropical agricultural crops. Extracts from native plants that show antifungal properties are proving to be highly effective against attine ants in tests for crop protection by Costa Rican researchers.

Leaf-cutter ants are so ubiquitous that you may soon take them for granted. But they have many secrets, so take your time with them. Once, I bent to inspect some leaf-cutter ants on the Osa Peninsula. They were chiseling their way through the leaves of an entire bough that had crashed to the ground from the top of their feeder tree. I was startled to hear a high-pitched squeaking sound, emitted with a whir of contentment. It felt like I was listening to a million little buzz saws. Some ants produce an audible squeak when alarmed, but this was eerily different. Their sound, a type of stridulation produced by scraping bodyparts, had strange acoustics. It was very loud a few inches from the leaves, but almost inaudible a couple of feet away, and silent to someone standing up. As a result, people usually miss it. This "near-field" ant sound has been recently researched and found to fade much faster than regular

Buttress roots absorb air under waterlogged conditions and provide props for vines.

A zip line reaches this tree platform halfway to the canopy.

sound. Ants hear through their knees, and most ant stridulation is designed to transmit through the ground and branches in a primitive way easily picked up by knee-joints. Amazingly, new uses are being found for this near-field sound. New technology using near-field sound is now being used in shopping malls to whisper special offers to shoppers close to the location of their items of interest.

Leaf-cutter ants, however, use this sound for defense. When the ant finishes clipping its leaf segment, it sounds out more and more urgently. This signals to a smaller type of leaf ant called the minima that it can hitchhike a ride on the leaf. There are three sizes of worker ants: The medias are the middle-sized workers that carry the leaves. The minimas have evolved to be much smaller so they can hitchhike on the media's leaf. An occasional soldier ant, a maxima, wanders through the leaf-line with its huge defensive jaws, though many of these soldiers remain underground ready to defend the nest. The brown minima shown in the image on page 265 has responded to the call and moved into position on the leaf edge.

When the leaf-clipping ant squeaks to the minima, it is calling for help: The minima's function is to fend off phorid flies from their lofty perch. Soldiers do this, too, waving their heads and jaws at any sign of fly attack. The phorids parasitize ants, bees, and millipedes, in this case laying eggs on the medias as they haul their leaves around. After the phorid fly hatches, the larva eats the media from within, leaving the brain until last. By signaling for help through this special near-field sound, the worker is able to get extra security for the way home.

Resources

HOW TO BE AN ECOTRAVELLER

*P*ura vida is the Costa Rican way, so you'll find a wide range of ecotravel options there, from wilderness spas to canopy zip lines in the cloud forest. Select those with sustainable practices so your choice helps ensure that the heavily encroached rainforests and reefs can enjoyed for generations to come.

To choose a sustainable vacation, you may want to check the selection of sustainable ecolodges and ecoadventures in the voluntarily compiled Certification in Sustainable Tourism Program (CST: www.turismo-sostenible.co.cr). Unfortunately, this is not a comprehensive listing, nor is it reliable. Organizations listed by CST include some hotel complexes and chains that are not primarily ecolodges, and CST does not yet list some ecolodges that have done much to foster conservation and to train and employ local community members. Therefore CST should not be regarded as the primary guide about where to stay. CST is being expanded by Rainforest Alliance's work with the Costa Rican government to help train small businesses and ecolodges to become more "nature-friendly" (www.rainforestalliance.com). This will enable more businesses to rank in the CST program. Rainforest Alliance has been helping to turn big business in this direction. The organization has changed Costa Rican banana production from a highly pesticide-dependent, ocean-degrading agribusiness, which once caused major health problems for workers, to a more ecofriendly one.

The idea of sustainability extends beyond the use of green architecture and recycling to the community as a whole. Sustainable ecolodges are both "green" and also contribute financially and in other ways to their local Costa Rican community. For example, Lapa Rios Lodge helped start and sustain the village school, and Selva Verde Lodge runs and houses a skills education center and library for the rural Sarapiquí community.

A large area of Costa Rica is dedicated to conservation and restoration of the wilderness, either in government-run conservation areas and their associated parks, or in private reserves (key destinations of both types are listed below). By visiting ecolodges and paying small park fees you are directly supporting the conservation of these important zones. You can also contribute financially to the purchase of rainforest for restoration and conservation through various organizations, some associated with ecolodges listed below. As you travel in the forest, you are likely to share trails with the tropical ecosystem researchers whose work it is to explore the mysteries of this fascinating wilderness, and some of them may be willing to discuss their projects if you are sensitive to their work.

If you take a moment to become still and open to what this wonderful country has to show you, to choose sustainable businesses, and to tread lightly on the environment, you will be richly rewarded.

Communications

For directory assistance dial 113.

Telephones and email can be unreliable in Costa Rica, and there may not be established mail routes to reach ecolodges deep in wilderness areas. This is a disadvantage for business transactions, but does mean that many lodges are TV and cell-phone free, providing the ideal getaway. Most ecolodges accept faxed credit card payments, or have city offices or US addresses to which payment should be mailed for secure deposit. If you send a fax payment, check that you receive confirmation in return, preferably by email.

FIRST AID

Medical Emergencies: *Hospital CIMA San José*
This new hospital is affiliated with Baylor University, Texas, and offers up-to-date
24-hour services. (tel 506-208-1000, emergency 506-208-1144,
www.hospitalsanjose.net, urgencias@hospitalcima.com)

Bug Spray

The activity of *Anopheles*, the mosquito that carries malaria, peaks at 1 AM, but there are some day-flying mosquitoes that can be a nuisance, such as blue devils. Fortunately, many ecolodges are in breezy locations and mosquitoes are kept at bay. It is advisable to use mosquito repellent and sleep under mosquito nets treated with permethrin repellents to avoid itchy bites and the danger of malaria or dengue fever. DEET and some other bug sprays are effective in keeping mosquitoes away. See the CDC website (www.cdc.gov) for information on DEET toxicity; lemon-eucalyptus-based repellents may be preferable. Consider purchasing clothes with repellent locked into the fabric (this treatment may need to be refreshed periodically), available from camping stores or Travelsmith.com. If you purchase your net, make sure you get the fine-net variety; larger holes will not be effective. Most ecolodges offer beds with mosquito nets, but bunkhouses in ecolodges often do not. Avon Skin-So-Soft is good for the biting no-see-ums that occasionally swarm at night.

Chiggers

Sulfur powder works well when dusted on socks and ankles to fend off chiggers, which cause itchy bites.

Dengue Fever

The day-flying *Aedes aegypti* mosquito carries dengue fever, a serious disease that can be fatal if caught more than once. This mosquito is currently found in densely populated areas, including all major Costa Rican cities and towns, although the disease tends to come in headline-hitting outbreaks. You can easily spot the mosquito's white-banded legs. Use bug spray to reduce risk.

Heat Stroke

Plan ahead to avoid heat stroke and the less dangerous, but still challenging, heat exhaustion. Wear a hat, sunscreen, loose clothes, and drink plenty of water. Avoid activity around noon when the sun is strongest. (Non-tropical countries do not experience this vertical sun, when the sun's rays are concentrated into a much smaller area and are therefore significantly more intense). Allow one liter of water per hour walked and take frequent breaks to cool down.

Heat stroke can be lethal. The individual suffering heat stroke stops sweating, and their temperature increases. They feel hot and dry and confused to the point that they may lose consciousness. If you see someone suffering these symptoms, get immediate medical attention while soaking the victim's clothes with cold water, giving them cool, not cold, water to drink if conscious, and fanning them.

Malaria

Costa Rica is generally thought of as a country without malaria. This used to be true, but unfortunately the disease is creeping back. There are some regions, usually on the borders, the coasts, and particularly in the southeast, where there is either endemic malaria or a number of cases recorded each year. Therefore, talk with your health provider before you travel, or check the CDC web site, www.cdc.gov. If you choose to forgo anti-malarials, it is wise to avoid malaria-prone areas and to use bug spray.

Snakes

Costa Rica is the ideal place to find a wide variety of poisonous and non-poisonous snakes. Generally, snakes will sense your footstep vibrations and depart rapidly. However, you may surprise a snake either coiled or crossing a path. Therefore look for coiled or sinuous shapes where you put your feet and hands both in daytime and at night (when some small but dangerous snakes may settle down on the warmer concrete of a bunkhouse floor).

For a snake bite, get medical attention immediately. In the San José area, one option is Hospital CIMA San José (tel 506-208-1000, emergency 506-208-1144, www.hospital sanjose.net, urgencias@hospitalcima.com). Try to remember the color, shape and markings of the snake but do not endanger yourself by trying to catch it. Keep the snake-bite victim calm to slow down the effects if the snake turns out to be poisonous. Lay or sit the person down with the bite below the level of the heart. Do not apply a tourniquet. Apply a dry dressing over the bite.

Swimmer's Ear
This itchy condition is caused by a fungal infection common in the tropics and can ruin a holiday. You can alleviate this condition by mixing equal parts of rubbing alcohol, vinegar, and water. Swab the ear with this acidic mixture, then dry carefully. This adjusts the ecological balance of the ear and helps prevent the fungus from growing. The fungus loves an alkaline (basic) humid environment, which the acidic vinegar and drying alcohol neutralize.

Toxic Plants and Animals
Avoid touching the "beach apple" or manchineel tree (*manzanillo*) growing among the mangroves behind the beaches, with its apple-like fruits. The sap is so toxic that it can cause blindness. When touched the leaves irritate the skin, and when burned on a campfire the twigs can cause lung problems.

Poison-dart frogs creeping around the forest floor look bright and cute, but their toxin is so potent that when absorbed through a scratch in the skin it can cause severe poisoning or death.

Venomous marine animals to avoid include jellyfish, the spines of lionfish, stingrays, and some corals. Cone shellfish are pretty but can be deadly, so don't pick them up: they have a harpoon that can stretch several inches from the edge of the shell to stab prey, and unfortunately also contains a toxic dose that can fell a human being.

Bullet ants are named for their painful punch. Learn to recognize the compact, bulky shape of this particular ant species and to avoid putting your hand on handrails and trees in which these ants may be nesting.

Tropical Diseases
Costa Rica ranks first in Latin America for the prevention and treatment of disease, according to the United Nations. However, Costa Rica is a tropical country with various diseases, including Chagas' disease, caused by a parasite picked up from a "kissing" bug that lives in the cracks of substandard adobe and thatch buildings. If you experience symptoms of fever, an unexplained swollen eye, unexpected pain, or other inflammation during your trip or after returning from Costa Rica, assist diagnosis by telling your medical specialist that you recently traveled to a tropical country.

Safety
In San José, Quepos, and Limón, theft and other crimes have become problems for tourists, so be on your guard against pickpockets, scams, and other dangers, and dress down accordingly. Rental cars are not recommended due to the poor quality of the roads.

Spanish
Costa Rican Spanish is flavored with elegance and respect. Listen for the sprinkling of *tiquismos*, unique Costa Rican and Central American expressions of endearment and courtesy. Spanish-language and Central American cultural programs are offered in many ecotravel destinations, including Monteverde. Check with your ecolodge if you want to take half-day classes at a language school or would like to include a short stay with a local family in order to speak Spanish and experience local life.

For limited Spanish speakers, most ecolodges can converse in English. Multilingual or English-speaking guides are available at many destinations on request. It is fun to go on a guided hike with a Spanish-speaking guide—the names of the plants and animals in Spanish evoke the love and care that Costa Ricans have for their environment.

Volcanoes
Costa Rica is known for its fascinating active volcanoes. You can watch volcanoes from a safe distance and during the less active periods. It is not advisable to attempt to walk up the trails close to any volcano summit unless the volcano is completely dormant. Pyroclastic flows of ultra-hot ash and volcanic gases have unfortunately reached nearby visitor observation sites during recent eruptions. At the volcano, activity can change at any time, so be prepared to revise your plans immediately if you hear rumbling or see sudden changes that may warn of an impending eruption. Check for current volcano warnings before you finalize your plans.

National and International Ecotravel, Bus, and Air Travel

Abercrombie & Kent
High-end nature tours.
US tel 800-554-7094
abercrombiekent.com
tel 506-735-5178

Aventuras Naturales
Avenida Central, Calles 33/35, San José
tel 506-225-3939, fax 506-253-6934,
US tel 800-514-0411
avenat@racsa.co.cr

Bay Island Cruises
Gulf of Nicoya tourist expeditions.
tel 506-258-3536, fax 506-239-4404

Butterfield and Robinson
High-end ecotours including kid-centered
ecoadventures.
US tel 800-678-1147
www.butterfield.com

Calypso Cruises
Arcadas building near the Gran Hotel,
San José.
Cocos and Gulf of Nicoya islands tourist
expeditions; sailing on the Gulf of Nicoya
through sister company Seadventures.
tel 506-256-2727, fax 506-256-6767,
US tel 866-978-5177

**Certification in Sustainable Tourism
Program (CST)**
www.turismo-sostenible.co.cr

Costa Rica Gateway
Specializes in birding trips and nature
tours to several acclaimed ecolodges.
tel 506-433-8278, 506-433-5634,
fax 506-433-4925, US tel 888-246-8513
www.crgateway.com
crgateway@racsa.co.cr

Costa Rica Transfers
A bus transfer service that provides rides
from the airport to secure bus stations
and books bus tickets for you.
www.costaricatransfers.com

Cotur
Tortuguero trips on Miss Caribe.
Calle 36, Paseo Colón/Avenida 1,
San José
tel 506-233-0133, fax 506-233-0778
cotur@sol.racsa.co.cr

Earthwatch
Field research organization offering many
expeditions focusing on conservation.
Grants for teachers and student groups.
P.O. Box 75, Maynard, MA 01754-0075,
US
267 Banbury Road, Oxford OX2 7HT, UK
126 Bank St, South Melbourne, Victoria
3205, Australia

Elderhostel
Ecotravel and education for seniors.
www.elderhostel.org

Fantasy Bus
San José-based tourist buses and ecotours.
Tourist bus destinations, natural history
tour planning, airport transfers, and
itinerary ideas.
tel 506-220-2126
www.graylinecostarica.com

Holbrook Travel
Recommended nature travel company
offering a variety of enrichment programs
to various countries, including to their
own Selva Verde Lodge near La Selva.
Elderhostel programs are also on their
itinerary. US tel 800-451-7111 or
352-377-7111, fax 352-371-3710
www.holbrooktravel.com
travel@holbrooktravel.com

Interbus
near Fuente de la Hispanidad, San Pedro
de Montes de Oca, San José
San José-based tourist buses and tours.
Tourist bus destinations, private ecotravel
itineraries, and airport transfers.
tel 506-283-5573
www.costaricapass.com (online
reservation service)

Liberia International Airport
(Daniel Oduber Quiros International
Airport, LIR), west of Liberia on Route 21.
International flights; regional flights to
Punta Islita, Samara, Tamarindo, and
other airstrips.

MINAE
(Ministry of Environment and Energy)
Government conservation office in San
José that coordinates some volunteer
conservation activities for visitors and
locals.
tel 506-257-2239
www.minae.go.cr

NatureAir
Domestic flights from Pavas, San José area (Tobias Bolaños Airport). Pavas is west of La Sabana. Allow about 15 minutes for airport transfer from San José International Airport to Tobias Bolaños Airport. NatureAir offers flights from Pavas to Granada (Nicaragua), Bocas del Toro (Panama), La Fortuna, Liberia, Tamarindo, Nosara, Carillo (Samara), Punta Islita, Tambor, Barra del Colorado, Tortuguero, Limon, Bocas del Toro, Quepos, Palmar Sur, Drake Bay, Puerto Jimenez, Carate, and Golfito.
tel 506-220-3054, 506-299-6000, fax 506-220-0413, US/Canada tel 800-235-9272
www.natureair.com
info@natureair.com
reservations@natureair.com

OTEC Tours (Organización de Turismo Estudiantil Costarricense)
Travel for Costa Rican students, including dive and horseback riding ecoadventures open to international students and teachers.
tel 506-257-7108, fax 506-233-2321

Public bus
Bus schedules and bus stop maps are available at the ICT office (see Tourist Office).

A Safe Passage
Transfers, including from San José international airport to your pre-booked public bus at the bus stop in Alajuela.
tel 506-365-9678
www.costaricabustickets.com
rchoice@racsa.co.cr

SANSA
Domestic flights from San José International Airport (SJO, Juan Santamaria International Airport). A shuttle bus takes passengers from international arrivals to the SANSA area at the other end of the airport. SANSA offers flights from San José to: Liberia, Tamarindo, Nosara, Samara, Punta Islita, Tambor, Barra del Colorado, Tortuguero, Quepos, Palmar Sur, Drake Bay, Puerto Jimenez, Golfito, and Coto 47.
tel 506-221-9414
www.flysansa.com

San José International Airport
(Juan Santamaria International Airport)
Alajuela, 16km from downtown San José

Sertu Tours
Caño Negro Wildlife Refuge; beach and marsh ecotours are among their listings.
tel 506-257-2363

Swiss Travel
Radisson Europa, 250m west of Centro Comercial El Pueblo, San José.
An established Costa Rican travel company that offers help in planning your own ecotravel.
tel 506-282-4898, 506-221-0944, fax 506-282-4890
www.swisstravelcr.com
info@swisstravelcr.com

Syracuse Tours
Private van shuttles and bilingual tours arranged to suit your personal itinerary.
www.syracusetours.com

Tilarán Transportation (bus)
tel 506-222-3854

Tourist Office (Instituto Costarricense de Turismo, ICT)
Below the Plaza de la Cultura
Calle 5, Avenida Central/2, San José
tel 506-222-1090, 506-223-1733,
US tel 1-866-COSTA-RICA
www.visitcostarica.com

VEASA air charter
(Vuelos Especiales Aéreos/SA)
tel 506-232-1010

Ecolodges, ecoadventures, national parks and private reserves for each region listed by chapter.

I. NORTHWEST

Guanacaste

Albergue de Montaña Rincón de la Vieja
Curubande-based ecolodge with treetop trails across seventeen platforms.
tel 506-256-8206, 506-256-7290, 506-695-5553
rincon@sol.racsa.co.cr

Guanacaste Conservation Area
(Area de Conservación Guanacaste/ACG) Apartado Postal 169 5000, Liberia, Guanacaste. Costa Rica Conservation offices in Liberia (506-666-0630), Santa Rosa (506-666-5051), and Pocosol (506-661-8150). Serving Guanacaste National Park (506-666-5051), Rincón de la Vieja Volcano National Park (506-666-0630), Santa Rosa National Park (506-666 5051), Junquillal Bay Wildlife Refuge, Horizontes Experimental Forest, Corredor Fronterizo Wildlife Refuge, Iguanita Wildlife Refuge, and Riberino Zapandi Wetlands.
www.acguanacaste.ac.cr
acg@acguanacaste.ac.cr

Guanacaste Dry Forest Conservation Fund
c/o Professor Daniel H. Janzen, Department of Biology, 415 South University Avenue, University of Pennsylvania, Philadelphia, PA 19104

Guanacaste National Park (Area de Conservación de Guanacaste/ACG) Santa Rosa field station: Center for Tropical Dry Forest Research.
tel 506-666-5051, 506-695-5598, 506-695-5577, fax 506-666-5020
www.acguanacaste.ac.cr
Guanacaste National Park satellite field stations: Cacao Biological Station, Maritza Biological Station, Pitilla Biological Station, Nancite Biological Station.

Hacienda Guachipelín
Ecolodge and canopy tour.
tel 506-442-2818, fax 506-442-1910
info@guachipelin.com
www.guachipelin.com

Hacienda los Inocentes Wildlife Conservation and Recreation Center
North of the Guanacaste National Park border.
tel 506-679-9190, 506-265-5484, fax 506-679-9224, 506-265-4385
www.losinocenteslodge.com
info@losinocenteslodge.com

Morgan's Rock Hacienda and Ecolodge
Nicaragua, just north of Guanacaste on the border.
tel 506-257-0766, fax 800-886-2609
www.morgansrock.com
info@morgansrock.com

Posada el Encuentro
Bed and breakfast in ecolodge and two cottages, with option of camping in the rainforest, tent supplied.
tel 506-382-0815, fax 506-666-2472

Rincón de la Vieja Volcano National Park (*see also under* Guanacaste Conservation Area)
tel 506-666-0630
For horses, call 506-666-5051

Santa Maria Volcano Lodge
Ecolodge on the Atlantic side with lush rainforest
tel 506-235-0642, fax 506-272-6236

Lomas Barbudal and Palo Verde

Lomas Barbudal Biological Reserve (*see also under* Tempisque Conservation Area) Maps from Friends of Lomas Barbudal office in Bagaces.
tel 506-671-1290

Palo Verde Biological Field Station (*see also under* Tempisque Conservation Area) Organization for Tropical Studies (Organización para Estudios Tropicales/OET). Mail payments to: OTS North American Headquarters, P.O. Box 90630, Durham, NC 27708-0630, USA Or make payments to: ESINTRO S.A. and deposit directly to Banco Nacional #606377-0 (US dollars), Banco Nacional #181973-9 (*colones*).
tel 506-524-0628, reservations 506-524-0607, fax 506-524-0629
US tel 919-684-5774, US fax 919-684-5661
www.ots.ac.cr
paloverde@ots.ac.cr

Palo Verde National Park (*see also under* Tempisque Conservation Area) Old Hacienda Palo Verde Park headquarters, tel/fax 506-200-0125

Palo Verde National Park office,
tel 506-671-1072

Rancho Humo
Ecolodge near Bagaces overlooking the
Tempisque River.
tel 506-255-2463, fax 506-255-3573

Tempisque Conservation Area Offices
Bagaces and Palo Verde Conservation
Area offices: Apdo 5251, Hojancha, (tel
506-659-9194); Apdo 14 5750, Bagaces
(tel 506-671-1290); Palo Verde (tel 506-
671-1072). Serving Barra Honda
National Park (tel 506-671-1290, 506-
671-1072), Cabo Blanco Absolute
Natural Reserve, Camaronal Wildlife
Refuge, Cipancí Wildlife Refuge, Cueva
Murcielago Wildlife Refuge, Curú
Wildlife Refuge, Diria National Forest
Wildlife Refuge, Guayabo Islands
Biological Reserve, La Ceiba Wildlife
Refuge, Las Baulas National Marine Park,
Lomas de Barbudal Biological Reserve
(tel 506-671-1290), Mata Redonda
Wildlife Refuge, Negritos Islands
Biological Reserve, Ostional Wildlife
Refuge, Palo Verde National Park (tel
506-671-1072), Romelia Wildlife Refuge,
Tamarindo Wildlife Refuge.
act@ns.minae.go.cr

Nicoya Peninsula

Agua Rica Diving Center, Tamarindo
Dive trips to Catalina Island and
snorkeling beaches including Playa
Conchal, Playa Carbon, and Playa Real.
tel/fax 506-653-0094
www.aguarica.net
agricadv@racsa.co.cr

Bahía Luminosa
Near Curú Wildlife Refuge.
tel 506-641-0386
marine fVHF channel 16
www.bahialuminosa.com
tropics@sol.racsa.co.cr

Barra Honda National Park (*see also
under* Tempisque Conservation Area)
Spelunking.
tel 506-685-5267, 506-233-5284,
506-671-1062

Bat Island
Dive and sport fishing boats leave from
Papagayo Peninsula marinas.

Las Baulas National Marine Park
Adjacent to Tamarindo Wildlife Refuge.
(*See also* National Parks and
Conservation Areas)

Leatherback turtles. The ranger station at
Playa Grande offers bilingual turtle-
nesting tours during the evening.
Reservations required
Ranger station tel 506-653-0470

Bill Beard Diving Safaris, Hermosa Beach
PADI, NAUI, NASE, and IANTD
Nitrox certification.
US tel 877-853-0538 or 954-453-5044,
fax 954-453-9740 (Fort Lauderdale, FL)
www.billbeardcostarica.com
costarica@diveres.com

Cabo Blanco Biological Reserve
In Cabuya, tel 506-645-5277
San Miguel Biological Station:
bunkhouse accommodation, tel 506-645-
5890

Catalina Islands
Dive and sport fishing boats leave from
Tamarindo and other Gulf of Papagayo
marinas.

Costa Pajaros (Bird Coast)
The shoreline of the northeast side of the
Gulf of Nicoya between Puntarenas and
the Tempisque River is a wading bird
haven.

Curú Wildlife Refuge
(*See also* National Parks & Conservation
Areas). Between Paquera and Tambor.
Office is near the beach at Curú Bay.

Florblanca Resort
North of Malpais near Cabo Blanco
Nature Reserve.
tel 506-640-0232, fax 506-640-0226
www.florblanca.com
florblanca@racsa.co.cr

The Four Seasons Resort, Papagayo
Peninsula.
Luxurious pampering, PADI dive
expeditions; a resort rather than a
sustainable ecolodge.
tel 506-696-0000, fax 506-696-0500

Hotel Lagarta Lodge
On the Nosara River above Ostional.
Complete with its own reserve;
certification for Sustainable Tourism
Level 2.
tel 506-682-0035, fax 506-682-0135
www.lagarta.com
lagarta@sol.racsa.co.cr

Hotel Punta Islita
Pacific Ocean spa near Islita; certification
for Sustainable Tourism Level 3.

tel 506-290-4259 fax 506-232-2183
www.hotelpuntaislita.com
info@hotelpuntaislita.com

Hotel Villa Baula
Beachfront ecolodge with charming
cabanas on Playa Grande, the
leatherback turtle nesting beach;
certification for Sustainable Tourism
Level 2.
tel 506-653-0644 and 506-653-0493,
fax 506-653-0459
www.villabaula.com
Info@villabaula.com

Isla Tortuga, offshore of Curú.
Cruises depart Bahía Luminosa or
Puntarenas.
Calypso Cruises tel 506-256-2727, US tel
866-978-5177, fax 506-256-6767
www.calypsocruises.com
info@calypsocruises.com

La Ensenada Lodge, Ensenada.
Costa Pajaros birdwatching, near
Guayabo Islands, Pajaros Island, and
Negritos Island Biological Reserves.
Restricted public access
tel 506-289-6655
www.laensenada.net

Ostional National Refuge
For olive ridley turtles, in Ostional
village, Nosara.
The ranger station is in Ostional village,
tel 506-680-0167
ADIO (Asociacion de Desarrollo de
Ostional) bilingual turtle-watching tours,
tel 506-682-0470
Sea turtle research station, University of
Costa Rica at Ostional, tel 506-682-0267

Rich Coast Diving
Full-service PADI dive center offering
scuba certification on Coco Beach.
tel 506-670-0176, US tel 800-4-DIVING
(Miami, FL)
www.richcoastdiving.com
dive@richcoastdiving.com

Sueno del Mar Bed and Breakfast
Tamarindo.
tel/fax 506-653-0284
www.sueno-del-mar.com
innkeeper@sueno-del-mar.com

Tamarindo Wildlife Refuge
Southern end of Gulf of Papagayo.
Adjacent to turtle nesting beaches.
www.tamarindo.com

Tempisque Conservation Areas, *see page 276.*

2. MONTEVERDE

Albergue Ecoverde
San Gerardo ecolodge.
tel 506-385-0092
www.agroecoturismo.net
cooprena@racsa.co.cr

Arco Iris Eco-Lodge
Santa Elena cabins.
tel 506-645-5067, fax 506-645-5022
www.arcoirislodge.com
info@arcoirislodge.com

Bajo del Tigre Reserve
(*See* Children's Eternal Rainforest)

Butterfly Garden, Cerro Plano
tel 506-645-5512

Children's Eternal Rainforest (Bosque
Eterno de los Niños, BEN)
Managed by the Monteverde
Conservation League.
Bajo del Tigre visitor center, Cerro Plano
tel 506-645-5305, fax 506-645-5104
Guides for Monteverde or Children's
Eternal Rainforest, tel 506-645-5112
Reservations for Poco Sol or San Gerardo
field station bunks, tel 506-645-5003,
506-645-5200
acmmcl@sol.racsa.co.cr

Canopy Tour, Monteverde
tel 506-291-4465, US tel 305-433-2241
www.canopytour.com

El Sapo Dorado, Cerro Plano
Chalet accommodations with excellent
cuisine.
tel 506-645-5010
www.sapodorado.com

Finca Ecologica Reserve, Cerro Plano
tel 506-645-5363, 506-645-5222

Friends of the Monteverde Cloud Forest
Accepts funding from US individuals for
the Monteverde Preserve.
PO Box 1964 Cleveland, OH 44106-
0164, USA

Galeria Colibri (Hummingbird Gallery)
By Monteverde Reserve entrance.

Hotel Belmar, Monteverde
Austrian chalet style hotel; certification
for Sustainable Tourism Level 4
tel 506-645-5201, fax 506-645-5135
www.hotelbelmar.net
info@hotelbelmar.net

Los Angeles Cloud Forest
(*See* Villa Blanca Cloud Forest)

Monteverde Conservation League
tel 506-645-5112, 506-645-5003

Monteverdeinfo.com
Santa Elena office by tree house.
tel 506-645-7070, fax 506-645-6060
montever@monteverdeinfo.com
monteverdeinfo.com

Monteverde Lodge and Gardens
Managed by Costa Rica Expeditions.
tel 506-257-0766, US tel 800-886-2609,
fax 506-222-0333
www.expeditions.co.cr
ecotur@expeditions.co.cr

Monteverde Preserve (Reserva Biológica
Bosque Nuboso Monteverde)
3-hour guided tours at 7:30 AM, 8 AM,
and 1 PM daily. 5-hour birding tour at 6
AM daily. 2-hour nocturnal tour at 7:15
PM daily. Student and researcher lodge
(La Casona) located at entrance.
Managed by Tropical Science Center
(Centro Científico Tropical/CCT).
CCT, PO Box 8-3870, ZIP 1000, San
José, Costa Rica
tel 506-645-5122, fax 506-645-5034
www.cct.or.cr/en; montever@cct.or.cr or
montever@racsa.co.cr

**Monteverde Preserve Backpacking
Shelters**
Alemán or La Leona shelter 3.5 hours
from main entrance; Eladios hut or
Portland Audubon Center 5 hours from
main entrance; El Valle shelter, 2.5 hours
from main entrance. Reservations
required. tel 506-645-5122
www.cct.or.cr/en
montever@cct.or.cr or
montever@racsa.co.cr

Orchid Garden (Orquídeas de
Monteverde), Cerro Plano
tel 506-645-5510

San Luis Ecolodge, San Luis
Lodge and research station with farm and
cloud forest activities; certification for
Sustainable Tourism Level 3.
tel 506-645-8049, 506-645-8051,
fax 506-645-8050
www.ecolodgesanluis.com
reservations@ecolodgesanluis.com

**Santa Elena Cloud Forest Reserve of
Monteverde**, Santa Elena
Administered by the Santa Elena

community high school from the Pension
Santa Elena. Half-day tours at 7:30 AM and
11.30 AM daily; 7:00 PM for 1.5-hour tours.
tel 506-645-5693, fax 506-645-5390
Reserve 6:30 AM departure from Pension
Santa Elena, tel 506-645-5051
Jeep pickup and guide, tel 506-645-5014
www.monteverdeinfo.com/reserve.htm
For guide reservations (specify Santa
Elena), email guide@monteverdeinfo.com
rbnctpse@racsa.co.cr

Selvatura
Santa Elena-based zipline canopy tour
with many other activities.
www.selvatura.com

Sendero Tranquilo Reserve, Monteverde
tel 506-645-5272, or call El Sapo Dorado
lodge if reserve office is closed: 506-645-5010.

Skywalk Skytrek, Santa Elena
tel 506-645-5238, fax 506-645-5786
www.skywalk.com
www.skytrek.com

Villa Blanca Cloud Forest Hotel and Spa
(Previously called Los Angeles Cloud
Forest Reserve)
San Ramon location near San José with
zip lines, reserve trails, and ecolodge
Certification for Sustainable Tourism
Level 4.
tel 506-461-0300, 506-461-0301,
fax 506-461-0302
www.villablanca-costarica.com

3. SAN JOSÉ &
CENTRAL PACIFIC
REGIONS

San José Area
Alajuela Butterfly Farm
By Los Reyes Country Club, Alajuela,
west of San José.
Living collection of butterflies at all life
stages. Bus pickups from San José hotels
occur three times a day.
tel 506-438-0400
www.butterflyfarm.co.cr

BioPark, *see* INBioParque

**Butterfly Gardens & Entomological
Museum**
In the basement of the School of Music
(Artes Musicales), University of Costa
Rica Campus, in San Pedro, San José.

Closed weekends.
tel 506-225-5555 x 318
Faculty of Agriculture Office,
tel 506-207-5647

Central Pacific Conservation Area (Area de Conservación Pacifico Central/ACOPAC)

Conservation Area offices: Santiago de Puriscal (506-416-7878), Manuel Antonio (506-786-7161), Carara (506-383-9953). Serving Cacyra Wildlife Refuge, Caraigres Protected Zone, Carara National Park, Cataratas Cerro Redondo Wildlife, Cerro Chompipe Protected Zone, Cerro las Vueltas Biological Reserve, Cerro Nara Protected Zone, Cerros de Escazú Protected Zone, Cerros de Turrubares Protected Zone, El Rodeo Protected Zone, Fernando Castro Cervantes Wildlife, Finca Barú Pacifico Wildlife Refuge, Finca Hacienda La Avellana Wildlife, La Cangreja National Park, La Ensenada Wildlife Refuge, Los Santos Forest Reserve, Manuel Antonio National Park (506-786-7161), Montes de Oro Protected Zone, Pájaros Island Biological Reserve, Páramo Wildlife Refuge, Peñas Blancas Wildlife Refuge, Playa Blanca Marine Wetlands, Playa Hermosa Wildlife Refuge, Portalón Wildlife Refuge, Punta Leona Wildlife Refuge, Puntarenas Estuary Wetlands, Quitirrisi Protected Zone, San Lucas Island Wildlife, Refuge, Surtubal Wildlife Refuge, Tivives Protected Zone, and Transilvania Wildlife Refuge.

Farmers' Market: Mercado Borbon
Calle 8 between Avenida 3 and 5, San José. NOTE: Dress down when visiting any markets.

Farmers' Market: Mercado Central
Calles 6/8 between Avenida Central and 1, San José.
Closed Sunday.

Farmers' Market
Calles 7/9 and Avenidas 16/20, San José.
Saturday morning.

Feria Organica: Organic Farmer's Market
Northwest of the US Embassy, San José. Tuesday and Friday afternoons, Saturday mornings.

Finca Rosa Blanca Country Inn
In the foothills of Santa Bárbara de Heredia north of San José, overlooking the central valley. Luxury inn with lush gardens brimming with tropical fruit, birds, and butterflies. Infinity pool. Certification for Sustainable Tourism Level 5.

tel 506-269-9392
www.finca-rblanca.co.cr
info@fincarosablanca.com

Hotel Bougainvillea
Surrounded by coffee plantations in Santo Domingo de Heredia near San José. Certification for Sustainable Tourism Level 3.
tel 506-244-1414, fax 506-244-1313
www.hb.co.cr/EN

INBioParque (BioPark), Heredia
tel 506-244-4730, fax 506-244-4790
www.inbio.ac.cr/inbioparque
inbioparque@inbio.ac.cr

Jade Museum (Fidel Tristán Jade Museum)
Costa Rica's best jade collection. 11th floor, INS National Insurance Institute building, east of the Barrio Amon at the north end of the Parque Espana, Avenue 7, Calles 9/11, San José. Closed weekends.
tel 506-223-5800 x 2584

La Paz Waterfall Gardens
Vara Blanca east of Poás Volcano. Vara Blanca location for Peace Lodge, waterfall gardens, butterfly gardens, and hummingbird gallery. Self-guided 3.5-km trails, buffet lunch, and shuttles.
tel 506-225-0643 or 506-482-2720, fax 506-225-1082
www.waterfallgardens.com

La Salle Museum of Natural Sciences
Paleontology, archeology, and zoology collections. A hundred yards/meters west of La Salle College, Calle Lang, southwest of La Sabana Metropolitan Park, San José. Closed weekends.
tel 506-232-1306

Lankester Gardens
Renowned orchid and butterfly garden run by the University of Costa Rica. Near Paraiso, 6km/3.7mi outside Cartago, southeast of San José.
tel 506-552-3247

National Museum
Bellavista Fortress, Central Avenue, 15&17 Street, San José.
Jade, gold, archeological finds, and colonial art and history. Closed Monday.
tel 506-221-4429, 506-257-1433

National Orchid Show, Zapote
A world-renowned orchid show at the Republic Tobacco, Zapote, San José in March. Information can be obtained from the ICT (see Tourist Office) and the Costa Rica Orchid Association, ACO.

tel 506-223-6517, 506-224-4278
www.ticorquideas.com

Pre-Columbian Gold Museum
By the Tourist Office, San José (*see* Tourist Office).
Please bring identification.
Closed Monday.
tel 506-243-4202, 506-223-0528,
fax 506-243-4220
museooro@racsa.co.cr

Serpentario
Avenida 1 between Calles 9/11, Barrio Carmen, San José.
Snakes and lizards in downtown San José.
Check for opening times before you go.
tel 506-255-4210

Simon Bolivar Zoo (Parque Zoologico Simon Bolivar)
Calle 13 north of Avenida 9, San José.
A sleepy, ancient zoo.

Tourist Office (ICT: Instituto Costarricense de Turismo)
Below the Plaza de la Cultura, Calle 5, Avenida Central/2, San José.
tel 506-222-1090 or 506-223-1733,
US tel 1-866-COSTA-RICA
www.visitcostarica.com

Spyrogyra Butterfly Garden
Flying butterflies near downtown San José, southeast of El Pueblo shopping center.
tel 506-222-2937
www.infocostarica.com/butterfly
parcar@racsa.co.cr

Zoo Ave
Excellent Alajuela-based conservation center with birds and other animals.
tel 506-433-8989
www.zooave.org

Central Pacific

Ballena National Park (*see also under* Osa Conservation Areas office, under chapter 6 resources)
Las Tres Hermanas and Isla Ballena for diving, humpback whales (November through March), turtles, and seabird nesting.
tel 506-735-5036, 506-735-5580

Carara Biological Reserve
Quebrada Bonita ranger station,
tel 506-383-9953

Cabinas las Olas
At Playa Avellanas near Carara Biological Reserve; certification for

Sustainable Tourism Level 2.
tel 506-658-8315, fax 506-658-8331
www.cabinaslasolas.co.cr
olassa@racsa.co.cr

Fantasy Bus Tours
Ecotourist bus serving the central Pacific coast.
tel 506-220-2126

Hacienda Barú Lodge and Wildlife Refuge
Near Ballena National Park at Dominical, west of San Isidro de El General on the Pacific Coast.
tel 506-787-0003, fax 506-787-0057
www.haciendabaru.com
info@haciendabaru.com

Hotel Punta Leona
Hotel complex south of Carara Biological Reserve on the beach. Certification for Sustainable Tourism Level 3.
tel 506-231-3131, fax 506-232-0791
www.hotelpuntaleona.com
info@puntaleona.com

Iguana Tours
Manuel Antonio National Park kayaking.
www.iguanatours.com

Juan Castro Blanco National Park (*see also under* Arenal Conservation Area: Northern Region, under chapter 4 resources)
tel 506-460-1412

Manuel Antonio National Park
tel 506-786-7161

Mystic Dive Center
Ventanas Beach, south of Dominical on the Brunca Coast at Ballena National Park.
Scuba, snorkeling, and PADI certification. Dive boats go to Caño Island and Ballena National Park.
tel 506-788-8636
www.mysticdivecenter.com

Oro Verde Private Nature Reserve
Birding spot (no ecolodge) near Ballena National Park.
www.costa-rica-birding-oroverde.com

Rainmaker Nature Reserve
tel 506-777-1250

Rancho Merced, National Wildlife Refuge near Ballena National Park

Si Como No Hotel
Resort-style hotel complex with small reserve. Certification for Sustainable

Tourism Level 4.
3 km from Manuel Antonio National Park.
tel 506-777-0777, fax 506-777-1093
www.sicomono.com
information@sicomono.com

Tárcol Lodge
Tárcoles River birdwatching haven.
tel 506-297-4134
www.costaricagateway.com

Tulemar
Bungalows and villas with restaurant near
the Manuel Antonio National Park offer
full kitchens and rainfall showers.
Certification for Sustainable Tourism
Level 1.
tel 506-777-0580 or 506-777-1325,
fax 506-777-1579
www.tulemar.com

Villa Lapas
Ecolodge and private reserve with canopy
zip line, canopy bridge walk, birdwatching guide, and other activities.
Near Carara Biological Reserve in Santa
Lucía. Certification for Sustainable
Tourism Level 1.
tel 506-637-0232, fax 506-637-0227
www.villalapas.com

4. MOUNTAINS

Guanacaste Mountain Range
Albergue de Montaña Rincón de la Vieja
Curubande-based ecolodge with treetop
trails across seventeen platforms.
tel 506-256-8206, 506-256-7290,
506-695-5553
rincón@sol.racsa.co.cr

Hacienda Guachipelín
Ecolodge and canopy tour.
tel 506-442-2818, fax 506-442-1910
www.guachipelin.com
info@guachipelin.com

Posada el Encuentro
Bed and breakfast in ecolodge, and two
cottages, with option of camping in the
rainforest, tent supplied.
tel 506-382-0815, fax 506-666-2472

**Rincón de la Vieja Volcano National
Park** (see listings under chapter 1 resources)
tel 506-666-0630; for horses, call
506-666-5051

Santa Maria Volcano Lodge
On the Atlantic side with lush rainforest.
tel 506-235-0642, fax 506-272-6236

Tilarán Range
Arenal Botanical Gardens
South of Nuevo Arenal.
Packed with rare tropical species, a
butterfly garden and hummingbird gallery.
tel 506-695-4273, fax 506-694-4086
www.exoticseeds.com
exoticseeds@hotmail.com

Arenal Tilarán Conservation Area
(Area de Conservación Arenal
Tilarán/ACAT)
Conservation Area office: Tilarán,
Guanacaste (506-695-5908, 506-695-
5180), Caño Island (506-735-5282,
acati@ns.minae.go.cr). Associated
mountain and non-mountain parks:
Alberto Manuel Brenes Biological
Reserve, Arenal Monteverde Protected
Zone (not part of the private Monteverde
Preserve), Arenal Volcano National Park
(506-695-5908, 506-695-5180), Curi
Cancha Wildlife Refuge, Miravalles
Protected Zone, Tenorio Protected Zone,
Tenorio Volcano National Park.

Arenal Volcano
tel 506-695-5908, 506-695-5180

Arenal Volcano Observatory Ecolodge
A research lodge in the danger zone.
Certification for Sustainable Tourism
Level 2.
tel 506-290-7011, lodge 506-692-2072,
fax 506-290-8427
www.arenal-observatory.co.cr
info@arenal-observatory.co.cr

Cabinas La Rivera
La Fortuna cabins.
tel 506-479-9048

Tabacón Hot Springs Resort and Spa
Arenal Volcano heats these natural hot
springs east of La Fortuna. Certification
for Sustainable Tourism Level 2.
tel 506-519-1900, US tel 877-277-8291,
US fax 877-277-8292
www.tabacon.com
ventas@tabacon.com

Tico Wind
Lake Arenal windsurfing.
www.ticowind.com

Central Range
**Bosque de Paz Rain and Cloudforest
Lodge and Reserve**
Birding and wildlife lodge, orchid garden,
hummingbird gallery and restaurant
located between Poás Volcano and Castro
Blanco National Park.

tel 506-234-6676, fax 506-225-0203
www.bosquedepaz.com
info@bosquedepaz.com

**Central Mountain Volcanic
Conservation Area** (Area de
Conservación Cordillera Volcanica
Central/ACCVC)
Conservation Area office: Apartado
Postal 10104 1000, San José (tel 506-
290-8202, fax 506-290-4869,
accvc@ns.minae.go.cr). Serving
mountain and non-mountain parks:
Bosque Alegre Wildlife Refuge, Braulio
Carrillo National Park (506-290-8202),
Central Volcanic Forest Reserve, Cerro
Atenas Protected Zone, Cerro Dantas
Wildlife Refuge, Cerros de la Carpintera
Protected Zone, Corredor Fronterizo
Wildlife Refuge, Cuenca Río Tuis
Protected Zone, El Chayote Protected
Zone, Grecia Forest Reserve, Guayabo
National Monument, Irazú Volcano
National Park (506-290-8202),
Jaguarundi Wildlife Refuge, La Marta
Wildlife Refuge, La Selva Protected
Zone, Poás Volcano National Park (506-
290-8202), Río Grande Protected Zone,
Río Tiribí Protected Zone, Río Toro
Protected Zone, Turrialba Volcano
National Park.

Guayabo National Monument
East of Santa Cruz below Turrialba
Volcano. The most significant
archeological site in Costa Rica. 4WD
vehicle required.
tel 506-290-8202

Irazú Volcano (*see also under* Central
Mountain Volcanic Conservation Area)
tel 506-290-8202

Lagunillas Lodge
Near Poás Volcano.
tel 506-389-5842

La Paz Waterfall Gardens (Peace
Waterfall)
Multiplex gardens, restaurant, and
rainforest experience.
tel 506-225-0643, fax 506-225-1082
www.waterfallgardens.com

Poás National Park
tel 506-290-8202

Rancho Naturalista
Well-known birding hot spot.
tel 506-297-4134, US tel 888-246-8513,
fax 506-297-4135
www.costaricagateway.com

Turrialba Volcano
tel 506-290-8202

Volcán Turrialba Lodge
For volcano risk-takers.
tel 506-273-4335
www.volcanturrialbalodge.com
info@volcanturrialbalodge.com

Talamanca Range
Tapantí National Park (*see also under* La
Amistad Conservation Area)
tel 506-771-3155

Albergue Monte Amuo
An hour's drive from Portero Grande.
tel 506-265-6149

Cerro de la Muerte
Field station on Cerro de la Muerte that
focuses on the páramo. *See under* Costa
Rica Trekking Adventures.

Chirripó National Park (*see also under*
Costa Rica Trekking Adventures)
tel 506-771-3155, bunk bookings
506-233-4160

Costa Rica Trekking Adventures
Backpacking hikes in Tapantí, Chirripó,
and Corcovado.
tel 506-771-4582, fax 506-771-8841
www.chirripo.com
selvamar@ice.co.cr

Durika Lodge and Biological Reserve
Ecolodge bordering La Amistad
International Biosphere Reserve, with
wilderness reserve, resident guide, hike to
indigenous communities, and organic
farm tour options.
tel 506-730-0657, fax 506-730-0003
www.durika.org
durika@racsa.co.cr

Genesis II Cloudforest Lodge
By Tapantí National Park.
tel 506-381-0739

Kiri Lodge and Reserve
Birding lodge near trout-fishing river.
tel 506-533-3040

**La Amistad International Biosphere
Reserve, Pacific Section** (Area de
Conservación La Amistad
Pacifico/ACLAP)
Conservation Area offices: San Isidro de
El General, Perez Zeledon (506-771-
3155, 506-771-4836), San Vito
(506-773-4060), Buenos Aires (506-730-
0846), Crestones Base (506-770-8040),

Carara (506-383-9953). Associated mountain and non-mountain parks: Chirripó National Park (506-771-3155), Joseph Steve Friedman Wildlife Refuge, La Amistad International Biosphere Reserve (Pacific Section 506-730-0846), Las Tablas Protected Zone, Palustrino Laguna del Paraguas Wetlands, Río Macho Forest Reserve, Rio Navarro Rio Sombrero Protected Zone, San Vito Wetlands (506-773-4060), Tapantí National Park (506-771-3155).

La Amistad Lodge and Reserve
San José office tel 506-228-8671,
fax 506-289-7858, lodge 506-200-5037
amistad@racsa.co.cr
www.laamistad.com

Las Cruces Field Station and Wilson Botanical Gardens
Ecolodge, field station, gardens, and rainforest preserves in the hills near San Vito. Run by the Organization for Tropical Studies (OET). OTS North American Headquarters and US payements: P.O. Box 90630, Durham North Carolina, 27708-0630, USA. Within Costa Rica make payments to ESINTRO S.A and deposit directly to Banco Nacional #606377-0 (US dollars), Banco Nacional #181973-9 (*colones*). Las Cruces tel 506-773-4004, central reservations tel 506-524-0607,
fax 506-524-0608
US tel 919-684-5774, US fax
919-684-5661
www.ots.ac.cr
lascruces@hortus.ots.ac.cr

Mirador de Quetzales
Just south of the 70km marker on the Interamerican Highway.
tel 506-771-4582, fax 506-771-8841

Savegre Mountain Lodge
Mountain quetzal research center, ecolodge, fruit orchards, and trout fishing at 2,200m/7220ft altitude
tel 506-771-1732, 506-390-5096,
506-771-2003, US tel 800-593-3305
www.savegre.co.cr

Talari Mountain Lodge
Birding lodge near San Isidro de El General.
tel 506-771-0341
www.talari.co.cr

Toucanet Lodge
In the valley of the Los Santos Forest Reserve close to cloud forest and páramo.
tel 506-771-4582, fax 506-771-8841
selvamar@racsa.co.cr

Trogon Lodge
Near Cerro de Muerte; with canopy tour across several platforms; high mountain area ecolodge.
tel 506-293-8181, fax 506-239-7657
www.grupomawamba.com

5. CARIBBEAN

Barra del Colorado
Barra del Colorado National Park (*see also under* Tortuguero Conservation Area)
tel 506-710-2929

Laguna del Lagarto Ecolodge
Barra del Colorado-based lodge in 500ha/1250ac virgin reserve. Certification for Sustainable Tourism Level 4. Also offers rainforest purchase to help conserve your own rainforest in the vicinity: www.protect-rainforests.org.
tel 506-289-8163, fax 506-289-5295
www.lagarto-lodge-costa-rica.com
info@lagarto-lodge-costa-rica.com

Tortuguero
Boca del Rio Lodge and Campground
Tortuguero camping.
tel 506-385-4676

Caño Palma Biological Station
Canadian Organization for Tropical Education.
Canadian tel 905-831-8809, fax 905-831-4203, Station tel 506-381-4116
www.coterc.org

Caribbean Conservation Corporation
www.cccturtle.org

El Manatí, Tortuguero
cell 506-383-0330, fax 506-239-0911

Laguna Lodge, Tortuguero
tel 506 709 8082, fax 506-709-8081,
San José tel 506-225-3740,
fax 506-283-8031
www.lagunatortuguero.com
info@lagunatortuguero.com

Mawamba Lodge, Tortuguero
San José office tel 506-293-8181,
fax 506-239-7657, lodge tel
506-223-2421, fax 506-255-4039
www.grupomawamba.com

Oasis Tours
San Juan River to Tortuguero from the Sarapiquí area.
tel 506-766-6108, cell 506-380-9493
www.tourism.com
oasis@tourism.com

Pachira Lodge, Tortuguero
tel 506-256-7080, US tel 800-644-7438,
fax 506-223-1119
www.pachiralodge.com
info@pachiralodge.com

River Boat Francesca
River trips from Tortuguero to Moín;
manatee tours from Tortuguero.
Fran & Modesto Watson
tel 506-226-0986
fvwatson@racsa.co.cr
www.tortuguerocanals.com

Tortuga Lodge,Tortuguero
Run by Costa Rica Expeditions.
tel 506-257-0766, US tel 800-886-2609,
fax 506-222-0333
www.expeditions.co.cr
ecotur@expeditions.co.cr

Tortuguero National Park (Area de
Conservación Tortuguero/ACTO)
Conservation Area office: Apdo 135
7200, Siquirres (tel 506-710-2929, 506-
710-2939, email acto@ns.minae.go.cr).
Serving: Acuíferos Guácimo y Pococí
Protected Zone, Barra del Colorado
Wildlife Refuge (506-710-2929), Cariari
National Wetlands, Corredor Fronterizo
Wildlife Refuge, Dr. Archie Carr Wildlife
Refuge, Tortuguero Protected Zone,
Tortuguero National Park

Tropical Wind
River trips from Moín to Tortuguero.
tel 506-709-8046, 506-709-8055,
506-758-4297, fax 506-790-3059
Tortuguero_info@racsa.co.cr

Pacuare Reserve
**Centro Agronomico Tropical de
Investigaction y Ensenanza (CATIE)**
Botanical garden.
tel 506-556-2700
www.catie.ac.cr
jardinbotanico@catie.ac.cr

**Pacuare Jungle Lodge and Aventuras
Naturales**
Sarapiquí area.
tel 506-225-3939, US tel 800-514-0411
or 800-773-4202
www.junglelodgecostarica.com
www.toenjoynature.com

Tropical River Foundation (Fundación
Ríos Tropicales)
Organizes world-class whitewater
kayaking and conserves threatened
Pacuare and Reventazón rivers.

tel 506-233-6455, fax 506-255-4354
www.riostropicales.com
info@riotropicales.com

Sarapiquí
**Agricultural College of the Humid
Tropical Region** (EARTH)
tel 506-713-0000, fax 506-713-0001
www.earth.ac.cr

Aguas Bravas
La Virgen, Sarapiquí, Toro, and Peñas
Blancas River whitewater rafting 12km
south of Puerto Viejo.
tel 506-292-2072, fax 506-229-4837

**Arenal Conservation Area: Northern
Region** (Area de Conservación Arenal
Huetar Norte/ACAHN)
Conservation Area Office: Apdo 10104
1000, San José, Costa Rica (tel 506-460-
1412, humedales@ns.minae.go.cr). Serving:
Arenal Volcano Emergency Forest
Reserve, Caño Negro Wildlife Refuge
(506-460-1412), Cerro El Jardin Forest
Reserve, Corredor Fronterizo Wildlife
Refuge, Cureña Forest Reserve, Juan
Castro Blanco National Park, Lacustrino
de Tamborcito Wetlands, Laguna Las
Camelias Wildlife Refuge, Laguna
Maquenque Wetlands.

Caño Negro Wildlife Refuge
Located outside the Sarapiquí area to the
north, but accessed by tours that also visit
the Sarapiquí.
tel 506-460-1412

El Gavilan Lodge and Reserve
Sarapiquí area.
tel 506-234-9507, fax 506-253-6556
www.gavilan.lodge.com
gavilan@racsa.co.cr

La Danta Salvaje Reserve and Lodge
tel 506-750-0012
ladanta@racsa.co.cr

La Selva
This large, well established research
station offers guided walking tours of the
wildlife in La Selva's extensive primary
and secondary rainforest and orchards.
Bunkhouses and mess hall offer good
basic services for ecotravellers and
researchers. University-run.
US tel 919-684-5774, San José office tel
506-524-0607, La Selva tel 506-766-
6565, fax 506-766-6535
www.ots.ac.cr/en/laselva
laselva@sloth.ots.ac.cr

Oro Verde
tel 506-743-8072, 506-843-8833
www.costarica-birding-oroverde.com

Rara Avis
Las Horquetas, located by Highway 4
south of Puerto Viejo.
tel 506-764-1111, fax 506-764-1114,
www.rara-avis.com
raraavis@sol.racsa.co.cr

Selva Verde Lodge
Full-service ecolodge near La Selva run
by Holbrook Travel. Certification in
Sustainable Tourism Level 2. Runs a local
resource center for the community.
tel 506-766-6800, fax 506-766-6011, US
tel 800-451-7111 or 352-377-7111
www.holbrooktravel.com
selvaverde@holbrooktravel.com

Tirimbina Reserve/Centro Neotropico Sarapiquís Ecolodge
Ecolodge with stunning indigenous-
inspired architecture. With
pre-Colombian tomb field, with stone
carvings and petroglyphs. Located at La
Virgen de Sarapiquí. Certification for
Sustainable Tourism Level 3.
tel 505-761-1004, fax 506-761-1415
www.sarapiquis.org
magistra@racsa.co.cr

Braulio Carrillo National Park

**The Atlantic Rainforest Aerial Tram
and Rainforest Lodge,** Braulio Carrillo
National Park.
tel 506-257-5961, fax 506-257-6053
www.rainforesttram.com

Braulio Carrillo National Park
tel 506-290 8202

Barva Volcano
Jungle Trails (Los Caminos de la Selva)
guided walks.
Calle 38, Avenidas 5/7, P.O. Box
5941-1000, San José
tel 506-255-3486, fax 506-255-2782

**Central Mountain Volcanic
Conservation Area** (Area de
Conservación Cordillera Volcanica/
Central ACCVC)
Conservation Area office: Apartado
Postal 10104 1000, San José (tel 506-
290-8202, fax 506-290-4869,
accvc@ns.minae.go.cr). Serving mountain
and non-mountain parks: Bosque Alegre
Wildlife Refuge, Braulio Carrillo National
Park (506-290-8202), Central Volcanic
Forest Reserve, Cerro Atenas Protected
Zone, Cerro Dantas Wildlife Refuge,
Cerros de la Carpintera Protected Zone,
Corredor Fronterizo Wildlife Refuge,
Cuenca Río Tuis Protected Zone, El
Chayote Protected Zone, Grecia Forest
Reserve, Guayabo National Monument,
Irazú Volcano National Park (506-290-
8202), Jaguarundi Wildlife Refuge, La
Marta Wildlife Refuge, La Selva Protected
Zone, Poás Volcano National Park (506-
290-8202), Río Grande Protected Zone,
Río Tiribí Protected Zone, Río Toro
Protected Zone, and Turrialba Volcano
National Park.

Río Danta Restaurant and Reserve
At Braulio Carillo National Park's border.
tel 506-293-8181, fax 506-239-7657
www.grupomawamba.com

Villa Zurqui
Regular inn near Zurqui entrance to
Braulio Carrillo National Park. Easy
driving distance from San José.
tel 506-268-5084, fax 506-268-8856
hvzurqui@racsa.co.cr

Limón Region

Almonds and Corals Beach Tent Camp
Gandoca-Manzanillo Refuge.
Certification for Sustainable Tourism
Level 4.
San José office tel 506-272-2024, 506-
272-4175, fax 506-272-2220; lodge tel
506-759-9057

ANAI (Talamanca Ecotourism and
Conservation Association)
Volunteer turtle research.
tel 506-224-6090, fax 506-253-7524
www.anaicr.org
anaicr@racsa.co.cr

ASACODE Reserve and Lodge
c/o ANAI in San José for more information.
tel 506-224-6090, fax 506-253-7524
anaicr@racsa.co.cr

**Aquamor and Talamanca Dolphin
Foundation**
PADI dive shop and dive boat
expeditions.
tel 506-759-0612, fax 506-759-0611
www.greencoast.com
aquamor1@racsa.co.cr

Aviarios del Caribe Lodge
Ecolodge whose owners specialize in sloth
rehabilitation. Located at the migratory
flyway on the Estrella River Delta near
Limón.
Tel/fax 506-382-1335
aviarios@costarica.net

Bastimientos National Marine Park,
Panama
Archipelago with many dive shops and
marine ecoadventures just across the
border near Sixaoloa.
ww.bocas.com/btisturi.htm

Cahuita National Park
tel 506-758-3170

Cahuita village phone (shared)
tel 506-758-1515

Cariblue Hotel
By Cocles Beach in Puerto Viejo near
Cahuita. With Certification for
Sustainable Tourism Level 2.
tel 506-750-0035, fax 506-750-0057
www.cariblue.com
cariblue@racsa.co.cr

Casa Camarona
By Cocles Beach in Puerto Viejo near
Cahuita. With Certification for
Sustainable Tourism Level 2.
tel 506-283-6711, lodge tel 506-750-
0151, fax 506-222-6184, lodge fax
506-750-0210.

Gandoca-Manzanillo Wildlife Refuge
(see under La Amistad Conservation Area)
South of Cahuita on the coast.

Hitoy-Cerere Biological Reserve (see
under La Amistad Conservation Area)
West of Cahuita on the foothills of the
Talamancas.

La Amistad Conservation Area:
Caribbean section (Area de
Conservación La Amistad
Caribe/ACLAC)
Conservation Area office: Apdo 10104
1000, San José, Costa Rica, (tel 506-758-
3170, 506-754-2133, humedales@
ne.minae.go.cr). Serving: Aviarios del
Caribe Wildlife Refuge, Barbilla National
Park, Cahuita National Park (506-758-
3170), Cariari National Wetlands, Cuenca
Rio Banano Protected Zone, Cuenca Rio
Siquirres Protected Zone, Gandoca
Manzanillo Wildlife Refuge, Hitoy Cerere
Biological Reserve, La Amistad
International Biosphere Reserve
(Caribbean section 506-758-3170),
Lacustrino Bonilla Bonillita Wetlands,
Limoncito Wildlife Refuge, Pacuare Matina
Forest Reserve, Rio Pacuare Forest Reserve.

Samasati Nature Retreat
Caribbean ecolodge with yoga, nature
watching, and spa. Certification for

Sustainable Tourism Level 3.
tel 506-224-1870, US tel 800-563-9643,
fax 506 224 5032
www.samasati.com
samasati@samasati.com

Selva Bananito Reserve and Lodge
On the northern edge of La Amistad
International Biosphere Park near Limón.
San Pedro office tel 506-253-8118, fax
506-280-0820, lodge tel 506-284-4278
www.selvabananito.com
conselva@racsa.co.cr

6. OSA PENINSULA AND GOLFO DULCE

Corcovado National Park
Adventuras Tropicales Golfo Dulce
(see Osa Natural)

Bosque del Rio Tigre Sanctuary and Lodge
Near Dos Brazos and the ex-gold-mining
area of Corcovado. Resident guide and
extensive birding and nature activities.
Puerto Jimenez office tel 506-735-5062,
cell 506-383-3905, US tel 888-875-9453
Post Office fax 506-735-5045
www.osaadventures.com
info@osaadventures.com

Corcovado Lodge Tent Camp
Near southwest border of Corcovado
National Park.
tel 506-257-0766, 506-222-0333,
fax 506-257-1665, US fax 800-886-2609
www.costaricaexpeditions.com
ecotur@expeditions.co.cr

Corcovado National Park (see also under
Osa Conservation Area)
Sirena field station and bunkhouse;
satellite field stations at Los Patos, San
Pedrillo, La Leona, El Tigre (Dos Brazos).
Reservations and camping permits from
the Puerto Jiménez office. Access by boat,
Sirena airstrip, or trails.
tel 506-735-5036, 506-735-5580
www.costarica-nationalparks.com/
corcovadonationalpark.html
corcovado@minae.go.cr

La Leona Ecolodge Tent Camp
Near southwest border of Corcovado
National Park.
tel 506-735-5704, 506-735-5705
www.laleonalodge.com
info@laleonalodge.com

Luna Lodge Reserve
Near southwest border of Corcovado
National Park.
tel 506-380-5036, US tel 888-409-8448
www.lunalodge.com
information@lunalodge.com

MINAE
Government Conservation Office in San
José.
tel 506-257-2239
www.minae.go.cr

Osa Aventura
Corcovado guided tours with Mike Boston.
tel 506-735-5670, fax 506-735-5717
www.osaaventura.com
info@osaaventura.com

Osa Conservation Area (Area de
Conservación Osa/ACOSA)
Osa Conservation Area office is located
by the airport in Puerto Jiménez, tel 506-
735-5036, 506-735-5580. Caño Island
office tel 506-735-5282, corcovado@
minae.go.cr. Serving: Ballena National
Marine Park, Caño Island Biological
Reserve (506-735-5282), Carate Wildlife
Refuge, Corcovado National Park,
Donald Peters Hayes Wildlife Refuge,
Golfito Wildlife Refuge, Golfo Dulce
Forest Reserve, Osa Wildlife Refuge (506-
735-5036), Piedras Blancas National
Park, Rancho La Merced Wildlife Refuge.

Osa Natural, Puerto Jiménez
tel/fax 506-735-5440
www.osanatural.com

Drake Bay
Albergue Jinetes de Osa
Dives to Caño Island and more.
tel 506-371-1598, US tel 800-317-0333
crventur@costaricadiving.ccosta
www.costaricadiving.com

Aquila de Osa Inn
Drake Bay and Caño Island diving, and
Corcovado expeditions.
tel 506-296-2190, fax 506-232-7722,
US/Canada tel 866-924-8452
www.aquiladeosa.com
info@aquiladeosa.com

Cabinas Jade Mar
tel 506 284-6681, fax 506-233-3333

Casa Corcovado Jungle Lodge
Caño Island diving, Corcovado
expeditions, and more.
tel 506-256-3181 fax 506-256-7409

www.casacorcovado.com
corcovado@racsa.co.cr

Cocalito Lodge
Birders', botanists', and nature watchers'
lodge.
tel 506-284-6369
Canada
tel 519-782-3978
www.costaricanet.net/cocalito
berrybend@aol.com

Delfin Amor Ecolodge
US tel 831-345-8484, US toll-free fax
866-527-5558, emergency lodge cell
506-847-3131
www.divinedolphin.com
delfinamor@divinedolphin.com

Drake Bay Wilderness Resort
Full-service ecolodge with diving,
kayaking, rainforest expeditions.
Elderhostel runs whale research
expeditions from here.
tel 506-770-8012, US tel 561-762-1763
www.drakebay.com
emichaud@drakebay.com

Golfo Dulce Lodge
At Playa San Josecito near San Pedrillo
ranger station. Certification for
Sustainable Tourism Level 3.
tel 506-821-5398, fax 506-775-0573
info@golfodulcelodge.com

Gulf Islands Kayaking
Office located in Canada.
Canada tel 604-539-2442

Marenco Beach and Rainforest Lodge
San José booking office tel 506-258-1919,
fax 506-255-1346, US tel 800-278-6223,
lodge tel 506-770-8002, fax 506-255-1346
www.marencolodge.com
info@marencolodge.com

Mirador Lodge
Drake Bay and Caño Island diving and
Corcovado expeditions with organic
gardening specialty.
tel 506-214-2711, US tel 877-769-8747,
US fax 509-356-5325, Canada fax 514-
372-0231, UK fax +44 (870)134 8876.
www.mirador.co.cr
info@mirador.co.cr

Punta Marenco Lodge
tel 506-841-9329, fax 506-268-2015
www.puntamarenco.com
ventas@puntamarenco.com

La Paloma Lodge
PADI-certified instruction.
tel 506-293-7502, fax 506-293-0954
www.lapalomalodge.com
info@lapalomalodge.com

Poor Man's Paradise
Reef and rainforest simplicity.
tel 506-771-9686, fax 506-770-2674
www.poormansparadise.com

Proyecto Campanario
Tent camp and reserve with educational
courses.
tel 506-258-5778, fax 506-256-0374
www.campanario.org
info@campanario.org

Rio Sierpe Lodge
Expeditions to Panama, Corcovado, and
Caño Island.
tel 506-253-5203, fax 506-253-4582
www.riosierpelodge.com
info@riosierpelodge.com

Caño and Cocos Islands
Aggressor Fleet
Cocos Island dive trips.
US tel 800-348-2628 or 985-385-2628,
US fax 985-384-0817
www.aggressor.com
okeanos@aggressor.com

Caño Island (*see also under* Osa
Conservation Area)
Many Drake Bay ecolodges offer dive
trips to Caño Island.
tel 506-735-5282

Cocos Island
Conservation Area office (Area de
Conservación Marina Isla de
Coco/ACMIC)
Apdo 10104 1000, San José, Costa Rica
tel 506-233-4533, 506-283-0022
acmic@ns.minae.go.cr

Hunter Fleet
Cocos Island and Malpelo Island dive
trips. Two boats. Nitrox training.
US tel 800-203-2120, 506-228-6613,
fax 506-289-7334
info@underseahunter.com
www.underseahunter.com

Mystic Dive Center
Ventanas near Palmar Sur.
Dive trips to Caño Island from the beach
by Ballena Marine Park.
tel 506-788-8636
info@mysticdivecenter.com
www.mysticdivecenter.com

Golfo Dulce
Bosque del Cabo
Ecolodge with thatched *cabinas* and
houses, swimming pool, bar, open-air
restaurant, guides and beaches. South of
Puerto Jiménez overlooking the gulf, the
Pacific, and Corcovado. Recommended.
tel/fax 506-735-5206
www.bosquedelcabo.com
phil@bosquedelcabo.com

Cecropia Foundation
www.elremanso.com
hector@cecropia.org

Corvocado Foundation, Puerto Jiménez
www.corcovadofoundation.org

Crocodile Bay Lodge, Puerto Jiménez
www.crocodilebay.com

Escondido Trex, Puerto Jiménez
Kayaking on the Golfo Dulce and Pacific.
tel 506-735-5210
www.escondidotrex.com
osatrex@racsaco.cr

Esquinas Rainforest Lodge
Near Piedras Blancas Reserve, northeast
Golfo Dulce.
tel/fax 506-775-0140, lodge 506-775-0901
www.esquinaslodge.com
esquinas@racsa.co.cr

El Remanso
South of Puerto Jiménez overlooking the
Pacific. Lodge offers a variety of
Corcovado area activities including
canopy and waterfall climbing adventures
with the conservation-focused owners.
Corcovado hikes.
tel 506-735-5569, fax 506-735-5126
www.elremanso.com
info@elremanso.com

Lapa Rios
Ecolodge overlooking the gulf with two-
story restaurant, gorgeous serenity pool,
large thatched cabins and access to guides
on a hillcrest. Corcovado treks. Certification for Sustainable Tourism Level 5.
tel 506-735-5130, fax 506-735-5179
www.laparios.com
info@laparios.com

Neotropical Foundation (Fundación
Neotrópica)
www.neotropica.org

Orchid Garden (Casa de Orquídeas)
Playa San Josecito north of Golfito.

Take a ferry from any of the Golfo Dulce
towns. Guides available Sunday through
Thursday.
tel 506-775-0353

Osa Conservation Area
(*see under* Ecolodges, Ecoadventures,
National Parks, and Private Reserves:
Corcovado)

Osa Natural
(*see under* Ecolodges, Ecoadventures,
National Parks, and Private Reserves:
Corcovado)

Piedras Blancas National Park
(*see under* Osa Conservation Area)
tel 506-735-5036, 506-735-5580

Piro Forest Reserve
South of Puerto Jiménez.
tel/fax 506-735-5013
www.tuva.org

Playa Nicuesa Rainforest Lodge,
Piedras Blancas National Park
tel 506-735-5237, US tel 866-348-7610,
512-342-7160
www.playanicuesa.com

Tiskita Reserve and Lodge
Near Pavones Beach south of Golfito.
tel 506-296-8125, fax 506-296-8133
www.tiskitalodge.co.cr
info@tiskitalodge.co.cr

TUVA Foundation (Fundacion Tierras
Unidas Vecinales por el Ambiente)
Osa Peninsula conservation organization
with extensive programs. Volunteer
opportunities. Apt. 54, Puerto Jiménez.
tel/fax 506-735-5013
www.tuva.org
info@tuva.org

Zancudo Boat Tours
Located at the Cabinas los Cocos south of
Golfito on the east of Golfo Dulce.
tel 506-776-0012
loscocos@loscocos.com

Index